Peace and Security

Peace and Security

The Next Generation

Edited by
George A. Lopez
and
Nancy J. Myers

ROWMAN & LITTLEFIELD PUBLISHERS, INC.
Lanham • Boulder • New York • Oxford

ROWMAN & LITTLEFIELD PUBLISHERS, INC.

Published in the United States of America
by Rowman & Littlefield Publishers, Inc.
4720 Boston Way, Lanham, Maryland 20706

12 Hid's Copse Road
Cummor Hill, Oxford OX2 9JJ, England

British Library Cataloguing in Publication Information Available

Library of Congress Cataloging-in-Publication Data

Peace and security : the next generation / edited by George A. Lopez and Nancy J. Myers.
p. cm.
Includes bibliographical references and index.
ISBN 0-8476-8594-2 (cloth : alk. paper).—ISBN 0-8476-8595-0 (pbk. : alk. paper)
1. International relations. 2. United States —Foreign relations—1945-1989. 3. World politics—1945–

JX1391 .I637 1997
327.09045 19 97-32889
CIP

ISBN 0-8476-8594-2 (cloth : alk. paper)
ISBN 0-8476-8595-0 (pbk. : alk. paper)

Contents

Key Concept Chart x

Introduction xiii

Acknowledgments xvii

PART ONE: CHALLENGES TO PEACE AND SECURITY

CHAPTER I. The Burdens of History: Nuclear Weapons, the Cold War, and Massive Defense Spending 3

Introduction 3

I.1 The Nuclear FAQ
Bulletin Editors

I.2 The Man Behind the Bomb 9
William Lanouette

I.3 How Soviet Physicists Caught Up 18
David Holloway

I.4 Four Trillion Dollars and Counting 25
U.S. Nuclear Weapons Cost Study Project

I.5 Midnight Never Came 37
Mike Moore

Chart: The Arms Race 50

Discussion Questions 51

CHAPTER II. The Proliferation Problem: Will "They" Get the Bomb? 53

Introduction 53

II.1 The Myth of the Islamic Bomb 56
Pervez Hoodbhoy

II.2	Engineer for Hire David Albright	64
II.3	Black-Market Bombs and Fissile Flim-Flam Kirill Belyaninov	68
II.4	Potatoes Were Guarded Better Oleg Bukharin and William Potter	76
II.5	Non-Proliferation Regime: Jury-Rigged but Working David Albright and Kevin O'Neill	79
	Chart: The Missile Threat	87
	Discussion Questions	88

CHAPTER III. Legacies of Insecurity: Human Costs, Societal Impacts, and Environmental Disasters 89

	Introduction	89
III.1	Victims of the Arms Race U.S. Nuclear Weapons Cost Study Project	92
III.2	Nothing Clean about Cleanup Linda Rothstein	94
III.3	Who the Hell Will Insure Us? Len Ackland	98
III.4	Poisoned Pacific Bengt Danielsson	101
III.5	Chernobyl: The Decade of Despair David R. Marples	105
III.6	Nuclear Language and How I Learned to Pat the Bomb Carol Cohn	114
	Map: A-Bomb Damage to Hiroshima	123
	Discussion Questions	124

CHAPTER IV. From Foe to Friends? The Soviet Successor States 125

	Introduction	125
IV.1	Russia Will Turn Inward Viktoria Tripolskaya-Mitlyng	128

IV.2 Baltic Pride, Russian Tears — 132
Nina Chugunova

IV.3 Kazakhstan Finds Its Own Way — 139
Leonid Zagalsky

IV.4 Power Play in Central Asia — 144
Mikhail Ustiugov

IV.5 Armenia's Energy Choice — 148
Astghik Vardanian

Map: New Nations of the Former Soviet Union — 155

Discussion Questions — 156

PART TWO: BUILDING PEACE AND SECURITY

CHAPTER V. Promoting Global Cooperation: Multilateral Peacekeeping and Sanctions — 159

Introduction — 159

V.1 Phantom Forces, Diminished Dreams — 162
Richard C. Longworth

V.2 We Are Dying of Your Protection — 167
Dzenita Mehic

V.3 A Stronger U.N. Strengthens America — 173
Jonathan Dean

V.4 Misreading the Public on Peacekeeping — 180
Steven Kull

V.5 On Sanctions, Think Small — 183
Ivan Eland

V.6 Who Suffers from Sanctions? — 188
Drew Christiansen and Gerard F. Powers

Chart/Map: Peacekeeping and Sanctions — 190

Discussion Questions — 192

CHAPTER VI. Arms and Security at Millennium's End — 193

Introduction — 193

VI.1 More Security for Less Money — 196
Mike Moore

VI.2 A Chinese View on Nuclear Disarmament 202
Dingli Shen

VI.3 World Court Says Mostly No to Nuclear Weapons 205
Mike Moore

VI.4 The Revolt Against Nuclear Weapons 208
Michael Krepon

VI.5 Comprehensive Test Ban Only a Beginning 211
William Epstein

VI.6 Four Steps to Zero 215
The Henry L. Stimson Center

Chart: A Sense of Proportion 221

Discussion Questions 222

CHAPTER VII. The Emergence of Global Citizenship 223

Introduction 223

VII.1 Scientists as Public Educators: 1945–50 226
Eugene Rabinowitch

VII.2 The Global Tide 230
George A. Lopez et al.

VII.3 A Movement Is Born 238
Nadezhda Azhgikhina

VII.4 The Revolutions of 1989 243
Mary Kaldor

VII.5 Squeezing Apartheid 248
Jennifer Davis

VII.6 Remember Your Humanity 253
Joseph Rotblat

Chart: Nobel Peace Laureates, 1945–1996 259

Discussion Questions 262

Index 265

About the Contributors 273

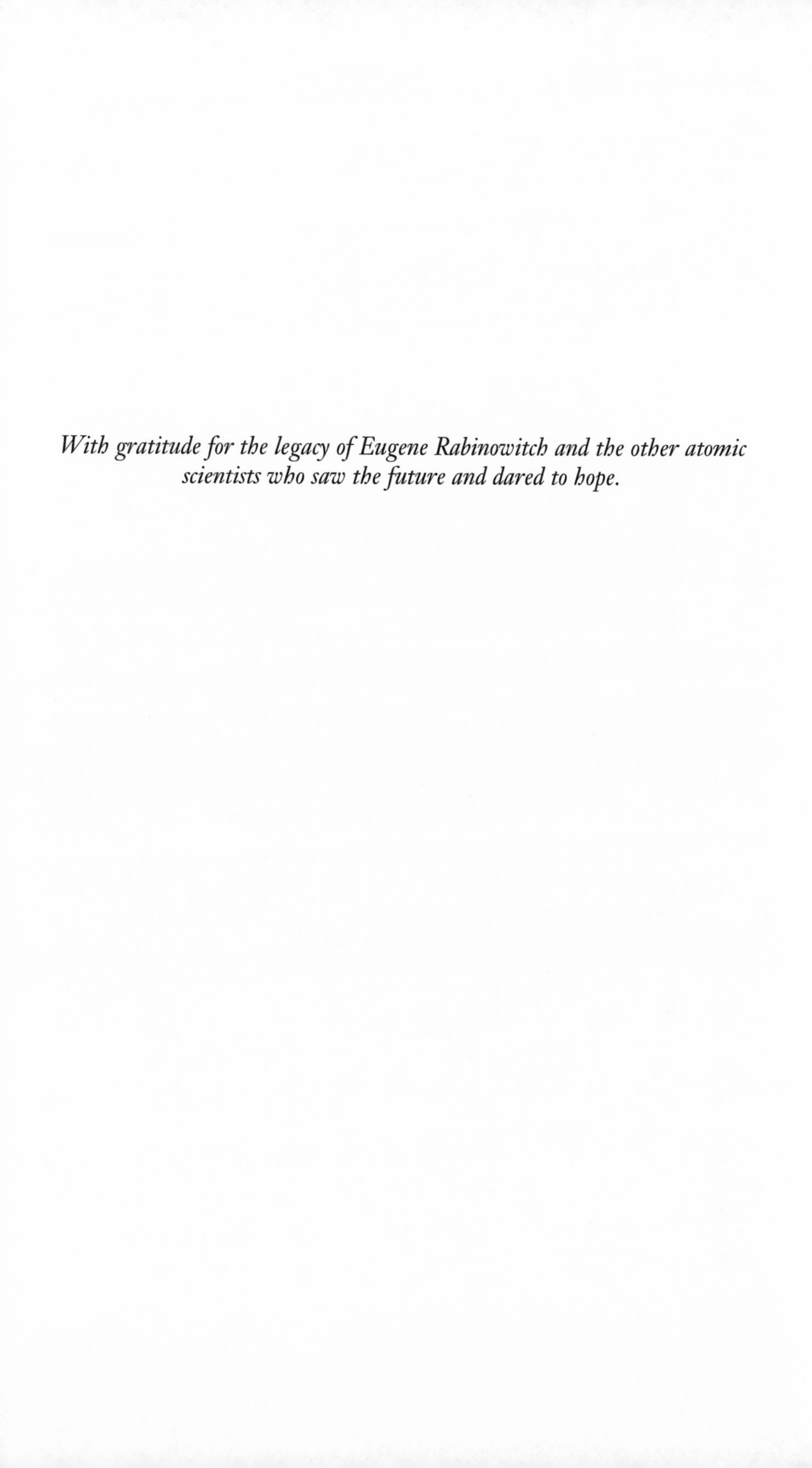

With gratitude for the legacy of Eugene Rabinowitch and the other atomic scientists who saw the future and dared to hope.

Key Concept Chart

	Chapter I	Chapter II	Chapter III	Chapter IV	Chapter V	Chapter VI	Chapter VII
alliances	I.5	II.5		IV.1, IV.4	V.5	VI.2	
apartheid							VII.5
arms control	Introduction, I.5	II.5	III.6	Introduction		VI.2, VI.5, VI.6	VII.1
ballistic missile defense	Introduction, I.4, I.5	chart		Introduction			
civil society				IV.2, IV.4, IV.5			Introduction, all articles, chart
comprehensive test ban			III.4			VI.5	
counterforce/ countervalue	Introduction, I.4, I.5		map				
defense conversion			III.2, III.3				
détente	I.5						
deterrence	Introduction, I.4, I.5	II.1				VI.2	
disarmament	Introduction, I.5, chart		III.2, III.3			VI.2, VI.4, VI.5, VI.6	VII.1, VII.4, VII.6
dual-use technology		II.2					
economic sanctions					Introduction, V.5, V.6, chart		VII.5
environmentalism			III.2, III.4, III.5	Introduction, IV.5			VII.2
ethnic groups			III.4	IV.2, IV.3, IV.5	V.2		
export controls		II.2, II.5					
extended deterrence	I.4, I.5						VII.4
feminism			III.6				VII.3
fissile materials		II.3, II.4	III.1, III.2, III.3			VI.5	
globalization							Introduction, VII.2
global warming				IV.4, IV.5			
"guns and butter"		II.1				VI.1, chart	

humanitarian intervention					Introduction, V.1, V.2, V.3, V.4		
human rights			III.1, III.3, III.4, III.5	IV.2, IV.5	V.2, V.3, V.6		VII.3, VII.4, VII.5
hydrogen bomb	I.1, I.4, I.5						
information technology					V.4		Introduction, VII.2
interdependence				IV.2, IV.4	V.3		Introduction, VII.2, VII.4, VII.5
international law						VI.3, VI.4	VII.1, VII.6
Islam		II.1		IV.3			
just-war thinking	I.2, I.3	II.1	III.6		V.6		
military-industrial complex	Introduction, I.4, I.5					VI.1	
mutually assured destruction	Introduction, I.4, I.5, chart		III.6			VI.3	
nationalism	I.2, I.3			Introduction, IV.1, IV.2, IV.3			
NATO	I.5			IV.1			VII.4
non-governmental organizations						VI.3, VI.4, VI.5	Introduction, all articles
nonproliferation	I.1	Introduction, all articles				VI.2	
peacekeeping					Introduction, V.1, V.2, V.3, V.4, chart		
sovereignty				IV.1, IV.2, IV.3	V.1, V.2, V.5		VII.5
strategic arms limitation	I.4, I.5		III.2, III.3			VI.6	VII.1
technology transfer		II.2, II.5		IV.4			
terrorism		Introduction, II.3, II.4					
Third World		Introduction, II.1	III.4		V.3, V.4		
war	I.2		map	IV.5			VII.1, VII.6

This volume covers a wide range of material, including detailed discussions of arms and security issues and events in particular countries. Instead of indexing all these details, we have selected concepts and terms that are central to the study of international relations, peace, and security and that may not be obvious in the titles of chapters and articles. We have cross-referenced these terms with the introductions, articles, charts, and maps to provide a useful reference tool for faculty and students and to supplement the organization by chapter.

Introduction

One of the more frequently cited quotes of the first fifty years of the nuclear era was Albert Einstein's assertion, "The unleashed power of the atom has changed everything save our modes of thinking."

The past half-century was marked by a striking contrast between the politically dominant modes of thinking, which sustained the development and massive deployment of nuclear weapons, and the voices of a number of scientists and scholars, often dismissed as naive, that were raised against these developments. With the hindsight granted by the end of the Cold War, many analysts now recognize that the alternatives posed by thoughtful critics of the arms race were not so far-fetched after all. Moreover, now that a superpower nuclear confrontation no longer seems imminent, many analysts are willing to re-examine the history and impact of the arms race, as well as its relationship to peace and security. This book responds to that rethinking.

For nearly 50 years following World War II, the political climate in each of the nuclear superpowers reinforced deterrence as the best strategy to avoid war, while retaining at various times the option to fight a nuclear war. The search for a security system that depended less on nuclear weapons and deterrence, and that rejected the war-fighting option, required poise and persistence. If such new modes of thinking were to attract serious attention, they needed to be nurtured through critical review and open discussion.

No other intellectual outlet was more consistent and convincing in providing such a forum than the *Bulletin of the Atomic Scientists*. Founded in 1945 by scientists who worked on the first atomic bombs, the *Bulletin*'s unique strength was that it took seriously the technical and scientific aspects of nuclear energy and weapons, but mixed such discussions with attention to the public and foreign policy import of such difficult topics.

The founders of the *Bulletin* emphasized the potential danger of the use of nuclear weapons, symbolized by the now-famous "Doomsday Clock" that appears on the magazine's cover. They were also eager to explore the new modes of thinking about international cooperation to which Einstein, one of their number, had referred. (The "modes of thinking" quotation originated in a 1946 funding appeal Einstein issued on behalf of his colleagues and their new magazine.)

During its tenure as a leading publication in the security studies community, the *Bulletin* has provided challenging articles about nuclear weapons and their impact on social, economic, and environmental realities, and about defense spending and policy. In the 1990s, the *Bulletin* has also focused on international trends and institutional arrangements needed for constructing a security system that does not depend on nuclear weapons.

In keeping with the global consciousness of its founders, the *Bulletin* publishes journalists and analysts from all over the world. These international voices and a number of U.S. experts examine today's security issues in historical perspective in this volume.

The Purpose of This Book

The post–Cold War era provides a unique opportunity to assess the cost of the arms race of the past five decades and to scrutinize the increasing range of options for creating a more secure and peaceful world. The selections in this volume are especially sensitive to the notion that the building of peace and security systems in the future depends on ideas that exclude massively destructive weapons.

In that sense, the volume has a bias. Readers will not find among the articles arguments for new weapons systems or military responses to various political problems, although the editors' introductions to each chapter sample some contending positions. The selections of particular chapters do not present unanimous views. But the *Bulletin*'s voice on issues of peace and security is clear.

We have developed this book in order to meet some specific needs in the peace and security studies fields:

- for a collection of serious, readable essays on the diverse issues that comprise the security puzzles of the post–Cold War era;
- for a book that seeks to educate the next generation of citizens about the myriad issues associated with the nuclear era, each of which involves technical, military, ethical, and political dimensions;
- for a volume that integrates the legacy of the Cold War with the current dangers and opportunities for the future.

It is clear even to those who do not share the views of the *Bulletin* that a number of the more challenging and credible ideas about dealing with the arms race, the huge defense budgets of the superpowers, and the meaning of the environmental, social, and political impact of the arms race have appeared in its pages. Thus, *Peace and Security: The Next Generation* provides a structure for thinking about peace, weapons, and security during the Cold War and its aftermath.

Secondly, although college and university students now coming of age as national and global citizens have had little direct experience of the Cold War, its residual problems and patterns will influence the political and economic agenda for years to come. Students need the information provided in this volume in order to assess future options for international security.

Finally, despite the end of the Cold War in geopolitical terms, many of the modes of thinking about nuclear weapons, military policy, and defense that characterized the Cold War have persisted. For many analysts, the intellectual location of strategic issues and nuclear weapons problems remains where it was a decade ago—solely in the realm of national security. Nuclear weapons are still widely accepted as part of the cost of preserving peace. Moreover, the decline in the real threat of nuclear war between the superpowers has not translated into a parallel trajectory for demobilization and decreased military spending.

The Organization of This Book

Consistent with Einstein's concern, we have designed this book to suggest new thinking about the problems of arms, security, and peace. In Part One, we present articles that address many of the challenges to peace and security that the arms race, militarism, and the Cold War at once reflected and generated. We begin in Chapter I with articles that survey the development and massive deployment of nuclear weapons during the Cold War. In Chapter II we examine various current aspects of nuclear proliferation and its political and economic contexts. Chapter III presents selections on the dark side of the security preserved by the arms race with some emphasis on its health and environmental effects. Finally in Chapter IV we address the chaotic aftermath of the collapse of the Soviet Union and the challenges it poses to peace and security.

Part Two of the book reflects various dimensions of a secure international order, one less dependent on massive weapons and more dependent on multilayered cooperation. Our consideration begins in Chapter V, with an analysis of two existing multilateral tools for preserving peace and security: the deployment of U.N. peacekeeping forces and the use of economic sanctions. In Chapter VI we explore the prospects for the abolition of nuclear weapons and reduced levels of military spending as a route to peace. In Chapter VII we conclude the volume with articles on the role of citizen movements and the concept of civil society in the emerging international order.

The Pedagogical Plan of the Book

Our goal in *Peace and Security: The Next Generation* is to provide a quality complement to most standard international relations textbooks and those used in American foreign policy courses. One essential way to attain this goal was to select some of the most engaging articles that have appeared in the *Bulletin* in the past few years. In addition we have created some special pedagogical features in this volume:

- At the beginning of the volume we have provided a chart matching key concepts of international relations and security studies with particular articles in the volume.
- Each chapter is introduced by an overview of the issues under investigation and a summary of the selected articles.
- At the end of each chapter we have provided a chart, table, or map that illustrates key parts of the chapter. We also provide a list of discussion questions related to the material.

The end of the twentieth century closes the curtain on an important era in human history, in which the major lessons were generated by the nuclear arms race. This volume provides an array of ideas and information that may set the stage for a new, more secure global experience based on a variety of humane arrangements, not on the threat of mass destruction.

Chicago, Illinois
January 1997

Acknowledgments

This volume had its beginnings in early 1995, in a series of discussions among the staff of the Educational Foundation for Nuclear Science, publisher of the *Bulletin of the Atomic Scientists*, and George Lopez, who serves on the magazine's editorial board. The challenge was to match the magazine's rich contemporary and historical resources to the needs and interests of faculty and students of international affairs.

Throughout the development of this volume, *Bulletin* editor Mike Moore and managing editor Linda Rothstein offered valuable suggestions on article selection and editing. As we began to envision specific outlines and chapters, we tested these with international affairs faculty through questionnaires, focus groups, and informal discussions. This important work was guided by the Educational Foundation's international programs director, Viktoria Tripolskaya-Mitlyng, and business manager Kathleen Weis. We were especially aided by detailed comments from Jeffrey Roberg of University of Wyoming, Debra Delaet of Drake University, Carter Whatley of Texas A&M, and others who offered comments through the publisher, Rowman & Littlefield.

The success of this volume, of course, lies in the outstanding quality of the work of some 40 authors, who agreed readily to the editing and use of their original work in this new context. None was more helpful than Joseph Rotblat, whose suggestions about chapter arrangement provided the final piece of a puzzle in assembling this collection. We are most grateful to all.

We offer hearty thanks to Jennifer Knerr of Rowman & Littlefield, who shepherded this project from its earliest stages with a rare combination of directive vision, editorial freedom, and discipline. This volume is a tribute to her creativity and professional guidance.

Finally, we thank the Samuel Rubin Foundation for a special grant to develop this book. We also appreciate the encouragement of the John D. and Catherine T. MacArthur Foundation, the W. Alton Jones Foundation, and others whose support of the Educational Foundation for Nuclear Science has made this venture possible.

George A. Lopez
Nancy J. Myers

Part One

Challenges to Peace and Security

Chapter I

The Burdens of History: Nuclear Weapons, the Cold War, and Massive Defense Spending

We take major technological advances and scientific breakthroughs for granted today. We do not find it strange, for example, to "surf" a "net" that we did not know existed five years ago on a tiny, powerful computer that was only a far-fetched dream ten years ago. Nor is it surprising that government-supported research and development had something to do with such advances. We regularly hear debates about the politics and economics of scientific research, whether in the space program or in the search for a cure for AIDS. Politicians do not argue about whether the government should spend money for such things, although they do debate amounts and priorities.

It has not always been this way. Our world is quite different from that of the late 1930s and early 1940s. In that era, society certainly recognized how it had benefited greatly from the inventions and scientific advances of the first part of the century. Yet at that time, the U.S. government had minimal involvement in major scientific research. A research project that would necessitate large-scale government investment was simply too large and complicated for most to imagine.

The very first such project was the effort to build the atomic bomb. The Manhattan Project, the code name given to this gigantic research and development project, involved an unprecedented alliance of science, government, and the military. And in both the United States during World War II and the Soviet Union soon after the end of the war, this alliance—with the important addition of industry—would become the cornerstone of the nuclear arms race and massive military spending.

The articles assembled in this first chapter provide complementary perspectives on how the nuclear arms race began, what sustained it, and how the dynamics of the Cold War had as much to do with the changing technologies of war as they did with ideological differences between the two superpowers. The essays illustrate that the arms race began, literally, one bomb at a time. In both countries it involved individuals of astounding scientific prowess who had, at the same time, profound aspirations for peace, security, and international cooperation. (In Chapter VII, Eugene Rabinowitch describes how some scientists organized to prevent further use of nuclear weapons.) Throughout this era, innovation, large-scale military spending, and the mutual hostility between the superpowers were woven together in the policy known as nuclear deterrence, the notion that neither power would launch an attack for fear that the other would destroy it in a counter-strike.

In this first selection of readings we present a glimpse of the U.S. and Soviet worlds that gave birth to the nuclear arms race, the Cold War, and large-scale military spending. To assist the reader just being introduced to the history, personalities, and trends of the nuclear era, we include a short fact-sheet, "The Nuclear FAQ," with answers to frequently asked questions about nuclear weapons. The two selections following it discuss some of the individuals noted in the FAQ.

As William Lanouette points out, the atomic bomb created by the Manhattan Project was the work of a number of physicists who attacked different dimensions of the puzzle of atomic energy. Lanouette focuses on one of the most intriguing personalities of the era, the Hungarian émigré Leo Szilard. Particularly noteworthy is the discussion of how the U.S. government, anxious to beat Hitler and the Germans in the presumed race to make the atomic bomb, forged an alliance among military officers, university researchers, and others to split the atom and then make the bomb.

On the Russian side, timing and motivation were different. David Holloway discusses how Stalin and his advisers were rather short-sighted about the importance of basic scientific research to the welfare of Soviet society. Yet, Stalin knew that serious, government-stimulated research was necessary for the Russians to develop an atomic bomb of their own. Holloway demonstrates how Soviet scientists were driven by patriotic concern. They did not want the United States to be the only global power with nuclear might.

Invention, modernization, and continued research cost money. Although the Manhattan Project was the first heavy U.S. investment in arms research, the pattern was quickly institutionalized and continued after the war. By 1959 President Dwight D. Eisenhower would question the wisdom of the development of this "military-industrial complex." Stephen Schwartz's article documents how and where the money of U.S. taxpayers—some four trillion dollars in all—supported the development of this complex, including the military structures that sustained it, throughout the Cold War and beyond.

Much of the information in the Schwartz article has been assembled only recently in an extensive study. No comparable studies yet exist of nuclear weapons spending in the Soviet Union, although the relative costs of the arms race in that society were even higher than in the United States. In fact, massive Soviet military spending helped break the back of that centrally planned economy by the late 1980s.

Many will continue to debate whether this was an appropriate price for avoiding World War III, or how much security was purchased with all those weapons and all that money. And so they should. It is clear, however, that these expenditures have altered the course of defense, science, economic development, and politics in ways that continue to the present day.

How close to war did the superpowers come during this nuclear competition? The *Bulletin of the Atomic Scientists* captured public attention with its symbolic clock, its hands poised close to midnight, which represented nuclear Armageddon. Over the years, scientists and editors used the clock to indicate the ebbs and flows of confrontation, détente, threatening advances, and significant agreements. In his article, current *Bulletin* editor Mike Moore surveys the Cold War as marked by the "Doomsday Clock." It is clear that throughout that period, science, invention, and political climate have combined to make the world either a more dangerous place or a safer one.

Today the clock continues to be an indicator of how the world is dealing—or not—with the challenge of building peace with security in the nuclear era. When the Cold War wound down in 1991, the *Bulletin*'s board of directors moved the clock back to an unprecedented 17 minutes before midnight. But in December 1995, they moved the hand forward again to 14 minutes before midnight. The world, they said, especially those powers possessing nuclear weapons, had not taken advantage of the opportunities presented by the end of the Cold War to increase global security by dismantling nuclear weapons and curtailing military spending.

The arms race chart at the end of the chapter shows the volume of nuclear weapons over the years and compares the U.S. and Soviet/Russian stockpiles. It does not show that the United States was far ahead of the Russians in both the sophistication of weapons and their deployment atop missiles, in submarines and ships, and on bombers. The chart also shows that, despite serious reductions by each country, more than 20,000 nuclear weapons still exist as the century draws to a close.

1.1 The Nuclear FAQ

BULLETIN EDITORS

Who Invented the Atomic Bomb?

The first nuclear device was detonated on July 16, 1945, at Alamogordo, New Mexico. The second and third bombs fell on Hiroshima and Nagasaki in Japan on August 6 and August 9, respectively. They were products of the "Manhattan Project," the $2 billion wartime effort by U.S. and British scientists and the U.S. Army to build a weapon that would "end the war." At its peak, about 160,000 people worked on the project in more than 25 sites across the United States. No one person can be completely credited with the invention of nuclear weapons. A few key figures:

In 1933, a Hungarian scientist working in England, Leo Szilard, first theorized that enormous amounts of energy could be released by a nuclear "chain reaction."

In December 1938, German scientists Otto Hahn, Fritz Strassmann, Lise Meitner, and Otto Frisch discovered nuclear fission in uranium, the heaviest natural element. The fissioning produced a tremendous release of energy; because a very small amount of uranium was involved, no one was endangered.

Szilard, who had come to America to conduct chain-reaction research, was convinced that Hitler would attempt to build an "atomic" bomb. He believed that the United States ought to do it first. However, Szilard lacked the clout to get a bomb project going. He and fellow Hungarians working in the States, Eugene Wigner and Edward Teller, persuaded Albert Einstein, the world's most famous scientist, to write a letter to President Franklin D. Roosevelt. Dated August 2, 1939, the letter said that it was conceivable that "extremely powerful bombs of a new type might be constructed." Einstein urged the government to help university scientists with their research into chain reactions. He also implied that Germany might be working on chain reactions.

In June 1942, the army took over the task of organizing all chain-reaction research into a full-blown bomb program, code-named the Manhattan Engineer District. Gen. Leslie R. Groves, the man who had just built the Pentagon, was in charge of the top-secret project.

Enrico Fermi, a Nobel Prize–winning émigré from Italy, presided over the first self-sustaining man-made nuclear chain reaction, which took place December 2, 1942, at the University of Chicago. University of California physicist Robert Oppenheimer became scientific director of Los Alamos National Laboratory.

How Do You Make an Atomic Bomb?

Nuclear weapons are not simple devices, contrary to frequent assertions that one could be built in a garage or basement.

To start, a potential weapons maker needs uranium. Lots of it. With that, the weapons maker can produce either uranium-235 or plutonium-239—the "fissile" isotopes that make a bomb go. Producing either in the quantities needed to make nuclear weapons is extraordinarily difficult and expensive. If a nation wants to mount a nuclear weapons program, it must be prepared to spend hundreds of millions of dollars, or even billions.

Once the fissile material is obtained, the remaining task is less difficult. A primitive nuclear weapon can be made by placing two "subcritical" masses of uranium into a gun-like tube and firing one mass into the other. The result: a supercritical mass, which produces an enormous explosion. The bomb that destroyed Hiroshima was such a weapon. Nevertheless, gun-type weapons are terribly inefficient, from a physics standpoint, and they require very large quantities of uranium-235 compared to an "implosion" bomb.

An implosion weapon consists of a small sphere of fissile material. The sphere—or "pit"—is generally plutonium-239, although uranium-235 can be used. The sphere is surrounded by high explosives arranged in such a way that it can be set off with amazing precision and symmetry, compressing the sphere evenly into a supercritical mass.

However a supercritical mass is achieved, neutrons emitted from the nuclei of either the uranium-235 or plutonium-239 are absorbed by the nuclei of similar atoms, splitting the nuclei and freeing yet more neutrons that penetrate yet more nuclei. The speed of this "chain reaction" is startling. Most of the energy of a nuclear weapon is produced within less than a microsecond (one millionth of a second).

This description is greatly simplified. In fact, modern nuclear weapons are extremely complex and embody neutron initiators to get the reaction going even more efficiently, and small amounts of tritium, an isotope of hydrogen, to "boost" the power of the weapon.

Which Countries Have Nuclear Bombs, and How Many Do They Have?

There are five "declared" nuclear weapon states: the United States, Russia, Britain, France, and China. In addition to the declared states, there are three "threshold" states: India, Israel, and Pakistan. Israel is widely assumed to have nuclear weapons; India and Pakistan are thought to have nuclear "capability." None of the threshold states have joined the Nuclear Nonproliferation Treaty.

In 1993, South Africa announced that it had secretly built six nuclear bombs, but had dismantled both the bombs and the weapons program.

In the 1980s, Iraq mounted an ambitious nuclear weapons program, but it was dismantled at U.N. direction after the Persian Gulf War.

North Korea was suspected of having a program, and it could possibly have several kilograms of weapon-grade plutonium stashed away. But the United States brokered a deal in 1994, in which North Korea would eventually shut down its inefficient and unsafeguarded nuclear reactors, to be replaced by safeguarded Western-style reactors.

Many experts believe that Iran wants nuclear weapons to counter Iraq's future ambitions, but most believe that Iran will not become a nuclear-weapon state for many years, if at all.

Here are the most recent estimates of how many warheads each nuclear power has for its armed forces:

Russia	12,000
United States	10,000
France	480
China	450
Britain	200

How Many Nuclear Tests Have There Been, and Where Did They Take Place?

As of January 30, 1996, there have been 2,044 nuclear tests. About one-fourth, or 528, have been conducted in the atmosphere; the rest were underground. In September 1996, the five declared nuclear powers signed a Comprehensive Test Ban Treaty, first proposed in 1954. Under the terms of the treaty, no further nuclear tests are to be conducted.

	Atmosphere	Underground	Total
United States	215	815	1,030
Russia	219	496	715
France	50	160	210
Britain	21	24	45
China	23	20	43
Grand Total*			2,044

*Please note that the grand total includes one underground test conducted by India on May 18, 1974.

1.2 The Man Behind the Bomb

William Lanouette

Leo Szilard, engineer, physicist, skeptic, and former student of Albert Einstein, was leading a weekly seminar at Berlin University in January 1933, but the worsening political situation made him edgy and uneasy. By month's end, he had two suitcases always packed so he could flee Berlin quickly. The Nazi-staged Reichstag fire was February 27, and when the "Jewish boycotts" started March 30, Szilard grabbed his suitcases and boarded a first-class wagon-lit on the night train to Vienna. First-class passengers were less likely to be interrogated, he said later, and he did not wish to discuss the small bundles of bank notes tucked in his bags.

From Vienna, working with the International Student Service, he began organizing a system to relocate "boycotted" faculty and students. Then from London, he continued a kind of one-man rescue operation, prodding academics, scientists, and funders into a network that would become the Academic Assistance Council (AAC) for refugee settlement. (The council still exists as the Society for the Protection of Science and Learning.)

In September 1933, Szilard was looking forward to hearing the nuclear pioneer Lord Ernest Rutherford, who was to deliver a public lecture at the British Association for the Advancement of Science. But on the morning of the lecture, Szilard awoke with a bad cold. He stayed home, but paged through the next day's London *Times* for the story, and read that Rutherford had said that "anyone who looked for a source of power in the transformation of the atoms was talking moonshine."

Leo Szilard found that paragraph "rather irritating because how can anyone know what someone else might invent?" Perhaps, thought Szilard, the famous Lord Rutherford was talking "moonshine."

Szilard later recalled that on Southampton Row, by his hotel, "as I was waiting for the light to change and as . . . I crossed the street, it suddenly occurred to me that if we could find an element which is split by neutrons and would emit two neutrons when it absorbed one neutron, such an element if assembled in sufficiently large mass, could sustain a nuclear chain reaction. I didn't see at the moment just how one would go about finding such an element or what experiments would be needed, but the idea never left me."

Suddenly an H.G. Wells novel he had read a year before had a grave new meaning. Atomic bombs were science fiction to Wells when he wrote *The World Set Free* in 1913, and they were frightful to contemplate when Szilard first read about them in 1932. But by the fall of 1933, Rutherford's challenge and Szilard's response were moving atomic bombs away from fiction to fact. Atomic bombs, and the chain reactions that would power them, became Szilard's "obsession."

"The thought did not come entirely out of the clear sky," he said later. But the ability to see both the mechanism and its fateful implications was Szilard's special insight.

First, if a neutron could strike an atom's nucleus with such force that it would emit two neutrons, then with each collision the freed neutrons might double in number. One neutron would release two, which would each strike an atomic nucleus to release four. These would each strike a nucleus releasing eight, then 16, 32, 64, 128, and so on. In millionths of a second, billions of atoms would split, and as they tore apart, the energy that held them together would be released.

Second, the amount of energy released could be huge, if Einstein had been correct in 1905, that energy would equal mass multiplied by the speed of light squared ($E = MC_2$). The number for mass is minute, but light speed is immense, and, at least in theory, the amount of energy latent in matter is also immense.

What allowed Szilard to put together the stray clues about a nuclear chain reaction, clues that other scientists working directly in atomic research had overlooked? No conclusive answer is possible, given the mysteries of Szilard's creative mind and the scant details he recalled. But this much is clear: While teaching discussion courses at the University of Berlin, Szilard had followed developments in nuclear physics by reading scientific journals. He also questioned anyone who knew about a subject, often with the precision of a prosecuting attorney. Unlike his colleagues in nuclear physics, Szilard was no experimentalist. Instead, he speculated haphazardly—intuitively—about the implications of other scholars' practical works, who moved each insight only as far as its next logical step and experiment. And Szilard had no other scientific or academic burdens and deadlines. No family. No close friends. No household chores. When he wanted to think about the chain reaction, he could. And did. For days and nights at a time.

He retreated to his room at the Imperial Hotel on Russell Square. Thinking. Scribbling calculations. Sketching hasty schematic patterns. For a week or more in the fall of 1933 he saw no one, broke his meditation only to eat meals sent up by room service, and each night fell exhausted into bed to sleep. Szilard soaked for hours at a time in his bathtub, dozed and daydreamed on his bed, and forced his impulsive vision into twin hypotheses. Not only did he see a chain-reaction mechanism to release the atom's energy; he also realized why a critical mass of material was necessary: Only with many atoms close together could the neutrons reach other nuclei and not escape.

Physics in the Bath

Having fled Nazi Germany that spring, Szilard also saw beyond his hypotheses to their political implications. Germany had quit the foundering League of Nations, and rhetoric at the Nazi party's rallies in Nuremberg was increasingly anti-Semitic and bellicose. No longer just a political aberration, the Nazi party was now the German state.

To save money, at the end of October Szilard rented a tiny room in the Strand Palace Hotel that had once been a maid's closet. His new room had no private bathtub, but shared one down the hall, and it was there that Szilard continued his brainstorming, usually beginning each day with a soak around nine to "dream about the possibilities" of nuclear physics.

"Are you all right, sir?" asked the maid, knocking on the bathroom door at about noon. Yes. Szilard was quite all right, thank you. He had just been thinking—in particular about beryllium, an extraordinarily light-weight steel-gray metal that he knew could give off neutrons. Other elements might also split and release extra neutrons, Szilard thought, and this possibility intrigued him.

Szilard tested his "nuclear chain reaction" idea with two physicists, George Paget Thomson at the Imperial College of Science, and Patrick M. S. Blackett in the physics department at the University of London. When neither evinced any enthusiasm for the concept, Szilard turned to British industry. His beliefs about the chain reaction as a commercial power source led him to file a patent on his concept on March 12, 1934.

He began to dream about the atom's commercial uses, perhaps replacing coal and oil as the world's industrial fuel; about its social implications, perhaps bringing abundant energy to developing countries now starved for water and minerals; and—unavoidably—about its potential as a weapon of mass destruction, perhaps giving Adolf Hitler "atomic bombs" to terrorize the world.

With no laboratory of his own to test his chain-reaction ideas, Szilard enlisted Fritz Lange and Lise Meitner in Berlin to arrange certain experiments into "the production of radioactive bodies." Szilard urged them to "take one after another all 70 elements [that he considered realistic possibilities] and bombard them with cathode rays [X-rays] and see if there is any activity by using a Geiger counter or the Wilson cloud chamber." In science at the time, such international collaboration was rare, although to Szilard it seemed the obvious thing to do.

Fellow Hungarian physicist Eugene Wigner and Szilard met in London early in the spring of 1934, and the two talked for hours about the chain-reaction patent. From Wigner, Szilard obtained new calculations and—most important to him—encouragement from a brilliant colleague whom he respected.

Throughout the spring and summer of 1934, Szilard repeatedly approached GE officials with vague requests that the company underwrite his research. Letters document Szilard's failure to communicate his intellectual excitement. He could scarcely focus on the chain-reaction concept himself, and during the six months he sought GE's help, he filed many "improvements" to his original patent: adding the names of elements likely to release neutrons, giving the size of the beryllium block to be used in experiments, proposing to mix the 70 likely elements together in order to isolate the radioactive ones systematically. While promising to tell the GE executives about the atom's new "industrial applications," Szilard would only describe his work on medical isotopes. The chain-reaction experiments, which Szilard called "the other more important issues," he kept secret, later assigning his patent to the British Admiralty.

Had Szilard been more practical and disciplined, his chain-reaction concept might have been confirmed first in the Bronx, at New York University's physics department, which in the summer of 1934 had invited him to work for a year as a research associate. At the time, Szilard's "Suggested Experiments for the Detection of Nuclear Chain Reactions and the Liberation of Nuclear Energy" were in a memo that proposed both commercial and university work. But Szilard was unsure if NYU's laboratories were properly equipped, and he miffed physicists there by demanding the right "to resign at the beginning of the term" if the equipment disappointed him.

Isotopes by Accident

Instead, Szilard talked his way into St. Bartholomew's Hospital research laboratory in 1934 where he and physicist Thomas Chalmers began studying beryllium—still Szilard's leading candidate for a nuclear chain reaction. They learned that beryllium emitted neutrons when exposed to radium's gamma rays, but nothing like a chain reaction followed.

Initially, Szilard aimed to bombard his elements with neutrons to create new compounds that would be medically useful. But a few days' work convinced Szilard and Chalmers that neutrons made some new compounds so unstable that their constantly changing states were difficult to control or calibrate. Faced with this unexpected result, many scientists would have abandoned the idea for some other project. But Szilard, in the words of his later colleague, physicist Maurice Goldhaber, "turned this apparent defeat around; it led him to a brilliantly simple method of isotope separation." They had just devised a way to isolate radioactive and non-radioactive forms of the same element.

Their results were published in *Nature* that September, giving researchers a simple method for separating isotopes. Known as the Szilard-Chalmers effect, this technique became widely used. With time they also recognized that slight amounts of the irradiated element sometimes remain in the original compound, so their method had medical uses after all—as "tracers" in the body.

Szilard was then alone among scientists in his belief that nuclear chain reactions might liberate the atom's energy; at the time, his friend and mentor Albert Einstein was touring the United States, where he told newspaper reporters that such efforts would be "fruitless."

Szilard spent the next three years traveling between England and the United States, trying to sell his ideas and existing on part-time research posts here and there. He crackled with ideas, but eschewed systematic research and managed, through a combination of imperiousness and impatience, to make himself unpopular with colleagues and possible benefactors. In 1935, Szilard's latest hosts at NYU seemed impatient with him, too. "They emphasize that I could leave here at twenty-four hours' notice if required," he wrote to a friend.

Meanwhile, in Italy, Enrico Fermi and his colleagues had, in early 1934, begun to bombard different elements with neutrons. The group discovered that a neutron added to an atom's nucleus did not always make it a heavier isotope of itself. It could sometimes become an isotope of a different element on the periodic table—indium (115), for instance, became tin (116)—a phenomenon that came to be called the Fermi effect. When Fermi heard about the Szilard-Chalmers work on isotope separation, he and his colleagues conducted similar experiments and rushed to publish their results.

In early 1938 the peripatetic Szilard settled, as much as he ever settled, at the King's Crown Hotel on 116th Street, just east of Columbia University in New York City. It would become a haven for much of the rest of his life.

Late in 1938, Enrico Fermi accepted a six-month teaching appointment at Columbia, shortly after receiving a Nobel Prize in physics for his work on neutron-induced nuclear reactions. So it was no surprise when Szilard ran into Fermi in the King's Crown lobby early in January 1939. The Fermi family arrived in New York City two days into the new year—Laura Fermi was Jewish, and fascist Italy had become dangerous. Szilard was at Columbia too, but he had no actual post. He poked around departments, including the lab of physicist Isidor Rabi, one of the world's great physicists. Szilard suggested many new experiments for Rabi and his colleagues. Rabi finally begged Szilard to stop. "You are reinventing the field," he said. "You have too many ideas. Please go away."

A Chorus of Confirmation

In late 1938, at the Kaiser Wilhelm Institute for Chemistry in Berlin, Otto Hahn and Fritz Strassmann bombarded uranium with neutrons and it broke into two parts—it "fissioned"—and in the process, released extra neutrons. Szilard had been right all along, although he had tested the wrong elements for his demonstration.

In January 1939, Niels Bohr, the Danish physicist and Nobel laureate arrived in New York, and he brought the news about successful fission at the Kaiser Wilhelm Institute. Lise Meitner and Otto Frisch had confirmed the process and cabled Bohr to tell him so.

Meanwhile, Fermi's colleagues, John Dunning and Herbert Anderson, duplicated the Meitner-Frisch experiment, confirmed uranium fission, and cabled the news to Fermi in Washington at a physics conference. Other physicists repeated the experiment and the *Washington Evening Star* carried a page-one article on the discovery. On February 5, the *New York Times* reported on the strange new results; the word was out.

The coming year would bring a frenzy of scientific and political activity. Indeed, during 1939, Szilard would almost single-handedly lead the physics community and the U.S. government to join forces in atomic energy research.

Now that fissioning had been achieved, multiple goals became urgent. There must be funding for nuclear research, there must be a program, and the science must be kept secret. But Frédéric Joliot-Curie and his colleagues in Paris published their fission findings in April 1939, in *Nature*. Szilard—who was already campaigning for secrecy—felt betrayed, although word was also leaking out in America.

Once Joliot's "Number of Neutrons Liberated in the Nuclear Fission of Uranium" appeared, several governments outside the United States took action. Britain's Ministry for the Coordination of Defence urged the Treasury and the Foreign Office to buy as much Belgian uranium as they could. In Russia, physicist Igor Tamm asked his students: "Do you know what this new discovery means? It means a bomb can be built that will destroy a city out to a radius of maybe ten kilometers." The French, too, realized where their research was leading.

By the summer of 1939, Siegfried Flügge at the Kaiser Wilhelm Institute in Berlin concluded that uranium fission might create an "exceedingly violent explosion." In September, Kurt Diebner, a German army physicist and ordnance expert, was made head of Germany's uranium project. It was the first country with a military unit to study the possible use of nuclear fission in weapons.

The First Design

Szilard's three-month appointment as guest researcher at Columbia ended that summer, but the quiet gave him time to think, and in four letters, he shared critical thoughts with Fermi. Those thoughts became the basis for the world's first successful chain reaction. Some 500 pounds of uranium had been borrowed from commercial suppliers. "I personally would be in favor of trying a large-scale experiment with a carbon-uranium-oxide mixture if we can get hold of the material," wrote Szilard on July 3. "I intend to plunge in the meantime into an experiment designed for measuring small capture cross sections for thermal [or slowed] neutrons."

Two days later, Szilard wrote to Fermi again, sending a corrected value for his neutron-density calculations. His mind swung between algebraic calculations and practical business. "It seems that it will be possible to get sufficiently pure carbon at a reasonable price," Szilard reported. The carbon and uranium should be "built up in layers" or stacked "in some canned form," making assembly and cleanup relatively easy.

Writing to Fermi "in a hurry" on July 11, Szilard was by now sure that he knew just how to create a chain reaction. Szilard later recalled, "I saw that by using a lattice of uranium spheres embedded in graphite, one would have a great advantage over using alternate layers of uranium and carbon." Szilard visited the National Carbon Company to ask about the purity of commercial graphite. His search for pure graphite was an important project, and it would have a decisive role in the near future.

Meanwhile, scientists in Berlin were beginning to publish their uranium discoveries, and the implications for great "energy liberation" were not lost on them. The news that German military expansion could easily overrun Belgium—its colony the Congo was the world's principal uranium source—moved Szilard and Wigner to new action. Should they warn the Belgian monarchs, and the U.S. government as well?

Einstein Joins In

Szilard and Wigner sought assistance from their former professor, Albert Einstein. On July 12, they met Einstein at his Long Island cottage. He had believed that the release of atomic energy was "only theoretically possible," but the conversation that day convinced him to act by writing his friends, the Belgian monarchs.

Although an avowed pacifist, he agreed to sound the alarm about atomic bombs, even if it proved to be a false one, in order to beat Nazi Germany to these awesome weapons. It took a scientist of Einstein's stature and personal conviction to take this risk, Szilard later noted. "The one thing most scientists are really afraid of is to make a fool of themselves," Szilard reflected. "Einstein was free from such a fear and this above all is what made his position unique on this occasion."

After several drafts, Szilard decided that Einstein's letter should not go to Belgium and the U.S. State Department, as they had first agreed, but directly to President Franklin Roosevelt. Then Szilard wondered, how long a letter did one write to the president, and, how did one deliver it? The final copy was dated August 2, 1939, and Alexander Sachs, a vice president of Wall Street's Lehman Corporation agreed to deliver it. He was not successful until October 11, and there was no real discussion until the next day.

Then Roosevelt was attentive, listened quietly, and interrupted. "Alex," he said, "what you are after is to see that the Nazis don't blow us up."

"Precisely," said Sachs.

Gen. Edwin M. "Pa" Watson, Roosevelt's secretary, telephoned Lyman J. Briggs, director of the National Bureau of Standards, then the government's principal physics laboratory, and asked him to chair an advisory committee on uranium. (Germany had done the same thing six months before.)

The plunge into bureaucracy began almost at once, in a first meeting with Bureau of Standards officials. Col. Keith Adamson, an army ordnance expert, thought Szilard's science was fantasy. At the scientists' ridiculously low $6,000 request for graphite and uranium, Adamson scoffed.

It generally takes two wars to develop a new weapon, he said, and besides, it was "morale," not research that led to victory. Shifting in his chair, the formal and ever-polite Wigner could not contain his impatience.

"Perhaps," he told Adamson in a high-pitched but steady voice, enunciating every syllable, "it would be better if we did away with the War Department and spread the military funds among the civilian population. That would raise a lot of morale."

"All right," Adamson snapped. "You'll get your money. We do have money for this purpose." Szilard was astounded by the offer. This promise of $6,000 would eventually swell to more than $2 billion before the first A-bomb was tested nearly six years later.

Inventing Secrecy

How to conduct nuclear research and keep the results secret? Leo Szilard brooded about privately funded research groups as he embarked on his many unsuccessful attempts to raise money for nuclear physics work.

Physicists Leo Szilard and Ernest O. Lawrence in 1935. They later became allies as they lobbied the United States to develop an atomic bomb. *American Institute of Physics*

Ironically, he said later, his bumbling helped keep Germany from winning World War II. If he had raised the money and painstakingly tested the 70 likely elements, Szilard concluded that he could have discovered as early as 1935 or 1936 that uranium released neutrons. And Germany, then planning for war, would be quick to acquire this knowledge for building an A-bomb. After the war, Szilard said jokingly that he, Enrico Fermi, and other physicists should receive the Nobel Peace Prize for not having conducted uranium experiments in the mid-1930s.

Beginning in 1936, Szilard pleaded with nuclear scientists outside Germany not to publish their neutron research. Such assertions, especially from an interloper in the field, were resented as being "unscientific." But Szilard kept pleading. He saw a war coming and feared that atomic weapons would determine the outcome.

"I am . . . in the uncomfortable position of a man who during a fire (either real or existent perhaps only in his imagination) tries to remove some jewelry which does not belong to him to some place of safety," he later admitted to Fermi's colleague Emilio Segré.

It was doubly ironic that, in November 1942, U.S. Army Security (and the increasingly testy and suspicious Gen. Leslie R. Groves) accused Szilard of not being secretive enough. Chicago's Manhattan Project leader, Arthur Holly Compton, told Groves about Szilard's early efforts to keep scientific secrets from Germany; Compton also reminded the general that Szilard had come to the United States on an immigrant visa from Germany before the Nazi takeover.

"I invented secrecy," Szilard said after World War II. From the moment in 1933 when he first conceived the nuclear chain reaction on Southampton Row, Szilard schemed to keep all related work a secret until 1945.

This article and the December 1992 *Bulletin* article from which it is excerpted are adapted from William Lanouette's *Genius in the Shadows: A Biography of Leo Szilard, The Man Behind the Bomb* (with Bela Silard), a Robert Stewart Book by Charles Scribner's Sons.

1.3 How Soviet Physicists Caught Up

David Holloway

At the end of World War II, Josef Stalin believed that postwar international relations would resemble those of the interwar period. Germany and Japan would rise from defeat. World capitalism would run into crisis, and sharp contradictions would emerge between the capitalist states. These contradictions would lead inevitably to a new world war.

Despite Stalin's grim long-range assessment, he saw no immediate danger. Atomic diplomacy by the United States seemed to him to be the greater threat. Atomic bombs were "meant to frighten those with weak nerves," he told Alexander Werth, the London *Sunday Times* correspondent in Moscow, in September 1946. If the Soviet Union were to compete in the tit-for-tat world of atomic diplomacy, it would have to have its own atomic bombs.

Although an atomic bomb program was launched during the war, its urgency and scope were greatly increased after Hiroshima. Lavrenti Beria, the most feared man in the Soviet Union after Stalin, would direct it. Massive secret facilities eventually would be built in many locations. But the heart of the program was to be Igor Kurchatov's Laboratory No. 2, located on the outskirts of Moscow, and its offspring, Arzamas-16.

Klaus Fuchs, the Soviet spy at Los Alamos, had provided a detailed description of the plutonium implosion bomb in June 1945. But neither Kurchatov nor Yuli Khariton, Kurchatov's closest associate, could be sure that Fuchs's information was completely reliable. Khariton and his team were assigned the task of verifying everything.

Investigating the implosion method called for repeated experiments with high explosives, which could not be done at Laboratory No. 2 because of its proximity to the city. Kurchatov therefore decided to set up a branch of the laboratory in an isolated area, where work on the design and development of the bomb could take place in total secrecy. Khariton would be the scientific director of the new laboratory.

By the spring of 1946, a site near the settlement of Sarov, about 400 kilometers east of Moscow, was chosen. It was on the edge of a large forest preserve, which provided room for expansion; and it was a beautiful spot. The town—or rather the carefully guarded "zone," which included the town and the research and development establishments—became known as Arzamas-16, after the city of Arzamas, 60 kilometers to the north. But it was sometimes known as the the "Volga office"—as well as "Los Arzamas."

The physicist Lev Altshuler moved to Arzamas-16 in December 1946: "On our arrival at the place we caught sight of the monastery churches and farmsteads, the forest, the Finnish houses nestling in the woods, the small engineering plant, and the inevitable companions of that period—the 'zones' [prison camps] populated by representatives of all the regions of the country, all the nationalities. . . . The columns of prisoners passing through the settlement in the morning on their way to work and returning to the zones in the evening were a reality that hit you in the eyes. Lermontov's lines came to mind, about 'a land of slaves, a land of masters.' "

Arzamas-16 was like paradise compared to half-starved Moscow, in Altshuler's view. Scientists and engineers "lived very well. Leading researchers were paid a very large salary for those times. Our families experienced no needs. And the supply of food and goods was quite different. So that all material questions were removed." Lazar Kaganovich, a member of the Politburo, complained in 1953 that the atomic cities were like "health resorts."

These conditions reflected Stalin's belief that Soviet scientists, if they were given the "proper help," would be able to overtake the achievements of foreign science. Privileged though they were, however, the nuclear scientists were surrounded by great secrecy and tight security. They could not talk to unauthorized people about their work, and nothing was published about the Soviet effort to build the atomic bomb.

"Beria's People Were Everywhere"

Within the project, secrecy was very strictly maintained. Reports were written by hand because typists were not trusted. If documents were typed—as, for example, the technical requirements for the first atomic bomb—the key words were written in by hand. Code words were used instead of scientific terms in secret reports and laboratory notes; neutrons, for example, were called "zero points." Information was strictly compartmentalized.

During Andrei Sakharov's first visit to Arzamas-16 in 1949, Iakov Zeldovich told him, "There are secrets everywhere, and the less you know that doesn't concern you, the better off you'll be. Khariton has taken on the burden of knowing it all." The need for secrecy was so deeply instilled that some people had recurrent nightmares about breaching security regulations, and at least one suicide was attributed to anxiety about misfiled documents.

Secrecy was reinforced by rigid security. Arzamas-16 was cut off from the outside world. A zone of about 250 square kilometers was surrounded by barbed wire and guards, and it was difficult in the early years to obtain permission to leave. Khariton was accompanied wherever he went by a bodyguard. (Kurchatov and Zeldovich—and later, Sakharov—also had bodyguards.)

The security services had informers in the project, and encouraged denunciations. "Beria's people were everywhere," Khariton later remarked. Once, when Khariton visited Chelyabinsk-40 to see how work on the plutonium production reactor was progressing, he attended a dinner to mark Igor Kurchatov's birthday. After the dinner—and a few drinks—Beria's representative said to Khariton: "Yuli Borisovich, if only you knew how much they write against you." Although he added, "But I don't believe them," the point had been made: there were plenty of accusations for Beria to use if he wanted to.

As the date of the first atomic bomb test grew near, the political climate in the country became increasingly oppressive. In August 1948 Trofim Lysenko achieved his final victory over the geneticists, and in January 1949 a campaign was launched against "cosmopolitans"—a euphemism for Jews.

The number of denunciations increased. In Anatoli Aleksandrov's words, "A great number of 'inventors,' including scientists, were constantly trying to find mistakes, writing their 'observations' on this score, and their number increased, the closer we came to completing the task." Such "observations" would not have been confined to technical matters. Mistaken technical choices were frequently explained in those days as the consequence of political error or disloyalty.

Kurchatov was open to the accusation that he had surrounded himself with colleagues who were Jewish, or who admired Western science too much, or had strong links with the West. Khariton was particularly vulnerable: he was Jewish, and he had spent two years in Cambridge where he had worked closely with James Chadwick, a key figure in the British nuclear project. Besides, both of his parents had left Soviet Russia. His father had been expelled by the Soviet authorities and had worked in Riga as a journalist until 1940, when the Red Army occupied Latvia. He was arrested by the NKVD and was sent to the camps or shot. Khariton's mother lived with her second husband in Germany in the 1920s; later she moved to Palestine.

Stalin and Beria wanted the atomic bomb as soon as possible, and they had to rely on Kurchatov and his colleagues to make it for them. They gave the scientists massive resources and privileged living conditions. Yet they harbored a nagging suspicion of the nuclear scientists. After all, if Soviet geneticists and plant breeders had tried to undermine Soviet agricultural policy as Lysenko said, might not the physicists sabotage nuclear policy?

Aleksandrov, who was the scientific director of the chemical separation plant at Chelyabinsk-40 in 1949, was coating the plutonium hemispheres with nickel when a group that included party official Mikhail G. Pervukhin, several generals, and the plant director, arrived. "They asked what I was doing," writes Aleksandrov:

"I explained, and then they asked a strange question: 'Why do you think it is plutonium?' I said that I knew the whole technical process for obtaining it and was therefore sure that it was plutonium and could not be anything else. 'But why are you sure that some piece of iron hasn't been substituted for it?' I held up a piece to the alpha-counter, and it began to crackle at once. 'Look,' I said, 'it's alpha-active.' 'But perhaps it has just been rubbed with plutonium on the outside and that is why it crackles,' said someone. I grew angry, took that piece and held it out to them: 'Feel it, it's hot!' One of them said that it did not take long to heat a piece of iron. Then I responded that he could sit and look till morning and check whether the plutonium remained hot. But I would go to bed. This apparently convinced them, and they went away."

Such episodes, according to Aleksandrov, were not unusual. Vasili Emelyanov recounts a similar incident. He once showed People's Commissar Avraami Zavenyagin a regulus of plutonium before the atomic test. "Are you sure that's plutonium?" Zavenyagin asked, looking at Emelyanov with fear. "Perhaps," he added anxiously, "it's something else, not plutonium."

"An Important Patriotic Duty"

The scientists were aware that failure would cost them dear, and they knew that Beria had selected understudies to take over the leading positions in case of failure. Terror was a key element in Beria's style of management as well as a pervasive factor in the Stalinist regime. But the scientists were not motivated by fear. Those who took part in the project believed that the Soviet Union needed its own bomb in order to defend itself, and they welcomed the challenge of proving the worth of Soviet science by building a Soviet bomb as quickly as possible.

According to Altshuler, "Our consent [to work on the bomb] was determined, first, by the fact that we were promised much better conditions for research and second, by an inner feeling that our confrontation with a very powerful opponent had not ended with the defeat of Fascist Germany. The feeling of defenselessness increased particularly after Hiroshima and Nagasaki. For all who realized the realities of the new atomic era, the creation of our own atomic weapons, the restoration of equilibrium became a categorical imperative."

Victor Adamsky, who worked in the theoretical department at Arzamas-16 in the late 1940s, has written that "all scientists held the conviction—and it now seems right for that time—that the state needed to possess atomic weapons, that one could not allow one country, especially the United States, to hold a monopoly on this weapon. To the consciousness of performing a most important patriotic duty was added the purely professional satisfaction and pride from work on a splendid task in physics—and not only in physics. Therefore we worked with enthusiasm, without taking account of time, selflessly."

Andrei Sakharov, who began work on thermonuclear weapons in 1948 and moved to Arzamas-16 in 1950, has said that "we (and here I speak not only in my own behalf, for in such cases moral principles are formulated in a collective psychological way) believed that our work was absolutely necessary as a means of achieving a balance in the world."

In spite of the presence of informers and the threat of repression, a spirit of cooperation and friendship existed at Arzamas-16. "It was necessary to secure the defense of the country," Khariton later said. "In the collective of scientists there was quiet and intense work. Close cohesion and friendship. . . . Although, of course, we had our sons of bitches." V. A. Tsukerman and Z. M. Azarkh write that "in the first, most romantic years of our work in the institute a wonderful atmosphere of good will and support was created around the research. We worked selflessly, with great enthusiasm and the mobilization of all our spiritual and physical forces."

"If You Want Peace, Prepare for War"

It is striking how the apparatus of the police state fused with the physics community to build the bomb. In the 1930s the physics community had enjoyed an unusual measure of intellectual autonomy, which was sustained by a set of social relationships. That autonomy was not destroyed by the creation of the nuclear project. It continued to exist within the administrative system that was set up to manage the project.

Before the war the nuclear scientists had paid close attention to research being done abroad and had striven to show themselves as good as their foreign colleagues. The American atomic bomb presented a formidable challenge to Soviet scientists and engineers, who now sought to prove their worth in this new competition. The fact that the Americans had already used the bomb may have lessened the sense of responsibility that Soviet scientists felt in making this destructive weapon. They were responding to the American challenge, not initiating the atomic competition. They believed the Soviet Union needed its own atomic bomb in response.

Discussion of moral qualms would of course have been dangerous; open opposition to the project, fatal. Terror encouraged people to put such questions aside and immerse themselves in their work. But the scientists did not have to work on the bomb; they could refuse to join the project, and some did, including Sakharov before 1948.

In his memoirs, Nikolai Dollezhal, the chief designer of the first reactor, discusses his own thoughts in 1946 when Kurchatov first drew him into the project. Dollezhal had regarded the bombing of Hiroshima as a "repulsive act of cynical antihumanism." If that was so, did the Soviet Union have the right to make and use the same weapon? His answer was yes, on two grounds:

First, making the weapon was not the same as using it against peaceful cities. The military and political leadership would choose the targets. And although Dollezhal knew something of the terrible purge of 1947, "Those affairs were internal—domestic, so to speak." The Soviet Union, as far as he knew, did not contravene the laws of war: unlike the Germans, they had not destroyed the noncombatant population; unlike the Allies, they had not carpet-bombed German cities.

Dollezhal's second argument was that possession of the bomb did not mean it would be used. All the main combatants in the war had had chemical weapons, but no one had employed them. That was because they feared retaliation. The Soviet Union needed all the means of attack possessed by the aggressor if it wanted to prevent such weapons from being used.

After the war, writes Dollezhal, cracks appeared in the foundation of the wartime alliance with the United States. Things that had not been spoken of in the critical moments of the war were now brought to light with merciless clarity: "The two systems were completely alien to each other ideologically—more than that, they were antagonistic, and the political trust generated by the wartime alliance was not long-lived or solid." The United States might declare the Soviet Union an enemy at any time in the future:

"The security of the country and patriotic duty demanded that we create the atomic bomb. And these were not mere words. This was objective reality. Who would forgive the leadership of the country if it began to create the weapons only after the enemy had decided to attack? The ancients had a point when they coined the phrase 'If you want peace, prepare for war.' "

From this reasoning Dollezhal drew the conclusion that work on the bomb was morally justified.

The attitude of Soviet scientists was shaped, finally, by the war against Nazi Germany. The participants in the atomic project had either fought in the war or contributed to the war effort by designing or producing weapons. They had taken part in a bitter and destructive war to defend the Soviet Union and, whatever they may have thought of Stalin's regime or his policies, they believed that their cause was just.

The war was hardly over before the atomic bomb posed a potential new threat. They had taken up arms against the German invader, and now they worked to provide their country with its own atomic bomb. The atomic project was in some psychological sense a continuation of the war with Germany.

This is adapted from an article in the November/December 1994 *Bulletin*, which in turn was adapted from *Stalin and the Bomb*, Yale University Press.

1.4 Four Trillion Dollars and Counting

The U.S. Nuclear Weapons Cost Study Project

STEPHEN I. SCHWARTZ, DIRECTOR

In the fall of 1951, Sen. Brien McMahon of Connecticut surveyed a world in which the Soviet Union and the United States had become adversaries. Crises in Europe, Greece, Iran, China, and now Korea suggested that the Russians were intent on global expansion. To meet the threat, U.S. political leaders were prepared to spend enormous sums on conventional weapons. McMahon believed that would put the country on a road with no good exit.

"At the rate we are moving," he told the Senate on September 18, "I can see ahead only two ultimate destinations: military safety at the price of economic disaster or economic safety at the price of military disaster."

But there was a better way. He had come, he said, to offer the American people "a message of hope," to outline a preparedness strategy that would bring the United States "peace power at bearable cost."

"Some people," he explained, "used to claim that A-bombs numbered in thousands or tens of thousands were beyond our reach. They insisted that the atomic weapon, although fearful and staggering, could never be decisive in winning a war or preventing it.

"I am here to report to the Senate and to the American people that the atomic bottlenecks are being broken. The day is coming when the quantity of atomic weapons we are capable of making could be sufficient, beyond any question, to serve as the paramount instrument of victory. There is virtually no limit and no limiting factor upon the number of A-bombs which the United States can manufacture, given time and given a decision to proceed all out."

And best of all, he noted, atomic bombs were inexpensive.

"If we mass produce this weapon, as we can, I solemnly say to you that the cost of a single atomic bomb will become less than the cost of a single tank. . . ."

Whatever can be said about the illusions and delusions involved in the notion of building national security on the foundation of nuclear weapons—and the *Bulletin* has said plenty over the past 50 years about that—it did not come cheaply.

Since the government first began work on the atomic bomb in 1940, the U.S. nuclear arsenal has cost at least $4 trillion in 1996 dollars—or approximately three times more, in 1996 dollars, than was spent on procurement for all of World War II. (Except where noted, all amounts are in 1996 dollars.)

This figure includes most, but not all, of the direct, indirect, and overhead costs required to develop, produce, deploy, operate, support, and control U.S. nuclear forces over the past 50 years. An additional $500 billion to $1 trillion could be added to this total once all known costs, especially those related to operating and maintaining the arsenal, are documented and analyzed. By way of comparison, the total figure will likely be approximately equal to the $5 trillion national debt.

In short, one-quarter to one-third of all military spending since World War II has been devoted to nuclear weapons and their infrastructure—far more than the government has ever officially acknowledged.

Four trillion dollars is not chump change. It is the amount of all outstanding mortgages on all buildings and homes in the United States. It is roughly equal to the amount Americans spend every year on everything. A stack of one million one-dollar bills would be eight-tenths of a mile high. A stack of four trillion one-dollar bills would reach the moon, encircle it, and start part way back.

Assembling the Pieces

This study is the first systematic effort to catalog the comprehensive cost of the U.S. nuclear weapons program, from its inception in 1940 to the present.

Earlier studies, government-funded and private, have examined portions of the program, usually focusing on a particular weapons system or set of programs. But few have tried to tally the five-decades total.

Our calculations include the costs borne by U.S. taxpayers to develop, field, and maintain the nuclear arsenal and to defend against attacks from nuclear-armed adversaries.

Defending against nuclear attack, for example, incurs huge costs. Although it is no longer intact, from the 1950s through the mid-1980s, the U.S. maintained an enormous air defense network with hundreds of radars and thousands of aircraft and anti-aircraft missiles, many armed with nuclear weapons.

In addition, ballistic missile defenses were widely researched, and a limited antiballistic missile (ABM) system was briefly deployed in North Dakota from 1975 to 1976. President Ronald Reagan's call for a Strategic Defense Initiative (SDI) in March 1983 accelerated spending for space-based defenses but produced no deployable systems.

Planning for civil defense was championed by many, but funding in this area was relatively modest. After a flurry of interest in bomb shelters in the early 1960s, interest waned and funding dropped after the Cuban missile crisis. In contrast, efforts to protect federal government officials during and after a nuclear war received substantial funding, which continues today.

With the collapse of the Soviet Union and the end of the Cold War, the United States began to concentrate on dismantling delivery vehicles and disassembling and storing warheads and bombs. Once the government decides how to dispose of hundreds of tons of uranium and plutonium now headed for storage, costs will increase.

While it is often said that the Cold War was won without a shot being fired, the nuclear weapons program nevertheless inflicted casualties, often on the very people the government sought to protect. A combination of secrecy, lax enforcement, neglect, and an overriding emphasis on production at all costs created an unprecedented legacy of toxic and radioactive pollution at dozens of sites and thousands of facilities around the country. It will take decades and cost hundreds of billions of dollars to clean up the mess at U.S. nuclear weapons production facilities—where it can be cleaned up at all.

Indifference also led to American citizens being needlessly exposed to high levels of radiation. Those most at risk were uranium miners and workers at reactors and processing buildings and facilities where uranium and plutonium components were fabricated, especially from the 1940s through the early 1960s. Also exposed were a quarter of a million military personnel who took part in "atomic battlefield" exercises in the Pacific and at the Nevada Test Site.

From 1951 to 1963, 100 nuclear bombs were detonated on or above the desert floor in Nevada. Fallout clouds drifted largely eastward, often depositing radioactive particles as far away as Canada and the East Coast. Among the hardest hit were inhabitants of northern Nevada and Utah. Although the Atomic Energy Commission (AEC) knew that fallout was dangerous, the agency consistently misled "downwinders," assuring them that they were safe, even as it undertook secret studies of fallout in milk, water, and foodstuffs to better track the path of the clouds. The AEC also engaged in self-described "body-snatching" to study fallout's effects on exposed people.

Also affected were thousands of Marshall Islanders, whose atolls the United States used to test 67 nuclear bombs from 1946 until 1958. In the process, their way of life was destroyed and several islands, including Bikini, were left uninhabitable. A 1952 test of the first thermonuclear or H-bomb vaporized the island of Elugelab.

Finally, there are the often overlooked managerial burdens, such as export controls to prevent nuclear proliferation, U.S. payments to the International Atomic Energy Agency (IAEA), arms control negotiation and implementation, and the cost of executive branch and congressional oversight of a multitude of nuclear weapons activities. No fewer than 25 cabinet and sub-cabinet agencies oversee the nuclear weapons program. In Congress, nearly 30 committees and subcommittees allocate funds, write laws and, to varying degrees, oversee the performance of the nuclear enterprise. Perhaps the largest of all management costs, and one of the hardest to pin down, is the cost of the elaborate secrecy and security measures used to prevent the dissemination of information about nuclear weapons and to protect the weapons themselves. These measures have direct and indirect costs, many of which may be immune to measurement in terms of dollars and cents.

The First Bombs

Created during World War II and used twice against Japan, nuclear weapons soon became a major component of U.S. national security policy. The enormous infrastructure built by the Army Corps of Engineers' Manhattan Engineer District—which included uranium enrichment plants, reactors, chemical separation facilities, and laboratories—cost more than $25 billion through December 1946. It quickly formed the basis for the weapons production complex of the Cold War.

The Manhattan Engineer District laid claim to huge areas of land in Washington State, Tennessee, and New Mexico, uprooting established communities and creating new ones for tens of thousands of workers. The White

House gave the project a blank check and its leaders actively discouraged Congress from asking what the money was for.

The Manhattan Project's total cost through August 1945 was $20 billion, or about $6.7 billion each for the Trinity device and the two bombs, "Little Boy" and "Fat Man," which were dropped on Hiroshima and Nagasaki, respectively. Nearly three-quarters of this amount was spent on processing or enriching uranium and producing plutonium at Oak Ridge, Tennessee, and Hanford, Washington.

Senior government officials optimistically estimated in May 1942 that it would cost about $148 million (about $1.7 billion in adjusted dollars) to construct and operate the facilities necessary to build "a few atomic bombs by July 1, 1944, and about twice as many each year thereafter." By mid-December 1942, that figure had more than doubled, to $4.6 billion in adjusted dollars. Congress was not informed.

Revving Up for Production

The nuclear weapons production complex consists of 19 sites occupying more than 3,900 square miles. Historically, the complex has involved several hundred facilities, most of them relatively small, as well as more than 900 uranium mines and mills. The complex includes 14 production reactors (in Washington and South Carolina), eight separation and reprocessing plants, and 239 underground storage tanks for high-level waste (in Washington, Idaho, and South Carolina). Poor record-keeping practices by the AEC and the Energy Department prevent a tabulation of total expenditures by site.

From 1951 to 1955, the AEC obligated $34 billion to refurbish and enlarge weapons complex facilities, principally to expand production of plutonium, highly enriched uranium, and other nuclear materials. In 1953, the AEC obligated $19 billion, only a little less than the entire Manhattan Project had cost.

The size of the weapons production complex remained more or less stable from the mid-1960s until the early 1980s, although costs increased by $14 billion under a Reagan administration plan to produce thousands of new weapons. In 1986, following the Chernobyl disaster, both citizens and public officials began to raise questions about safety—for example, the Hanford N-reactor was dangerously similar to the Chernobyl reactor. These concerns reached a peak in 1988 and 1989, and the complex largely ground to a halt as the Cold War ended.

The last new nuclear weapon was assembled at the Pantex Plant in Amarillo, Texas, in 1990. U.S. military production reactors for plutonium and tritium have not operated since mid-1988, and the last U.S. nuclear test was conducted in 1992.

Ironically, production costs increased as the size of the stockpile declined. In 1967, the arsenal peaked at 32,500 weapons and production spending, not including materials production, was $3.7 billion. Just two years later, the arsenal had declined to an estimated 26,600 weapons, but spending had reached $4.8 billion.

As a result of the Reagan administration's renewed emphasis on nuclear weapons, annual spending on bomb and warhead research, development, and production reached an all-time high of $5.8 billion in 1985, but the size of the arsenal had dropped to 23,500 weapons. By 1995, with some 14,000 warheads in the active and inactive stockpile, annual spending for research, development, testing, and production totaled $3.4 billion—higher in real terms than 20 years ago, when the arsenal was nearly twice as large and bombs were still being built.

Delivering the Goods

Over the past 50 years, the United States has purchased and fielded 12 distinct types of nuclear-capable bomber aircraft. Excluding Air Force B-29s—most of which were built and used as conventional bombers during World War II—the United States built nearly 4,700 nuclear bombers at a cost of more than $225 billion. About 67,500 nuclear-tipped missiles of 50 types were procured, at a cost of about $371 billion. These included approximately 6,135 ballistic missiles—3,160 intercontinental ballistic missiles (ICBMs) and 2,975 sea-launched ballistic missiles (SLBMs).

The most expensive nuclear bomber is the relatively new "Stealth" or B-2A *Spirit*, which, including research and development, cost $2.7 billion per plane. The most expensive ballistic missile is the MX or Peacekeeper, at $207 million a copy. The least expensive was the Minuteman missile, at $33–37 million each. The Trident II SLBM, the only ballistic missile still in production, costs $61 million a copy.

Over the years, about 116 weapon systems were built to deliver a total of about 70,000 warheads and bombs. The air force had 42 types of nuclear weapons, the navy and marines, 34, and the army, 21. Twenty-five others were developed but canceled before production began.

Officials made it seem that they knew exactly what number of bombers or missiles would deter the Soviet Union, but in fact, decisions about the size or mix of the arsenal were often arbitrary. The size of a weapons program was ultimately determined by factors that included congressional and military in-fighting, erroneous or politicized intelligence estimates, interservice—and occasionally intraservice—rivalry, jobs in congressional districts, corporate lobbying, and cycles of technological obsolescence and innovation, to name but a few. The triad of bombers and air- and sea-based missiles is often touted as a pragmatic and time-tested means of deterring an adversary, but in reality the triad exists largely because each service wanted a "piece of the action" in both the budgetary and mission-oriented sense.

Launch on Warning

The most important element of the nuclear weapons establishment is command, control, communications, and intelligence (C^3I). It encompasses not only the equipment, personnel, and procedures needed to enable the use of nuclear weapons, but also the equipment and personnel needed to prevent their unauthorized use.

C^3I is the brain and nerve center of U.S. nuclear forces; without it they would be useless. Ironically, this critical part of the nuclear infrastructure has never received the financial or institutional support needed to effectively carry out its mission.

Building bombs and delivery vehicles was only the beginning of the effort to create a credible nuclear threat. The commitment to base national security on nuclear weapons opened a Pandora's box of complex and expensive operational burdens. The United States needed spy systems capable of gauging the strength of enemy nuclear forces and providing precise targeting data, warning systems capable of detecting an imminent enemy attack, command systems capable of protecting the president and other key nuclear decision-makers during wartime, communications networks that could transmit the "go-code" to dispersed nuclear forces, and defensive systems capable of protecting U.S. military forces and the general population from destruction by incoming enemy forces.

These requirements were coupled with another key goal: preventing false alarms or unauthorized acts that might lead to accidental war. The burden of safety grew heavier during the 1960s as the United States and the Soviet Union put vast numbers of missiles on hair-trigger "use-'em-or-lose-'em" alert. Thousands of warheads stood ready for launch on a moment's notice; the missiles carrying them could fly half way around the globe in less than 30 minutes.

Despite impressive efforts to make it safe, a posture of rapid reaction was inherently dangerous. The speed of delivery systems put pressure on military

"Okay, I shouldn't have fired the missile, but hey! The keys were in the ignition!" *Frank Cotham*

and civilian commanders to make fateful decisions in minutes, and to do so on the basis of incomplete intelligence and warning.

Only some of command and control's demanding goals could be met. Successes included the development of spy satellites, at a cost of some $270 billion, to identify the locations of all Soviet missile launch pads, bomber bases, and submarine pens, as well as most other major military installations. In the mid-1960s, satellites managed by the National Reconnaissance Office provided timely intelligence on the strength of enemy nuclear forces, debunking fears of a "missile gap." As satellites became more sophisticated, they employed new types of sensors—including cloud-piercing radar and the capacity to eavesdrop on Soviet military communications.

Satellites also created new opportunities for strategic arms control. They enabled the United States to enter into and verify agreements meant to slow the strategic arms race and codify deterrence.

Despite the end of the Cold War, the United States still uses its strategic forces to target 2,500 sites in the former Soviet Union. Another 800 targets in China are covered by U.S. "strategic reserve forces." A small but growing number of targets in Iran, Iraq, North Korea, Syria, and Libya are being added to the target list. The strategic reserve could be prepared within hours to launch against Third World targets or elsewhere. Plans to use strategic forces in regional contingencies are known as "Limited Attack Options" and "Selected Attack Options."

U.S. strategic planners assumed that a Soviet nuclear attack could come as a complete surprise. This "bolt-from-the-blue" scenario drove the United States to develop stealthy submarines and hardened underground silos that could withstand an attack and retaliate. But it was more difficult to design command posts and communications networks that might survive.

Throughout the Cold War, classified studies consistently showed that a surprise attack could decapitate the U.S. command system and destroy the communications links used to send the go-code to retaliatory forces. Top political leaders, senior military commanders, and their fixed and mobile command posts and communications links were all vulnerable to sudden destruction by a few tons of Soviet weapons.

The historical significance of this finding is hard to overstate. It led the United States to depend heavily on "launch on warning"—authorizing and implementing the launch of forces immediately after detecting the launch of enemy missiles. It also led to the delegation of launch authority to senior military commanders in the nuclear chain of command. This increased the risk of unauthorized launch or a launch on false warning.

One major conclusion from this history emerges: the United States never achieved a safe and stable nuclear posture. The classic notion of stable deterrence was that neither adversary would initiate a nuclear attack as long as there was a credible threat of retaliation. Virtually all policy-makers embraced this idea—but its feasibility was another matter.

The defense establishments concluded that riding out an attack and then retaliating was not practical for a variety of reasons, including the inherent vulnerability of command and control. The United States underinvested in command protection and compensated with operational shortcuts based on launch-on-warning.

The Soviets also eventually gravitated to a quick-launch policy, after first investing hundreds of billions of dollars more than the United States in protecting command and control. They had an extensive complex of deep underground command posts, a nationwide grid of radio stations, and enormously redundant back-up nuclear control posts. The Soviet expenditure in these areas no doubt exceeded that of the United States by a factor of three or more—yet they too failed to achieve the desired result. Rapid reaction became the hallmark of both U.S. and Soviet nuclear posture.

All of this occurred without public debate or consent. Provocative and risky deterrent practices, ranging from strategic targeting to launch-on-warning to pre-delegation, were developed with little oversight. Civilian and military officials failed to supervise strategic planning or deal decisively with deficiencies in the safety and performance of nuclear command, control, communications, and intelligence systems. As Robert Dahl, the eminent political scientist, put it: "No decisions can be more fateful for Americans, and for the world, than decisions about nuclear weapons. Yet these decisions have largely escaped the control of the democratic process."

Retirement Pay

Until the early 1990s, the costs of retiring and dismantling nuclear warheads and bombs were largely subsumed under ongoing production costs. Fissile materials (plutonium 239 and highly enriched uranium) were routinely recycled into new weapons. Now, retirement costs are increasing as arms reduction agreements and unilateral measures shrink the size of the arsenal. The stockpile is expected to decline from an estimated 21,000 warheads and bombs in 1990 to around 7,500 warheads (3,500 strategic warheads, 2,500 "hedge" or inactive reserve, and 950 non-strategic with about 550 "spares") by 2003.

Between 1980 and April 1994, over 18,000 warheads and bombs were dismantled at the Pantex Plant near Amarillo, Texas. The current rate of dismantlement is about 1,400 warheads a year. More than 8,900 pits (plutonium cores from bombs and warheads) are stored in Pantex's munitions bunkers, known as "igloos." Highly enriched uranium components ("secondaries") are shipped to the Y-12 Plant at the Oak Ridge Reservation in Tennessee for additional processing and storage. Since production halted in mid-1990, Pantex's and Y-12's expenditures for these activities have totaled nearly $4 billion.

It is not yet possible to estimate with precision the ultimate costs of storage, processing for disposal, and final disposal of surplus fissile materials. An estimate based on current assumptions about storage, processing, and repository disposal of surplus plutonium, is about $15 billion. The cost of disposing of highly enriched uranium is especially difficult to determine. In theory, this material has a positive market value as power-reactor fuel, but the actual costs of disposition will depend on policies relating to the use of military fissile materials by the commercial uranium industry.

Between 1988 and 1995, the On-Site Inspection Agency (OSIA) has spent about $441 million verifying various arms control and reduction measures, including the Intermediate Nuclear Forces Treaty, START I, and the Partial Test Ban Treaty. These activities will continue as long as the treaties remain in force.

Significant retirement costs that have yet to be tallied include the decommissioning of more than 80 naval reactors and submarines (estimated by the General Accounting Office in 1992 to cost $2.7 billion), destroying ballistic missiles and missile silos, and the storage and security costs of weapons held at various military depots before shipment to Pantex.

Assisting Russian Dismantlement Efforts

Since 1991, Congress has provided $1.5 billion to help the former Soviet Union dismantle parts of its nuclear arsenal and safeguard its nuclear materials in the "Cooperative Threat Reduction" program, commonly known as "Nunn-Lugar." Not all of this money has been appropriated, but efforts to date have yielded significant results.

Funds from the program have helped Ukraine deactivate and disable at least 40 SS-19 and 46 SS-24 ICBMs armed with about 700 warheads, all formerly pointed at the United States or its allies. Of those 700 warheads, as of March 1995 nearly 400 had been returned to Russia, where all but 30 had been dismantled. By late 1996, Nunn-Lugar funding had helped eliminate 176 ICBMs in Ukraine that carried 1,240 warheads, at a cost of $149,193 per warhead.

Additional Nunn-Lugar funds will assist in the destruction of bombers and missile launchers, and provide $70 million to help eliminate 104 SS-18 ICBMs in Kazakhstan that carry more than 1,000 half-megaton warheads (at a cost of $70,000 per warhead). In 1995, some members of Congress objected to these efforts, arguing that they are too costly, and claiming that the Russians are diverting funds to produce new weapons. But most members of Congress agree that the long-term security benefits of the program outweigh its minimal costs.

Nunn-Lugar funds also covered the U.S. purchase of a quantity of highly enriched uranium from Kazakhstan, to prevent it from being stolen. In a secret operation code-named Project Sapphire, 31 U.S. scientists, technicians, and military personnel flew to Kazakhstan in October 1994 to process and package 600 kilograms (about 1,300 pounds) of highly enriched uranium stored at the Ulba Metallurgical Facility. The cost (excluding a payment to Kazakhstan rumored at around $30 million, but never officially disclosed) was nearly $7 million, which covered the military transport flights in and out of Kazakhstan, personnel costs, and four separate trips by the Energy Department's Safe Secure Trailers from Dover Air Force Base in Delaware to the Y-12 Plant at the Oak Ridge Reservation in Tennessee.

Secrecy v. Democracy

U.S. nuclear secrecy was founded on the unprecedented idea that nuclear weapons information is "born secret." Nuclear secrecy covers a wide variety of activities, including research and development, fissile materials production, war plans, and intelligence gathering and analysis. Cost figures are elusive because military secrecy programs aggregate both nuclear and non-nuclear efforts.

Potentially, the largest management cost of all—and the hardest to pin down—is the cost to a democratic society of the secrecy and security measures used to restrict the dissemination of information. These costs are intangible but real.

Even after its recent, highly publicized disclosures of formerly restricted data, the Energy Department still retains at least 280 million more pages of classified information, the majority of which concern its nuclear weapons programs. The cost of tracking and safeguarding these documents is bound to be high. Security costs could account for $75 billion of the nearly $400 billion spent by the Energy Department and its predecessor, the AEC, for nuclear weapons research, development, testing, and production activities.

Lost opportunity costs, especially the loss of public trust, is another intangible. So are issues such as the constitutional questions raised by the delegation of presidential launch authority and the harassment of workers who reveal unsafe or illegal practices. During the anti-Communist purges early in the Cold War, 494 scientists working for the AEC lost their clearances—and presumably their jobs—in the course of reviews of their loyalty.

Nuclear secrecy also played a role in the creation of the so-called "nuclear allergy," an affliction first contracted by New Zealand, which has a long-standing policy of refusing entry to its ports of nuclear-powered and/or nuclear-armed ships. Stonewalled by the navy's "neither confirm nor deny" policy (concerning the presence of nuclear weapons in any particular location), in 1985 New Zealand refused entry to all U.S. vessels and has only recently begun to relax that policy. Sweden, Denmark, and Japan all have similar concerns and have raised them with the U.S. government. This unfortunate antagonism of our allies has largely abated, mostly due to President George Bush's unilateral 1991 decision to retire most nonstrategic naval nuclear weapons and to store those that remain in shore depots.

Finally, nuclear secrecy often plays a detrimental role in foreign policy, by skewing decisions based on narrow interests and then shielding those decisions from public view. For example, the law prohibiting U.S. foreign aid to a country that has or is seeking to acquire nuclear weapons was written in a way that excluded Israel, which was (and remains) an unacknowledged nuclear power and the recipient of the majority of U.S. foreign aid.

During the war in Afghanistan, the Reagan and Bush administrations funneled aid to the *mujahideen* through Pakistan, using secrecy to sidestep the fact that Pakistan had a burgeoning nuclear weapons program, and was thus ineligible for such aid. The government also skirted the law when it helped France with its nuclear weapons program. To bypass laws prohibiting the sharing of sensitive nuclear weapons information, U.S. officials met annually with French nuclear officials and, in a carefully structured series of questions and answers, indicated *without explicitly saying so*, the best means to resolve a problem. This process was dubbed "negative guidance."

Today—and Tomorrow

Although this study is largely historical—and still in progress—important lessons for the public and policy-makers have emerged. These lessons include:

- The constitutional systems of checks and balances was rarely applied to the nuclear weapons program. A cloistered bureaucracy, largely unaccountable to Congress, managed the program. In addition, Congress frequently neglected its oversight function, allowing decades of wasteful spending.
- The government has systematically undercounted the true costs of the nuclear arsenal.
- Emphasizing deterrence over safety led the United States to underfund critical command, control, and communications programs and prevented the creation of a stable nuclear alert posture.
- Production took precedence over health and safety, leading to environmental degradation and the endangerment of nuclear weapons personnel and the civilian population.
- Pervasive and often unnecessary secrecy drove up costs, prevented the American people (and sometimes Congress) from knowing the full ex-

tent and cost of nuclear weapons programs, and helped undermine the people's trust in government.

- The cost of building weapons was relatively low, but the cost of deploying nuclear forces on land, in the air, and under the sea—and insuring their safety and linking them with a command and control system—were and are very high.
- Threat inflation—driven by Cold War fears, partisan politics, skewed intelligence estimates, and service rivalries—led the United States to build and deploy excessive numbers of weapons, wasting tens of billions of dollars on systems developed under inadequately scrutinized rationales.

The project's final report, the work of a committee of 12, is forthcoming. This is adapted from the November/December 1995 *Bulletin.*

1.5 Midnight Never Came

MIKE MOORE

The best-known symbol of the Nuclear Age—the *Bulletin*'s "Doomsday Clock"—had a hard-to-ignore debut. Early *Bulletins* were newsletters, lacking magazine-style covers. But when the June 1947 *Bulletin* arrived, it had a first-ever cover—a pay-attention-to-me jack-o'-lantern orange cover. Imprinted over the orange: a boldly simple seven-inch by seven-inch clock face. The hour hand was at 12; the minute hand at about seven minutes to. Humankind, the clock said, was in dire straits.

The clock, said an editorial in the July 1947 issue, "represents the state of mind of those whose closeness to the development of atomic energy does not permit them to forget that their lives and those of their children, the security of their country and the survival of civilization, all hang in the balance as long as the specter of atomic war has not been exorcized."

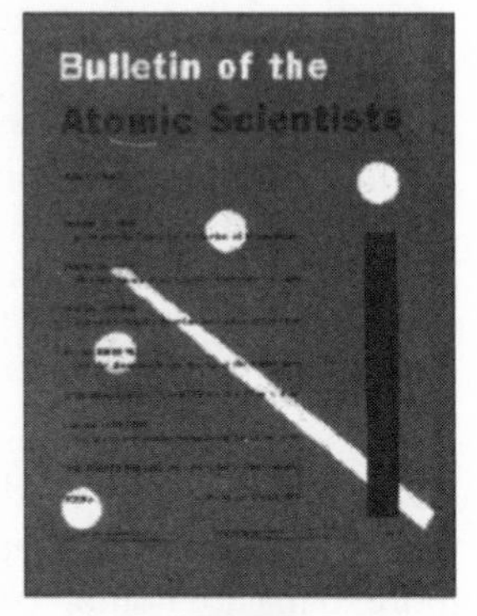

1947

And so the *Bulletin* Clock (first called "The Clock of Doom" and then "The Doomsday Clock") entered folklore as a symbol of nuclear peril and a constant warning that the leaders of the United States and the Soviet Union had better sit up and fly right.

It Moves!

The clock was the creation of a Chicago artist known as Martyl, the wife of physicist Alexander Langsdorf, a *Bulletin* founder. Years later, Martyl said she hit upon the idea "to symbolize urgency." She got that message across by using just the final quadrant of a clock face, which clearly suggested that the end of time was nigh. As for putting the minute hand at seven—that was, she said, merely a matter of "good design."

The minute hand stayed at seven minutes to the hour until the fall of 1949, when President Harry S. Truman announced that the United States had evidence that there had been an atomic explosion in the Soviet Union.

1949

The Soviets promptly disputed Truman. In a statement issued by Tass (and reprinted in the October issue of the *Bulletin*) the Soviet government claimed that U.S. experts had confused a large conventional explosion with an atomic explosion. That was understandable, explained Tass; the Soviet Union was blasting a lot as it built hydroelectric stations, canals, and the like. And, too, did not Western reporters recall that the Soviet Union had announced in November 1947 that it already had the weapon "at its disposal"?

The editors of the *Bulletin*, always mindful that Soviet leaders often lied, didn't buy the Tass explanation. Truman was right; the Soviet Union had set off an atomic detonation, and that was proof that the East-West nuclear arms race, long predicted by the *Bulletin*, was well under way.

"We do not advise Americans that doomsday is near and that they can expect atomic bombs to start falling on their heads a month or a year from now," wrote Editor Eugene Rabinowitch in an October 1949 essay. "But we think they have reason to be deeply alarmed and to be prepared for grave decisions."

In the October 1949 issue, the *Bulletin* moved the clock's minute hand for the first time, to three minutes to midnight.

Birth of the "Evil Thing"

The Soviet atomic explosion caught the Truman administration flat-footed. Gen. Leslie R. Groves, the director of the wartime Manhattan Project, had repeatedly predicted that it would take the Soviet Union a generation or more to make a bomb. Truman was even more confident; he believed that the Soviet Union lacked the scientific and industrial competence to *ever* mount a successful atomic bomb program.

The *Bulletin* was founded in December 1945 on the contrary notion. Back then, most of the scientists connected with the *Bulletin* believed that Soviet scientists and Russian industry were fully capable of building an atomic bomb in just a few years. (In November 1945, Harold C. Urey, a *Bulletin* founder, told the Senate Special Committee on Atomic Energy that "we should not think of a longer time than about five years.") The way to avoid a destructive nuclear arms race, the *Bulletin* said, was to put the control of nuclear energy, including weapons, into the hands of an international agency.

That didn't happen, of course. And now the Soviet fission explosion had given new urgency to a secret, high-level U.S. debate that had been simmering since the early days of the Manhattan Project: should the United States build a "Super," a "hydrogen bomb" far more powerful than the largest fission weapon?

A host of scientists advising the government opposed the Super. Morally, it would be so large as to be potentially genocidal. From a utilitarian point of view, it would serve no clear military purpose; fission bombs would be all anyone really needed. Physicists I. I. Rabi and Enrico Fermi, both key scientists during the Manhattan Project, described a hydrogen bomb as an "evil thing." James Conant, an adviser to Roosevelt and Truman on nuclear matters, said the "world is loused up enough"—it didn't need a hydrogen bomb.

In the end, anti-Super reservations were washed away in a tide of *Realpolitik*. Truman's key political advisers, including Secretary of State Dean Acheson, were convinced that the Soviets could—and would—build an H-bomb. Given that, it would be intolerable for the United States not to. (Today we know that the Soviets did indeed push ahead from fission to fusion, with scarcely a pause.)

On October 31, 1952, the United States tested its first true thermonuclear device, a thuggish thing called "Mike" that had a yield nearly a thousand times greater than the Hiroshima bomb. The islet of Elugelab in the Pacific, upon which it was detonated, disappeared, leaving a crater 160 feet deep and more than a mile wide. Nine months later, in August 1953, the Russians exploded a less powerful but still awesome thermonuclear device.

The September 1953 *Bulletin* cover was remade at the last minute, as soon as word of the Soviet test got out, and the minute hand moved to two minutes to midnight. In the following issue—October 1953—Editor Rabinowitch said:

1953

"The hands of the Clock of Doom have moved again. Only a few more swings of the pendulum, and, from Moscow to Chicago, atomic explosions will strike midnight for Western civilization."

Massive Retaliation and a "Cohesive Force"

In the 1950s, the U.S. consumer society boomed as a prosperous suburban lifestyle spawned highways, barbecue grills, TV sitcoms, and children. But abroad, the news was mostly bad. The Soviets were building nuclear weapons at a rapid pace, and they had even produced a few intercontinental ballistic missiles. (Emphasis on "few." Ardent Cold Warriors, including Democratic presidential candidate John F. Kennedy, charged that a complacent President Eisenhower had let the Russians pull ahead in ballistic weapons, thus producing a "missile gap." But it was a phantom gap, the product of misinterpreted intelligence, over-reliance on worst-case scenarios, anti-Soviet hysteria, and cynical domestic political calculation.)

In Europe, homegrown attempts to introduce democratic reforms in Hungary, encouraged by "liberation" rhetoric from Washington, had been aborted by Russian tanks. And in divided Germany, U.S.–Soviet relations were in perpetual crisis over the future of West Berlin, a let-it-all-hang-out oasis of capitalism in the heart of drab East Germany.

On the other side of the world, the Korean Peninsula, where the United States (with help from U.N. and South Korean allies) had fought North Korean and Chinese soldiers, was still a potential flashpoint. The Korean war had not quite ended; it was merely on hold.

Farther south, Communist China and the old Chinese warlord, Chiang Kai-shek, were at one another's throats. At the end of a bloody civil war, Chiang and his remaining troops had taken refuge on the island of Formosa, just off the Chinese mainland, and war in the Formosa Straits seemed perennially possible. As Chiang's protector, the United States would surely be involved.

In the Korean War, Eisenhower hinted broadly that he might use nuclear weapons to bring the war to an end. As for the war of nerves in the Formosa Straits, the president got the message across that the United States would not shrink from using nuclear weapons to protect Chiang.

1960

Despite the tumult and bloodshed, Rabinowitch found reasons in January 1960 to be moderately encouraged by the way the decade had unfolded, at least on the nuclear front. In the pre-nuclear era, turmoil in many parts of the world would have led to a major war. But now, "war threats and counter-threats have become bluffs and counterbluffs."

Rabinowitch was right. Talk was often bellicose—"massive retaliation" and "we will bury you" are only two of the truly memorable phrases from the decade. But the Soviets and the Americans had clearly become cautious vis-á-vis one another's vital interests. Direct confrontation between the superpowers was generally to be avoided; confrontation by proxy was just rearing its head.

The minute hand was again put at seven minutes to midnight, its original setting.

Fear Keeps the Peace

People sometimes assume that the minute hand of the clock is moved frequently. In fact, the clock has been reset just 15 times in 50 years. Clock moves reflect major trends, not transient events. For instance, the Cuban missile crisis in October 1962 failed to produce so much as a blip in the clock. The crisis—a frightening exception to the still developing "rule" that the United States and Soviet Union should not directly confront one another—came and went too fast for the *Bulletin* to act on it.

1963

A year after the missile crisis, in October 1963, the *Bulletin* moved the minute hand back in recognition of the signing of the Partial Test Ban Treaty, an agreement banning atmospheric nuclear testing. Rabinowitch explained in his editorial that the treaty was not a "significant step toward disarmament"—after all, underground tests would continue. Nor would the treaty prevent additional nations from acquiring nuclear weapons, Rabinowitch added. Indeed, he believed that China would shortly join the nuclear club. (China's first test of a fission device came in October 1964.)

Nevertheless, the treaty, said Rabinowitch, was tangible evidence that the "cohesive force" was still alive and well. Both sides of the East-West confrontation continued to experience "naked fear for survival," and that fear helped keep the peace. The treaty also suggested that "the forces of realism" were winning; on both sides of the East–West divide, "obstinate dogmatism" was in retreat.

The minute hand was moved back to 12 minutes to midnight.

A "First Step"

[In 1968 the clock was moved forward again, to seven minutes to midnight, reflecting disappointment over missed opportunities.] But in Geneva, a process had been going on since the mid-1960s that looked promising. On the theory that it only takes one spark to start a forest fire, nations—nuclear as well as non-nuclear—were attempting to limit the "horizontal" spread of nuclear weapons.

1969

Many of the non-nuclear weapon states were also fearful of "vertical" proliferation in the United States and the Soviet Union, while they remained enamored of nuclear power, which was seen as the cure for virtually all ills. In 1968, a deal was finally struck: Under the terms of the Nuclear Non-Proliferation Treaty (NPT), the nuclear weapon states would help non-nuclear weapon states develop nuclear power. In turn, the "have-not" states would agree not to develop or obtain nuclear weapons.

Finally, the five nuclear weapon states promised to work toward a cessation of the nuclear arms race and eventual disarmament. More than 100 nations signed the NPT, although some of the holdouts were worrisome—especially Israel, India, Pakistan, South Africa, Argentina, and Brazil.

But even with holdouts, Rabinowitch was heartened by the deal, if not overwhelmed. In the April 1969 issue, he wrote: "This treaty reasserts the common interests of all signatories in avoiding new instabilities, bound to be introduced into the precarious balance of nuclear terror with the emergence of new nuclear nations.

"The great powers have made a first step. They must proceed without delay to the next one—the dismantling, gradually, of their own oversize military establishments. Otherwise the hope raised by the treaty will prove futile."

The minute hand was moved back to ten minutes to midnight.

Parity Cometh

In 1964, Stanley Kubrick released *Dr. Strangelove*, a wickedly funny satire of deterrence theory, and Sidney Lumet gave audiences *Fail Safe*, an earnest and plodding essay on the same topic. Both films explored scenarios in which U.S. bombers erroneously attack the Soviet Union with nuclear weapons. In *Fail Safe*, Moscow and New York are destroyed; in *Strangelove*, the planet is fatally irradiated by a secret Soviet "Doomsday Machine."

In a sense, Kubrick and Lumet were cockeyed optimists. Sure, things didn't turn out so well for a few million people (*Fail Safe*) or a few billion (*Strangelove*), but in each case, a fictional president had hours to correct the original attack-the-Soviets mistake. But in the real world, the time scale was about to be reduced to minutes. There would no time for reflective assessment, no time for call-backs.

By the mid-1960s, the United States and the Soviet Union were working on antiballistic missile systems (ABMs), with the Russians showing far more enthusiasm for the concept than the Americans. To Soviet leaders, a defense system seemed reasonable, even morally compelling. But in the United States, a host of influential policy-makers, including Defense Secretary Robert S. McNamara, argued that an effective ABM system would be dangerous.

Mutual terror, went the argument, was still the great peacekeeper. As long as both sides knew that each could destroy the other, no matter who struck first, an uneasy peace would prevail. But ABMs had the potential for disrupting that rickety balance of terror. They would encourage a rapid acceleration of the nuclear arms race, because increases in offensive weapons were the surest and cheapest way of offsetting advances in defensive systems.

And in moments of high East–West tension, the side that believed that it had the most effective ABM system might be tempted to launch a first strike, confident that it could ride out the weakened retaliatory attacks with minimal damage.

But in an obscene game of chicken, the side that feared a preemptive first strike might well launch its own preemptive attack. Meanwhile, the other side, assuming that the enemy would reason thusly, would have even more reason to strike first.

Fear of Russian progress on ABMs inspired the United States to enhance its offensive forces by developing missiles that carried "multiple independently targetable reentry vehicles"—MIRVs. The last stage of an ICBM was merely a "bus" carrying several warheads, each of which could be released at a different time in a preplanned sequence. Thanks to in-flight course corrections by the bus, the warheads would have different ballistic trajectories and different targets.

In this new post-*Strangelove* world, an enemy who struck first would have a clear advantage, said nuclear strategists. Because one MIRVed ICBM could theoretically knock out several enemy missiles in their silos, the side that struck first could retain many of its missiles for a possible second strike.

The only way to level the "bolt-from-the-blue" playing field was for the target nation to launch its missiles *before* they could be destroyed in their silos. In a MIRVed use-'em-or-lose-'em world, the U.S. and Russian command authorities might have just minutes to make a launch–no launch decision, even if the information they had was muddled and ambiguous.

By the late 1960s, U.S. and Soviet leaders had come to suspect that the two nations were lurching toward an abyss. In an attempt to pull back from the edge, the Strategic Arms Limitation Talks (SALT) began in Helsinki in November 1969.

The central idea of SALT was that the United States and the Soviet Union would give up their respective dreams of achieving clearcut nuclear superiority. Instead, they would begin a process designed to produce a rough sort of "parity." In turn, that might bring a measure of predictability and stability to East–West relations.

1972

In 1972, two agreements were signed. One, the Anti-Ballistic Missile Treaty, effectively put an end to most ABM work, thus making an out-of-control nuclear arms race less likely. In effect, the treaty said that each nation must remain vulnerable to the other side's missiles; continued willingness to abide by a mutual suicide pact had become the Golden Rule of deterrence theory.

Meanwhile, the five-year SALT Interim Agreement froze the number of ballistic missile launchers—that is, the number of land-based missile silos and submarine-based missile launch tubes—at 1972 levels. It was an exceedingly modest start toward nuclear arms control; it did not actually limit the number of missiles each side could have or the number of warheads that a given missile might carry.

Bernard T. Feld, a member of the *Bulletin*'s Board of Directors, was generally pleased with the ABM Treaty, but wary of the Interim Agreement. Feld, whose sarcasm was not always hidden, wrote the clock editorial for the June 1972 issue:

"Now we have been presented with the greatest step towards world peace since the Sermon on the Mount, and we are torn between the impulse to cry 'bravo' and the desire to shout 'fraud.' "

MIRVed missiles were meant to counter the ABM "threat," he said. But now the ABM threat had faded—yet MIRVs remained. That was "because we are too far along with deployment and the Russians too far behind—an asymmetry that we do not want to give up and they do not want to freeze. So we have accepted that we will both go to MIRV, after which it will be too late to avoid MIRV without unacceptably intrusive inspection."

1980

The ABM Treaty was fine, but the Interim Agreement was thin gruel. Nonetheless, the United States and the Soviet Union *had* accepted the principle of parity, and that was a foundation to build upon. The minute hand was moved back to 12 minutes to midnight.

In September 1974 the minute hand was moved up to nine minutes to midnight. The optimism of 1972 had been "premature," said editor Sam Day.

And in 1980, the clock was moved forward again, to seven minutes to midnight, where it had started in 1947. Editor in Chief Bernard Feld offered a gloomy assessment of the world situation: an accelerating arms race, increased competition among nations for ever more scarce resources, and a "spreading trend toward irrationality in the national and international conduct of many states."

"War-fighting," Anyone?

Just 12 months later, the outlook for the world seemed even dimmer. The Soviet Union had dispatched tanks, troops, and dive bombers to Afghanistan in December 1979 to prop up a puppet government, further poisoning a none-too-cordial relationship between Moscow and Washington. President Jimmy Carter, who had sent SALT II to the Senate for ratification, condemned the Soviets for "invading" their neighbor, cancelled U.S. participation in the upcoming Olympic Games in Moscow, and asked the Senate to postpone action on SALT II.

More chillingly, the Carter administration, in an attempt to bring order to decades of jury-rigged nuclear-response plans and to enhance the "credibility" of deterrence, had devised a wider range of nuclear options, including the implementation of command-and-control measures that would—in theory—insure that the United States could fight a "protracted nuclear conflict."

Then in November 1980, former governor and movie star Ronald Reagan, a defense hawk who had campaigned on the premise that the United States had become dangerously weak vis-à-vis the Soviet Union, was elected president. SALT II was "fatally flawed," said Reagan, and the Soviets routinely flouted SALT provisions. In contrast, the United States, which played by the rules, had laced itself into a straitjacket. The way to end the Cold War, Reagan said, was to *win* it. Feld wrote in the January 1981 issue:

"Nuclear weapons—more and more unambiguously aimed at war-fighting rather than war-deterrence—are now being rapidly deployed by the East and West in Europe. The Russian SS-20 and the U.S. MX blatantly announce a new race in improved missile accuracy and mobility, heralding the acceptance of counterforce first-strike by both sides.

1981

"These ominous signs of deterioration are cast into starker relief by the flat unwillingness of either the United States or the Soviet Union to reject publicly, and in all circumstances, the threat of striking the other first. Both sides willfully delude themselves that a nuclear war can remain limited or even be won. In 1980, both sides officially declared nuclear war 'thinkable.' "

The minute hand was moved up to four minutes to midnight.

Ideologues Take Control

The early Reagan years alarmed the *Bulletin*'s editors, along with millions of other people in the United States and Western Europe. Reagan, who may have believed more ardently than any previous president in the ultimate abolition of nuclear weapons, nevertheless expanded and accelerated a weapons buildup that Jimmy Carter had begun. Reagan also seemed to enjoy tossing incendiary rhetoric into the dry-as-straw East–West barn. In his first presidential news conference, he asserted that Soviet leaders "reserve unto themselves the right to commit any crime, to lie, to cheat."

While the comment would not have raised an eyebrow if a historian had uttered it, it seemed recklessly provocative coming from the commander-in-chief of the most powerful nation on earth. Two years later, Reagan trumped his any-crime-any-time comment by calling the Soviet Union the "Evil Empire" in a speech redolent of Old Testament rhetoric about the final showdown between the forces of Good and Evil.

In 1983, Reagan announced the Strategic Defense Initiative (SDI), resurrecting the long-dead fantasy of unfurling an anti-ballistic missile umbrella over the United States. The president's March 23 speech came as a surprise to almost everyone, including some of Reagan's closest advisers. The space-based SDI plan was quickly dubbed "Star Wars," after the movie trilogy of that name.

1984

Reagan's Star Wars plan, if developed and deployed, would surely violate the ABM Treaty, critics said. It would lead to a resumption of an all-out nuclear arms race. And—as a final irony—it almost surely would not work in the event of an all-out attack. The *Bulletin*'s first unsigned clock editorial appeared in the January 1984 issue:

"As the arms race—a sort of dialogue between weapons—has intensified, other forms of discourse between the superpowers have all but ceased. There has been a virtual suspension of meaningful contacts and serious discussions. Every channel of communications has been constricted or shut down; every form of contact has been attenuated or cut off. And arms control negotiations have been reduced to a species of propaganda."

The minute hand was moved up to three minutes to midnight.

Breakthrough

In the late 1970s, in an attempt to enhance deterrence and the U.S. commitment to defend Europe, the West European members of NATO obtained a

U.S. promise to deploy 464 ground-launched nuclear-tipped cruise missiles on NATO soil, as well as 108 nuclear-armed Pershing II intermediate-range ballistic missiles.

In theory, the missiles would counterbalance a nasty-looking Soviet force of 243 triple-warhead SS-20 missiles aimed at NATO targets. They would also be bargaining chips. Deployment—even the threat of deployment—would give the West additional leverage in pushing for a treaty that would sharply constrain such weapons worldwide.

In the early 1980s, as deployment of the new missiles loomed and NATO and Soviet rhetoric became more alarming, popular opposition in Western Europe became a force to be reckoned with. In the fall of 1981, more than 250,000 people turned out for a protest in Bonn; the following month, some 400,000 protested in Amsterdam.

Deploying Pershing missiles that could hit Soviet targets in five to 10 minutes was utterly mad, said the protesters in Europe and in the United States. It would make the Soviets even more edgy, ultimately leading to an unintentional but devastating nuclear war. ABC-TV's two-part movie, *The Day After*, linked Pershing deployment to a civilization-ending war. It played to huge audiences on two continents.

The fact that the United States and the Soviet Union eventually signed an Intermediate-range Nuclear Forces (INF) Treaty in December 1987—which eliminated all such weapons (including Pershing IIs and SS-20s) rather than merely cutting their numbers—struck many people, including the editors of the *Bulletin*, as near-miraculous. But it wasn't quite that. Public opinion in Western Europe and the United States had made it plain to the Reagan administration that people were fed up with having to live at Ground Zero. Public pressure to do something about the nuclear arms race had become a potent political movement.

As surprising as Reagan's agreement to the INF Treaty may have been, it was even more startling to learn that the Soviet Union, long victimized by constipated and unimaginative leadership, finally had a top man—Mikhail Gorbachev—with the wit and the imagination and the courage to finally end the Cold War. The editorial in the January–February 1988 *Bulletin* said:

1988

"For the first time the United States and the Soviet Union have agreed to dismantle and ban a whole category of nuclear weapons. They have crafted provisions that enable each to be confident that the other will comply with the treaty's terms. The agreement they have fashioned can serve as a model for future accords. That agreement would not have been possible without the leadership displayed by General Secretary Mikhail Gorbachev and President Ronald Reagan. We applaud them."

The minute hand was moved back to six minutes to midnight.

The Great Melt

The Berlin Wall came down at the end of 1989, symbolizing the end of the Cold War. Gorbachev had long realized that the Soviet Empire, which had rested on a foundation of fear and intimidation for more than four decades, could not be sustained. His goals were to shore up Soviet society, to repair the collapsing Soviet economic machine, to introduce democratic reforms, to end Soviet isolation from the Western world, and to bring new life—"new thinking"—to the desperately outdated Communist Party.

Meanwhile, new thinking was far advanced in Poland, Czechoslovakia, Hungary, East Germany, and Romania. Men and women who had danced tepidly to Moscow's balalaika since the end of World War II would do it no longer. Revolution was in the air from the North Sea to the Black Sea. And Gorbachev was not about to send tanks into Eastern Europe, as his predecessors had, to keep the East Bloc nations in line. The editorial in the April 1990 *Bulletin* remarked:

"Now, 44 years after Winston Churchill's 'Iron Curtain' speech, the myth of monolithic communism had been shattered for all to see, the ideological conflict known as the Cold War is over, and the risk of global nuclear war being ignited in Europe is significantly diminished."

The minute hand was moved back to 10 minutes to midnight.

The Coup that Failed

The old era ended abruptly. Few had anticipated it; even fewer seemed to have a clear notion of what would—or should—come next. From a Washington perspective, change was good as long as it didn't get out of hand. The Reagan and Bush administrations had come to see Gorbachev as an ally, as a friend, as a bulwark against chaos in a troubled Soviet Union.

Back home in Russia, Gorbachev didn't have a prayer. He was said to be chiefly responsible for every problem and disgrace tormenting the Soviet Union—ranging from the nation's decline as a world power to its free-falling economy to an increase in public drunkenness to the imminent dissolution of the Union itself.

By the beginning of 1991, the general secretary was foundering, although official Washington seemed not to know it. The end came in late August, when reactionaries mounted a near-bloodless coup. The coup failed to install a government of revanchist communists, but Gorbachev was finished, although he remained in office through the remainder of the year.

Discredited and virtually deposed, yes. But Gorbachev had not been a failure. Beginning in 1985, when he took over as general secretary, Gorbachev had forced democratic reforms onto the moribund Soviet system. Although the reforms helped foment the turmoil that led to his downfall, they had become so ingrained by August 1991 that a successful right-wing coup was not possible. As unpopular as Gorbachev had become, the rightist alternatives looked worse to most Russians.

Shortly before the coup attempt, Gorbachev had signed the Strategic Arms Reduction Treaty, the Reagan-era successor to SALT and the first nuclear arms agreement that mandated steep rollbacks in so-called "strategic" weapons. And in September and October, as the Soviet Union sputtered to an end, Presidents Bush and Gorbachev announced a series of unilateral but parallel initiatives taking most intercontinental missiles and bombers off hair-trigger alert, and withdrawing thousands of tactical nuclear weapons from forward bases. The *Bulletin* editorial in the December 1991 issue said:

"The 40-year-long East–West nuclear arms race has ended. The world has clearly entered a new post–Cold War era. The illusion that tens of thousands of nuclear weapons are a guarantor of national security has been stripped away. In the context of a disintegrating Soviet Union, large nuclear arsenals are even more clearly seen as a liability, a yardstick of insecurity.

1991

"We believe that Presidents Bush and Gorbachev have guided their respective nations to a historic intersection of mutual interests. Continuing boldness and imagination are called for. Men and women throughout the world must vigorously challenge the bankrupt paradigms of militarism if we are to achieve a new world order. The setting of the *Bulletin* Clock reflects our optimism that we are entering a new era."

The minute hand of the clock was pushed back to 17 minutes to midnight.

[In December 1995, the *Bulletin* moved the minute hand forward to 14 minutes to midnight, signaling missed opportunities for disarmament and the growing danger of nuclear terrorism.]

This is adapted from the November/December 1995 *Bulletin*.

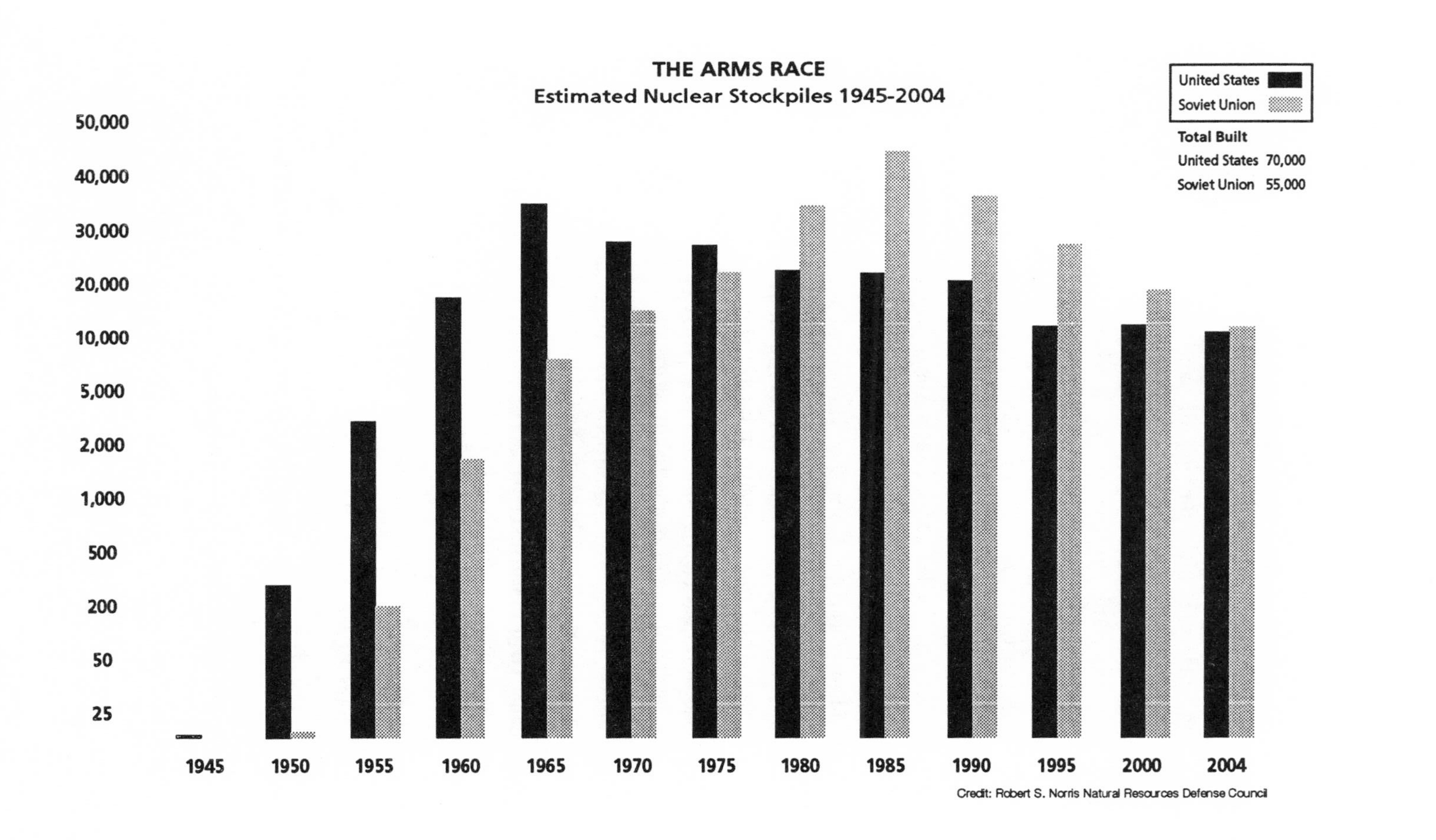
THE ARMS RACE
Estimated Nuclear Stockpiles 1945-2004
United States
Soviet Union
Total Built
United States 70,000
Soviet Union 55,000
50,000
40,000
30,000
20,000
10,000
5,000
2,000
1,000
500
200
50
25
1945
1950
1955
1960
1965
1970
1975
1980
1985
1990
1995
2000
2004
Credit: Robert S. Norris Natural Resources Defense Council

Chapter I
Discussion Questions

1. During the Cold War, the United States and the Soviet Union were very different political and economic systems. Yet both developed massive nuclear weapons systems and used these as the basis of much of their defense policy. Based on your reading of the articles in this chapter, discuss some of the differences and similarities in the early stages of the two countries' development of nuclear arms.

2. The title of this chapter is "The Burden of History." As you understand the issues discussed in the various articles, what particular burdens fall to the current generation of national and global citizens as a result of the weapons development and defense policies discussed in this chapter?

3. One of the most dominant concepts—and policies—of the nuclear era was deterrence. Strictly speaking, deterrence—the notion that out of fear of nuclear destruction, neither superpower would launch an attack on the other—was *the* central security concept of the Cold War. Based on your assessment of the readings in this chapter, how well did the concept and policy of deterrence fulfill its role in preventing war? in providing security for states? in actually guiding the actions of each of the superpowers in their defense policies?

4. The hands of the *Bulletin*'s "Doomsday Clock" ranged from 2 to 17 minutes before midnight during the first 50 years of the nuclear age. From your reading of Mike Moore's article about the Cold War as marked by the clock, as well as the other essays in the chapter, what were the three worst periods of global insecurity, with the highest likelihood of nuclear war? What were three periods of greater security and less tension between the superpowers? By comparing the worst and best times, is it possible to point out the kind of conditions that generate insecurity and those that generate more security among nations?

Chapter II

The Proliferation Problem: Will "They" Get the Bomb?

Preventing nuclear proliferation—keeping additional nations from acquiring nuclear weapons—has been a challenge since the beginning of the nuclear age. In fact, some of the Manhattan Project scientists who built the first atomic bombs also warned about the dangers of the spread of nuclear weapon technology. In Chapter VII, Eugene Rabinowitch laments the failure of their campaign to place nuclear technology under strict international control and thus prevent proliferation.

The U.S. nuclear monopoly was short-lived. The Soviets developed an atomic device in 1949, with considerable assistance from spies in the West but also through their own efforts. In 1952, Great Britain developed the bomb, followed by France in 1960 and the People's Republic of China in 1964. In all, these five "acknowledged nuclear powers" have produced more than 127,000 nuclear weapons—although nearly all were made by the United States (55 percent) and the Soviet Union (43 percent).

These five countries and a number of their allies have also led the effort to close the doors to the nuclear club. The mechanisms developed to do this are collectively called the nuclear non-proliferation regime: an array of commercial practices, technological safeguards, organizations, and legal measures designed to keep nuclear weapons, their technology, and the materials needed to generate nuclear explosions off the international market.

The governments of nations that possess nuclear weapons have been most effective in preventing the spread of nuclear technology and material when they have adhered to this goal in their trade and aid. But they are also supported by a strong international framework that has withstood a variety of pressures over the years.

The cornerstone of the regime is the Nuclear Non-Proliferation Treaty

(NPT), which was first signed in 1968, came into force in 1970, and was made permanent in 1995. The NPT prohibits the transfer of nuclear weapons, weapons-grade nuclear material (plutonium and highly enriched uranium), and weapons technology, but it obligates nuclear states to share technology and expertise for nuclear energy production and other peaceful purposes. It also admonishes nuclear weapons states to reduce their arsenals and eventually abolish nuclear weapons. To the dismay of many non-nuclear or "unacknowledged" nuclear states, this aspect of the treaty has not been effectively enforced—a principal reason that India has not joined.

The other aspects of the treaty are implemented by the U.N.'s International Atomic Energy Agency (IAEA), headquartered in Vienna. Originally designed to stimulate peaceful uses of atomic energy, the IAEA has become the primary institution for assessing whether countries are living up their pledge not to develop and produce nuclear weapons. This once obscure agency made headlines in the 1990s with its inspections and exposures of clandestine nuclear programs in Iraq and North Korea.

Pressures on the non-proliferation regime have increased over the years. Protracted regional conflicts and the state of near permanent war-readiness of nations in the Mideast and South Asia have led these states to search for a military or political advantage through acquiring nuclear weapons. Thus, a number of countries in these regions have long been suspected of operating not-so-clandestine nuclear development programs.

Other nations have sought to enhance their economic and political prestige, if not their leverage with the Western powers, by developing nuclear weapons. Such motivations, bolstered by various security and military concerns unique to each state, prompted nations as diverse as Algeria, Argentina, Brazil, Iran, and South Africa to pursue nuclear programs—although all but Iran have abandoned their programs. Meanwhile, Israel, India, and Pakistan have refused to join the NPT and have become unacknowledged nuclear weapons states. The dynamics of the global market and a vibrant black market for nuclear technology from the 1970s onward have exacerbated the proliferation problem from the supply side.

Iraq is a prime example of how market forces combine with political and military pressures in the quest for nuclear weapons. Iraq began working on nuclear weapons during its war with Iran in the 1980s and, while still a friend of the West, used above-board trade as well as more devious technology transfer to march to the verge of nuclear development. If the Gulf War and IAEA inspectors had not intervened, Iraq probably would have produced a few primitive nuclear weapons by now.

The demise of the Soviet Union posed a new set of problems. Suddenly, three newly independent nations—Belarus, Kazakhstan, and Ukraine—along with Russia, were de facto members of the nuclear club. In fact, Ukraine had more strategic nuclear weapons on its soil than did France, Britain, or China. But although Ukraine and Kazakhstan used these weapons as political and economic leverage for a time, the weapons were never under the new governments' control. All three nations eventually sent the weapons back to Russia and joined the NPT.

That process was a notable non-proliferation success story, the result of cooperative action by former foes. Financed in part by U.S. funds provided under the Nunn-Lugar bill, U.S. and Russian military personnel and engineers have deactivated thousands of weapons in the former Soviet Union in the past five years, both to prevent proliferation and to assure compliance with arms control treaties. The Russian arsenal, once 45,000 strong, now stands at 12,000. The United States, for its part, has reduced a stockpile that reached 32,500 in the 1960s to 10,000.

Readings in this chapter sample the range of human, political, and technical dynamics that contribute to the quest for nuclear weapons.

Iraq notwithstanding, Pervez Hoodbhoy argues that Western fears of an "Islamic" bomb may be greatly exaggerated. Two factors, he asserts, could further diminish Islamic nations' interest in nuclear weapons: the nuclear disarmament of Israel and increased democratization within these nations. Indeed, democratization appears to have played a role in other nations' decisions to renounce nuclear weapons: notably, South Africa, Argentina, Brazil, and the former Soviet states.

Articles by David Albright and Kirill Belyaninov show how human foibles—from economic need to naïveté—enter into the potentially explosive nuclear equation. Oleg Bukharin and William Potter report on an actual theft of material that might be usable in weapons, although such cases are still apparently rare. Finally, David Albright and Kevin O'Neill explain the components of the current nuclear non-proliferation regime and assess how well it is working. They conclude that while the regime is imperfect, things could be much worse.

How much of a threat to the United States is the proliferation of nuclear weapons? The chart, "The Missile Threat," at the end of this chapter shows that only China and Russia possess missiles with a range long enough to target the United States. For some this is a source of relief. But others believe that the greatest proliferation threat is from terrorists who come into possession of nuclear weapons or material—and whose target may very well be the United States.

II.1 The Myth of the Islamic Bomb

Pervez Hoodbhoy

The "Islamic Bomb" is the title of a 1979 BBC television documentary, of a book by Herbert Krosney and Steven Weismann, of another by D. K. Palit and P. K. S. Namboodiri, and it is used often in a hostile context in various discussions and writings. Although imprecisely defined, the "Islamic bomb" is roughly understood to be a nuclear weapon acquired for broad ideological reasons—a weapon that supposedly belongs collectively to the Muslim *ummah* or community and, as such, is the ultimate expression of Islamic solidarity.

Concern about the Islamic bomb is at the heart of the intense effort to prevent the spread of nuclear weapons to Muslim countries. The official justification is a general one: proliferation must be curbed globally. But unofficially, the Islamic bomb gets special attention.

Terrorism is given as one reason. Another is the threat of Khomeini-style Islamic fundamentalism sweeping unchecked across the world, locked in *jihad* with infidels, willing and able to use the ultimate weapons of mass destruction in hope of reward in the Hereafter. A third reason, related to the second, is "Islamism"—the fear that Muslim solidarity will lead to, in times of crisis, the transfer of nuclear arms from nuclear to non-nuclear Muslim countries. A final reason involves location: the region is the jugular vein of the West; no countries in such a strategic location should be permitted to threaten oil interests.

The Islamic bomb is seen as a law-and-order problem, requiring appropriate police action or punitive measures. Media images have created fearsome scenarios, including a Saddam Hussein caressing the nuclear button. There is a growing current of opinion, voiced unofficially, that in the post-Soviet world, war must be waged against the Islamic bomb and Islamic fundamentalism. As Red and Yellow perils fade into history, the "Muslim peril" (with the Islamic bomb in the background) has stepped into view.

But this perception is not helpful—in fact, it is extremely dangerous. Most discussions of the subject are either alarmist or narrowly technical, focusing on supply-side measures such as export controls and embargoes, or even on direct military action.

I believe, however, that proliferation—as a global phenomenon—is fundamentally a political problem and must be tackled as such. This does not mean that one must wait for all disputes between peoples or nations to be resolved before doing anything. But it does mean that the world community must take immediate and urgent steps to decrease the tensions that inspire countries to seek nuclear weapons, or—in the case of those with weapons—to contemplate their use.

Defined

The Islamic bomb evokes fearsome images: the power of nuclear annihilation in the hands of dictators, holy war and warriors, and terrorists. But Muslims, whether moderate or extreme, resent the use of the phrase even if they support, at some level, the idea of a bomb for Muslims. Why talk of an Islamic bomb but never of a bomb labeled with another faith?

Irrespective of whether or not an Islamic bomb can or cannot, or should or should not, exist, the concept behind the term is of Muslim origin. The idea of a nuclear weapon for collective defense of the entire Muslim *ummah* was, after all, articulated and advocated by Muslim leaders who recognized its popularity and determined to benefit from it.

The bomb looms large in the popular Muslim consciousness as a symbol of Islamic unity, determination, and self-respect. It is seen by many as a guarantee against further humiliating defeats, as the sure sign of a reversal of fortunes, and as a panacea for the ills that have plagued Muslims since the end of the Golden Age of Islam. Such sentiments are echoed by Muslims from Algeria to Syria, and from Iraq to Pakistan. A country that could turn this symbolism into reality would have the support of hundreds of millions of Muslims the world over. It is therefore natural that Pakistan, a Muslim country that is now a de facto nuclear state, should indeed enjoy considerable financial and political benefits from oil-rich Arab countries.

Such "evidence" seems to indicate that the Islamic bomb could become a reality, if not immediately, then in the not-too-distant future. But this would be a wholly incorrect deduction. There cannot be an Islamic bomb unless certain drastic developments occur.

While religious and political leaders proclaim the existence of one Muslim *ummah* and speak rhetorically of its common defense, the fact is that this goal is more elusive now than ever. Unity has never been a Muslim strong point. Today the Sunni–Shia split is as hostile as ever, and it has been augmented by numerous and frequently violent quarrels among Sunni sects.

At the political level, history bears witness to the negligible role that the collective Islamic consciousness has played in matters involving real issues of power. Much as Christians have fought each other for power over the centuries, Muslim dynasties have also battled. Today, oil-rich Arab countries pay lip service to the Palestinian cause—which they regard as an Islamic cause—

while investing their dollars in the United States, Israel's prime supporter and underwriter of its expansion into areas captured through war. The systematic destruction of Beirut in 1982, the Indian security forces' crimes against Kashmiri Muslims, and the Serbs' genocide inflicted upon Bosnian Muslims—all have failed to elicit a significant response from the Muslim community at large.

There are many examples of national fervor or a common language functioning as a far more powerful source of group identity than shared faith. For example, the Pakistan army was a violent instrument of oppression for Bengalis; Syrians organized the Tel-al-Zaatar massacre of Palestinians; and Iraq, Iran, and Turkey have jointly persecuted Kurds. The list is long.

In truth, pan-Islamism, the dream of nineteenth-century reformers like Jamaluddin Afghani, is a myth whose pursuit has yielded naught. As a modern corollary, the Islamic bomb is a meaningless notion. Individual Muslim countries may desire nuclear weapons, and some have been engaged in that enterprise for many years, but the motivations are essentially secular and nationalistic, although cloaked in Islamic garb. Just as Israel's nuclear weapons are intended to serve the state of Israel and not Judaism, so too the weapons sought by Pakistan, Iran, Iraq, and possibly other Muslim countries, are intended to serve the purposes of their states.

Disarming the Disarmed

Israel, which shares high-level defense technologies and intelligence data with the United States, is determined to be the sole nuclear state in the Middle East—by use of force, if necessary. Mordechai Vanunu's revelations suggest that Israel may possess about 200 warheads, some of them "boosted" weapons with H-bomb power. It also possesses an advanced delivery system with the Jericho and other missiles. To Muslims, U.S. complicity is evident both in Israel's nuclear arming and in helping Israel keep its adversaries denuclearized. When Israel was expelled from the IAEA for bombing the Osirak reactor in Iraq, the United States temporarily withdrew from the organization.

If past history is any guide, fears of possible future Israeli military action—directly or indirectly supported by the United States—against Iran, or even against the Pakistani enrichment facility at Kahuta, are not baseless. But will the Israeli strategy of nuclear espionage and military force continue to work indefinitely? Apparently many Israelis think it will, or they see no alternative.

But some Israelis recognize that Israel's nuclear monopoly may eventually break; advances in technology will make it impossible to keep nuclear weapons away from its adversaries. Moshe Arens, for example, has stated that Israel's adversaries will possess nuclear weapons within ten years. For Israeli hawks, this means that Israel must develop a second-strike capability. A second-strike capability would mean still more warheads, hardened underground missile silos, and possibly nuclear-armed surface vessels or submarines.

Roots of Antagonism

In the days preceding the U.S.-led assault on Iraqi forces in Kuwait, a besieged Saddam Hussein stitched the Muslim battle cry *Allah-o-Akbar* onto the Iraqi flag and prayed before television cameras. It was an anxious appeal to the power of political Islam and its ability to mobilize opposition to the West. Twenty years earlier, this leader of secular Arab nationalism would have raised the banner of pan-Arabism, a movement that met disgrace after repeated defeats of Arab forces on the battlefield. But now Hussein's call was for *jihad*, and the language used by Baghdad radio throughout the war was laden with Islamic symbolism. For example, as in the Arab–Israeli war of 1973, Iraqis killed in war were described as *shaheeds* (martyrs) rather than as patriots. This strategy worked even though the war was lost; Hussein succeeded in evoking a powerful emotional response among millions of Muslims the world over.

This raises questions that seem to have no reasonable answers: Why did many Muslims, possibly a majority, choose to ignore Hussein's invasion of Kuwait and his bloody crimes against other Muslims in Iraq and in Iran, and, instead, align themselves emotionally against the U.S.-led alliance? Why do neo-fundamentalist Islamic movements have so much support when, in fact, most of their targets are other Muslims? Fundamentalist *mujahideen* factions in Afghanistan have turned the city of Kabul into a battleground, and they are busily employed bombing neighborhoods, looting, maiming, and raping each other's followers in the name of Islam. A growing religious movement in Pakistan—the *Anjuman Sipah-e-Sahaba*—is seeking the expulsion of Shias from Islam, and they regularly commit assassinations and murders to achieve this end. Anger, violence, and fanaticism seem to have penetrated every Muslim country.

One consequence of Muslim extremism has been a growing (and reactionary) tendency in the West to view most, if not all, Muslims as fanatics maddened beyond reason. But this is irrational. Violence and extremism are not the monopoly of Islamic fundamentalism; they are common to fundamentalism of every faith. Moreover, in quantitative terms, the suffering inflicted on humanity by modern Western civilizations has been far greater, largely because they have wielded far greater powers of destruction. Nevertheless, political Islam has an extraordinary power to mobilize Muslims the world over. Why is it so militantly anti-West in character?

Irreligious Bombs

The answers, I believe, have relatively little to do with matters of faith and much more to do with the tangible, direct experiences of Muslims in this century. Militant political Islam has emerged as a response to the abject failure of Muslim society to provide the essentials needed for dignified human existence. Grossly unequal distribution of wealth in Muslim countries, suppression of fundamental human liberties, mistreatment of minorities and women, and populations soaring out of control have produced a nightmare. Muslim states have massacred their own citizens by the thousands in Iraq, Syria, Iran, former East Pakistan, and Timor. There are dictators and coups, nepotism and corruption. Heads of government in Muslim countries rarely retire to play golf; instead, they often meet death through assassination.

Plagued by religious and ethnic hatreds, and pushed backward by reactionary internal forces, the crisis of Muslim society has never been deeper. Eqbal Ahmed, writing in a Pakistani daily, observes: "It is difficult to recall a more demoralized and corrupt community in the annals of history. Each of the 30-odd 'Islamic' governments are dominated by self-serving rulers. All are addicted to armaments and to dependence on suppliers. All are littered with machines but command no technology. Not one is home to a university or research center of repute. They lack the will no less than the know-how to transform wealth into capital, importance into influence, resource into power."

Beyond doubt, the forcible dispossession of the Palestinians from their homeland created the greatest Muslim hostility to the West. Israeli policy, aimed at eliminating the Palestinians from the remnants of their homeland, is seen as having been consistently supported by the United States. Once a largely secular and nationalist Arab cause, the Palestinian issue ranks as the single most prominent Islamic issue.

In the latter part of this century, a dangerous and vicious pattern was established in the Muslim relationship with the West. Muslims see themselves as bullied by Western military might; this leads to a general perception that the West is dominating and subverting Muslim societies through economic and cultural power. Therefore the Muslims, as would any other people who feel besieged, tend to fall back and reinforce their own identity through opposition to the West and through appeals to past Islamic glories.

A consequence of the Muslim siege mentality—a trait they share with Israelis—has been mass paranoia. Wild theories of international conspiracies against Islam are believed by astonishingly large numbers of Muslims. Preachers and politicians denounce the West as the cause of all the ills of the Islamic world. Western culture, which invades every Muslim home via the mass media, is roundly condemned although it is allowed to continue, and is sometimes even welcomed, producing a curious form of cultural schizophrenia.

If the drive for nuclear arms is not derived from religion, a more general question remains. Why do some nation-states seek nuclear weapons? Perceptions of threats are undoubtedly important, but they are not necessarily the sole motivation. Prestige and power may be extremely important as well.

In a global climate of hostility, antagonism, and internecine wars, massive supplies of conventional but highly destructive arms from the industrial North are avidly sought by many countries of the South. The Gulf War reinforced this message; it was an important stimulus for the proliferation of all types of weapons. A few months after the war, one of the most successful exhibitions of military aircraft—in terms of numbers of buyers from developing countries—was held at Le Bourget, north of Paris. Patriot missiles, F-16s, helicopter gunships, and smart missiles are in great demand. Nuclear weapons—providing "more bang for the buck"—would be even more attractive if they were available.

Islam or no Islam, many Muslim countries want nuclear weapons for specific national reasons. Following the logic of modernization, they—as well as other developing countries—are imitating what the developed North has already done. Thus, Muslim states are indistinguishable from other modernizing states that have, or aspire to have, weapons of mass destruction. If a Muslim state acquires a nuclear arsenal, it is very likely to behave as would any other nuclear state. Islamic unity would probably have no real significance.

Bombs Made Easy

Can international controls effectively limit the spread of nuclear weapons? Having greatly extended its influence in the Security Council after the disintegration of the Soviet Union, the United States clearly hopes to use the United Nations as a means to this end. Other means include the International Atomic Energy Agency (IAEA) and the Nuclear Suppliers Group. New monitoring procedures will be implemented to check that countries that have signed the Nuclear Non-Proliferation Treaty (NPT) comply with treaty rules. Careful export controls and new monitoring methods may limit the rate of proliferation, but it is obvious that these procedures are effective only to a point.

It is becoming easier and easier for even rather poor countries with marginal technological infrastructures to develop the rudiments of a nuclear weapons program—provided that they are sufficiently motivated to do so. Pakistan has proved this point. It has a per capita GNP of less than $400, about 74 percent of its people are illiterate, and the quality of its educational system ranks close to the poorest in the world. The university system has essentially collapsed over the last two decades. The industrial base is narrow—80 percent of its exports are agriculturally based, and the manufacturing sector accounts for only 20 percent of its gross domestic product.

If Pakistan can do it, so can many other countries. Among Muslim countries, Iraq and Iran are the most likely to follow suit. Their financial resources are far greater than Pakistan's and their technical manpower base is at a roughly comparable level. According to nuclear weapons experts who examined the evidence compiled by the U.N. Special Commission on Iraq at the time of the Gulf War, Iraq was about three years away from producing its first atomic weapon. The destruction of its nuclear facilities, both during and after the war, has been a major setback to its efforts. But even so, the possibility exists that once sanctions are lifted, Iraq will be able to rebuild its program in a few years.

Relative to Iraq, Iran is better placed, should it seriously seek to develop nuclear capabilities. At the time of the Shah, as part of a grandiose program to install tens of reactors for nuclear power generation, thousands of Iranian scientists, engineers, and technicians were sent to the United States and other Western countries for training. After the revolution, the program was scrapped, but the manpower still exists in Iran to some degree, and a revival of interest is apparent from the September 1992 deal Iran made with China for the purchase of a test reactor.

Searching for Solutions

Nuclear weapons states must take effective steps toward global denuclearization. There is no other way. While the NPT is important as a means to decrease the chances of nuclear conflict, and should be signed by all nations, it must be regarded as only an interim arrangement. There is absolutely no reason why the world should—or will—accept that only those states that currently possess nuclear weapons have the right to possess them indefinitely. Nuclear-weapons states could demonstrate their commitment to eventual global denuclearization—and endow their anti-proliferation efforts with moral authority—by reducing weapon inventories.

Proliferators must be penalized impartially. Pakistan, Iran, and Iraq cannot be treated differently from Israel. Such a stand is morally indefensible. It would be a supreme irony if the United States were to recruit Israel—a clandestine nuclear weapon state—to enforce non-proliferation.

It is highly unlikely that an Islamic bomb will ever exist. It is improbable, but not impossible; it could conceivably come into existence if Muslims feel their backs are to the wall. Islam could provide a sufficiently strong legitimizing principle if the whole Muslim nation perceives itself as under attack. There is a suspicion among Muslims that, like the Jews of the 1940s, they are becoming targets for ethnic cleansing. The genocide in Bosnia, the mass expulsion of Palestinians demanded by right-wing parties in Israel, and the collective punishment inflicted on Iraqi civilians are widely perceived to be just such ethnic cleansing. The same suspicions may underpin the search for Muslim power.

The West must not feed the Muslim psychosis. A political, not punitive, approach is needed—one that emphasizes positive diplomacy and the need for regional arrangements. Muslim countries need to be empowered, to regain hope for the future, and to have recourse to justice in their disputes with other nations. This demands a new global democracy which gives them and other nations of the South real political and economic power.

At the same time, democratic movements for peaceful social change in countries of the South need to be strengthened. No proliferator, and in particular, no Muslim country among them, provides its citizens an existence in which human dignity and liberty are respected. Addiction to armaments, callous and brutal elites, islands of splendor amid vast seas of poverty and human misery, wide-spread corruption and nepotism, and grandiose prestige projects are all too common. These countries, lacking internal dynamism and the strength to confront internal weaknesses, resort to conspiratorial arguments. The South's claim to a higher degree of morality and spirituality is a sham; the treatment of its own citizens testifies to that.

The task of limiting proliferation is a daunting one, and the outcome is uncertain. It is true that the end of the U.S.-Soviet confrontation has created a dramatic new possibility for a world with far fewer nuclear weapons. But this historic opportunity could easily be lost and supplanted by nuclear anarchy, a likely consequence of rapidly spreading, widely available, multi-purpose technologies along with an emerging global scientific culture. Paradoxically, though the chance of many nuclear detonations has shrunk essentially to zero, the chance of a single or few detonations is likely to grow. This is no time for complacency.

This is adapted from the June 1993 *Bulletin*.

II.2 Engineer for Hire

David Albright

In the mid-1980s, Bruno Stemmler was unhappy with his job. He had worked as a physical chemist for MAN Technologie in Munich, Germany, since 1969. But he was embroiled in a conflict with management over what he regarded as inadequate compensation for his discoveries and perhaps inadequate appreciation of his talents.

Stemmler had been involved in the design and testing of gas centrifuges used to produce enriched uranium for nuclear reactor fuel, although the same centrifuges can be used to produce weapon material. MAN is an important partner in the European centrifuge enrichment consortium, Urenco, which sells non-weapon-grade low-enriched uranium to nuclear power plants.

Lured by the chance of finding new work, Stemmler visited Iraq in the fall of 1988 and the spring of 1989. Both visits were secret. In Iraq, he was soon recruited to provide technical assistance to the Iraqi centrifuge program. He planned to make additional trips—even to stay for some months—but early one morning in the summer of 1989, German investigators armed with a search warrant arrived at his home. After searching his house, the authorities took him away for questioning. They accused Stemmler of giving secret information about German centrifuges to the Iraqis, who were known to be trying to acquire nuclear weapons.

In the end, Stemmler was never charged, let alone tried, for any criminal act. But in December 1989, the German news weekly *Der Spiegel* printed a story about him and his colleagues. Stemmler never discovered the source of this story, but he said it was published when the investigation was almost finished. After the story appeared, MAN suspended him; Stemmler said the bad publicity worried MAN, which was afraid it would lose business in both Germany and the United States.

Tricks of the Trade

Stemmler never built an atomic bomb for Iraqi scientists, nor did he build centrifuges. What he did provide was technical assistance and guidance in certain important areas of Iraq's centrifuge program, including design and assembly. According to Stemmler, the service he rendered was not then a violation of German export law. Today, it would be.

Since much of the difficulty in developing centrifuges involves identifying problems and knowing "tricks," expert assistance can significantly shorten the time it takes to develop them. Export controls on the sale of nuclear-related equipment can help limit the spread of weapons. But scientists and technicians can play an equally important role, and thus their know-how is increasingly subject to export controls as well. But to make controls more effective, scientists like Stemmler should be suspicious about foreign employers with ready cash, since their abilities with even seemingly innocuous older technologies—like the centrifuges of the 1960s and 1970s—present a genuine danger.

Stemmler said he understands that now, and he often told me that he regrets that he did not think about the potential consequences of his actions in Iraq. But, he says, he was "never told that he was being taken to Iraq to talk about centrifuges." Once there, however, he felt justified discussing unclassified centrifuge technology with the Iraqis because the climate was very different when he first agreed to go. The West had supported Iraq in the Iran–Iraq war, which had just ended. And Iraq, then considered a friend of the West, was involved in a massive rebuilding program. Stemmler said he "never had the impression that Iraq was against the United States."

In addition, the Iraqis told him that their "only desire [was] to make nuclear fuel" for civil applications. During my first meetings with him, Stemmler often said that the Iraqi centrifuge could only have produced low-enriched uranium, not the highly enriched material needed for an atomic bomb. But as he learned more about other nuclear weapons programs, he was less confident about the latter claim. Information about Russia's centrifuge program was becoming available, including the revelation that Russia had produced about 1,200 metric tons of weapon-grade uranium with a less sophisticated machine than the design Stemmler saw in Iraq.

Impressions of Baghdad

Each of Stemmler's trips to Iraq lasted four or five days. During his stay he was questioned by a total of about 15 Iraqi centrifuge experts in a guarded ministry building near the al-Rashid Hotel (where he stayed) in downtown Baghdad. He said that the chief Iraqi expert, who was also the host for his visits, was called Muhammad, but he was not sure if that was his real name.

Stemmler said that the Iraqis showed him general assembly drawings of centrifuge designs and asked him about various components. He later described each drawing as roughly the size of his kitchen table (about three by four-and-a-half feet). Stemmler was surprised to see the drawings. He said, "I was relatively sure it was a Urenco machine"—and he knew that Urenco designs were classified.

Stemmler wanted to sell the Iraqis a license to use a patented process for applying a homogenous oxide coating on maraging steel that he and a few colleagues at MAN had developed. Maraging steel is used in the spinning components of centrifuges. Although maraging steel oxidizes naturally when formed into components or tubes, Stemmler had found that if the natural oxide layer is removed and replaced with a carefully applied uniform coating, the maraging steel components will resist corrosion a lot longer.

Because the process also turns the centrifuge rotor dark, the surface of the rotor radiates heat better. This is extremely important because the rotor operates in a vacuum, making heat transfer difficult. If excess heat is not properly dissipated, it interferes with the centrifuge's ability to separate uranium. Earlier rotors were painted black, but maraging steel rotors spun so fast that the paint flew off. Stemmler's oxidation process solved this problem.

The process had other potential applications. Stemmler hoped that he could find someone who would buy the patent—MAN had relinquished any claim, and he and his co-inventors retained ownership. Also, it was not classified.

Nevertheless, the patent was a major source of the conflict between Stemmler and MAN. Stemmler said that he and his co-patent holders wanted more money for the use of the process than MAN was prepared to pay. Stemmler said he wanted 50,000 Deutsche marks, but MAN offered only 15,000. He said that MAN claimed that it was using a variant of Stemmler's process in its production of maraging steel centrifuges. Stemmler said that the MAN process was actually equivalent to his, not a variant, and that he and his colleagues deserved more compensation. Stemmler said in early 1992 that he expected this dispute to go to court. One of his co-inventors told me in September 1993 that they still had not received any money from MAN.

During his first meeting in Iraq, Stemmler described the patent and the equipment that would be needed to properly oxidize maraging steel components. He told his hosts that oxidation furnaces and the necessary inserts could be obtained from Degussa, a German firm in Frankfurt that had supplied MAN many years earlier.

Stemmler told me during one of our last meetings that when he went to Iraq the second time, the Iraqis were having trouble oxidizing components evenly. He said Iraq had acquired a small oxidation furnace between his first and second visits, but had not been able to master the process. He said he gave them some hints about how to solve the problem.

Even after providing all this information, Stemmler still "hoped to get a contract to teach the Iraqis how to do the coating properly." Achieving a homogeneous layer can be very difficult, and according to Stemmler, it "takes a long time to develop a feeling for the process." He expected to visit Iraq a third time, and he hoped for a direct contract with Iraq that would have involved spending many months in Iraq "making experiments together" with the Iraqis.

After the Gulf War, I showed Stemmler pictures of oxidized rotors that had been found in Iraq by the IAEA and U.N. inspectors. He said that the Iraqis had not done it correctly.

On many occasions, Stemmler said that the Iraqi centrifuge experts displayed a lot of theoretical knowledge about centrifuges, but they lacked practical experience. He saw only primitive measuring and experimental equipment. Iraq also lacked "sufficient technical services and technicians to back up the engineers." Stemmler believed that the Iraqis were particularly interested in his practical experience.

He thought at the time that Iraq was many years away from serial production of maraging steel centrifuges. Stemmler said it is a "long distance from design to a practical machine."

Stemmler's assessment of the program is consistent with the findings of the IAEA Action Team. In its June 22, 1993, Fact Sheet, the IAEA Action Team for Iraq concluded: "The Iraqi centrifuge program was in a very early stage using clandestinely obtained European designs and illicitly obtained materials to build a few research machines."

Stemmler's Contribution

During my interviews with Stemmler, he was inconsistent in evaluating his own contribution to the Iraqi program. At times he tried to minimize the importance of his assistance. He said that he did not provide the most modern specifications, or Urenco-specific values. In some cases, he said, he tried to give them minimal information that was not usable for their specific machine. He also said he told the Iraqis several times that he did not want to work on centrifuges.

At other times, he said he believed he had helped to improve the Iraqi centrifuge design, although he said he did not provide the Iraqis with classified information.

Stemmler's colleagues do not agree on the potential value of his contribution. In general, his colleagues respect his theoretical abilities. But some say that he had difficulty turning his ideas into practical products. This shortcoming, they say, contributed to his problems at MAN.

Nevertheless, Iraq succeeded in obtaining a design and then in getting help to improve and build on that design from some of its original developers. Despite the design's "crudeness," the machine could have made weapon-grade uranium, although probably at a slower pace than planned.

Even though Stemmler did not receive a contract, Iraq paid him 120,000DM in two equal payments (equivalent to about $75,000 at today's rate of exchange). Sometimes he felt that was a lot of money, sometimes a little. As a fraction of the total amount Iraq spent on its centrifuge program, Stemmler's payment was insignificant. But he believed that he would have received a lot more money if he had actually negotiated a contract and gone to Iraq for several months.

Stemmler believes he broke no laws. Nevertheless, he has suffered greatly because of his activities. As public concern heightened about the spread of nuclear weapons, Stemmler had to bear responsibility for his actions.

The negative stories in the press made it impossible for him to find work. Virtually every time we met he talked about his latest attempt to find employment to support his wife and teenage daughter. He told me that when he called one German company about a job, he was confronted as the man who had helped Iraq build nuclear weapons. As a result, he was looking for work in Brazil and the United States. He hoped to find work in Brazil on a project to develop a more efficient distillation process for producing alcohol-based fuel for Brazilian cars.

Stemmler's case shows how technical knowledge can be misused and scientists can allow themselves to be manipulated. Export controls on know-how need to be strengthened. But efforts to control proliferation will increasingly depend on finding ways to increase the awareness of experts like Stemmler about the potential danger of the information they carry in their heads.

This is adapted from the December 1993 *Bulletin*.

II.3 Black-Market Bombs and Fissile Flim-Flam

KIRILL BELYANINOV

"There is one more piece, but nobody wants to take it. Too much hassle. We've been sitting on it for six months already," Nikolai said as he swung open the rusted door of an old garage. Tripping over things and swearing under his breath at the electricity that had just gone off, he led us inside. In a corner, covered with old rags and gas canisters, stood what appeared to be a nuclear warhead.

"SS-20, fully assembled." The middleman pointed at the red-stenciled military markings. "Seventy thousand dollars and you can take it now."

That was in August 1993. Vladimir, Dmitri, and I—three undercover journalists from *Literaturnaya Gazeta* and *Novaya Ezhednevnaya Gazeta* in Moscow—had been investigating the nuclear materials black market for six months already, and we were ready to wrap it up. We took a Polaroid photo of the alleged warhead and told Nikolai we'd double-check its authenticity with our "Moscow sources." Nikolai agreed, under the condition that we have an answer in three days.

By that point Nikolai was just one of several brokers we had scrupulously cultivated. We spent almost every day calling dealers, waiting, hearing promises, running to the lab to drop off radioactive samples, waiting, picking up samples all while crafting credible lies for the shadowy middlemen. We each knew what would happen if a dealer discovered our true identities.

In the Beginning

Crossing over to a market economy begins with crossing borders. Budding businessmen from the small but proud and independent Baltic states were the first to understand this. They started the flow of large quantities of scrap metal, timber, oil, and salvage to the West in the last three or four years.

There was a puzzling element to this tide of goods, however: none of the Baltic republics actually had any raw materials, and the only way to get to the nearest oil well was by plane. The traffickers found a way around this dearth of natural resources. The descendants of Estonians and Lithuanians who had been deported to Siberia after World War II were well-established in Russia's machine-building plants in the Urals. As they returned to Estonia or Lithuania, they brought along materials stolen or purchased from the factories.

The Latvians took a different tack: they slowly began selling off their republic's property, from copper and bronze monuments to door handles of Roman Catholic cathedrals. The theft of a heavy copper plaque from a Republican parliament building in Riga was the crowning achievement of local dealers. The guards must have been sleeping very soundly that night.

By 1992, tiny Estonia had become a huge exporter of scrap metal. Its neighbors, Latvia and Lithuania, were forced to find new ways of procuring convertible currency, because all their efforts to compete with Estonia had ended in failure. After studying possible markets, the black marketeers found a product: radioactive materials.

There were a few drawbacks—like potential danger to one's life. But the export of radioactive materials promised colossal profits, and it did not require renting an entire train, as was the case with transporting metals. A container with one kilogram of a substance containing uranium could easily fit into the trunk of any car.

The initial search for customers in the summer of 1991 was haphazard. Using reference books, dealers looked up small and mid-size Western companies doing business with Russia in almost any field and sent them offers by fax. When a Norwegian firm—having received an offer from Volgograd of red phosphorus, several tons of heavy water, and 10 kilograms of cesium—created a serious scandal, the radioactive materials market went deeply underground.

While the Western press zealously analyzed rumors of a secret black market for nuclear weapons, and while Western police arrested dozens of middlemen from Eastern European countries caught with samples of uranium and plutonium, the Russian leadership denied the existence of such a market with equal zeal. This denial was especially easy because none of the serious Western investigations into the black market produced any hard evidence.

"I can declare with complete confidence that we did not register one incident of sale of nuclear weapons," said Andrei Chernenko, the former director of the Public Relations Center of the KGB, in fall 1992. "All the disappearances of radioactive materials from the enterprises of the nuclear complex are purely accidental." Other Russian officials readily supported his statement.

Plutonium in a Cookie Box

The middleman sighed, anxiously scratched behind his ear, and asked, "You know the conditions, don't you?"

It was May 1993, the middle of our investigation. We had been invited to an apartment building in the center of Moscow around noon, where we met the middleman in a first-floor apartment furnished with only a few desks and an old fax machine.

The broker reached inside a sturdy bank safe and took out a cardboard cookie box. Inside the box lay a lead sheet rolled into a pipe and pinched at one end. Small, dirty, white flakes slowly fell on the table from the open end as he lifted it out of the box. Two of his recently hired bodyguards—who apparently had not yet learned the scientific nuances of "X-ray salesman" work—quickly jumped back.

"Don't worry," the middleman said. "We put some laundry detergent in there so that the sample does not accidentally fall out of the container, that's all."

They brushed aside a pile of documents on a dusty table to make room for the "container." The radiation monitor squealed loudly.

"It's plutonium 239, just what you ordered," the middleman confirmed. "The conditions are standard: you can take the sample for exactly 24 hours. Tomorrow you will tell us whether you will take the entire shipment or not. Then we can discuss delivery methods."

As he spoke, he handed me the cookie box—the immediate means of delivery. The following day we took the pinched lead pipe in its cookie box to the director of the Moscow Center of Radio Analysis Control, Sergei Belopukhov.

"Of course there is plutonium here," Belopukhov said. "But the sample also contains plutonium 242, plus cesium, americium, thorium, and some fission fragments. Well, it's your usual reactor utility waste. It's ideal material for terrorists, but you can't make a real bomb out of this."

Rules of the Game

When Dmitri, Vladimir, and I began this investigation, we didn't have any grandiose goals. We didn't set out to prove that it's possible to carry abso-

Frank Cotham

lutely anything out of most factories, either. But this sad truth has been proven time and time again in the past five years when entire trains carrying conventional weapons have vanished from the tracks, only to reappear in one of the Commonwealth of Independent States' "hot spots" a few weeks later. Our task was much easier: we simply tried to verify rumors.

Our first attempts in February 1993 did not bring any results. All we managed to learn was that everyone had heard about the nuclear materials market, but no one had ever met a live plutonium salesman.

Our stunning lack of success was caused in part by a rule we were unaware of: to get into the nuclear materials trade, generally you must be referred to a dealer by two of his colleagues.

Results finally started coming about two months later, when people in the halls of the trading exchanges began to recognize us as part of the "in" crowd. One of our first offers came from a broker at the Moscow Raw Materials Exchange who offered us 5 kilograms of 80 percent enriched uranium 235. We met him later during rush hour on a busy downtown street. Out of his briefcase he took a laboratory-type container with a sample and an absolutely official-looking certificate of quality from the lab at the State Institute of Rare Earth Metals (GIREMET).

The Moscow Center of Radio Analysis Control analyzed this sample as well and confirmed the information on the certificate. Then the real difficulties started. Because we couldn't afford to buy the enriched uranium, we said that we would pay for the 2.5-gram sample only after seeing all the "merchandise." When the middleman heard that, he lost interest in the deal and soon vanished altogether.

A few days later, his colleagues descended on us with offers of "merchandise" samples and GIREMET certificates. They also promised to deliver uranium or plutonium abroad. However, subsequent analysis of their samples at the Moscow Center of Radio Analysis Control showed that there was uranium in only one container—and it was only 2–3 percent enriched. Other samples from various brokers contained metallic powder, powdered sugar, and a few grams of cesium. One container was empty.

Trading Air

The flim-flam men are called "ventilators" because they trade air. Trading air as a commercial activity arose in Russia only recently. It quickly became popular in the growing circles of Russian dealers.

The structure of this business is very simple: a middleman finds a customer who wants to buy several kilograms of, let's say, plutonium. He offers a sample for analysis and receives a deposit. Almost anything can serve as a sample, from a few grams of the real substance—easily procured from numerous institute laboratories—to an empty lead container. A lead container can be X-rayed for a few hours to guarantee a high radiation count.

All transactions in these circles are conducted in U.S. dollars. After receiving a deposit, the middleman disappears for a week. While the disheartened buyer searches high and low for his broker, waving the empty container and the fake certificate in the air, his money is earning money. It's being used as capital for black market retailers, private lenders, or exploiters of dollar-ruble exchange rates. The profit isn't high; if the middleman receives a deposit of $2,000–3,000, he makes $200–300 at most. But he suffers absolutely no losses. The middleman finally meets with his client, apologizes profusely for the mistake, and returns the entire sum to his buyer.

More complicated versions of this trade require a more sophisticated knowledge of banking and criminal law. A year ago, certain Lithuanian and Estonian banks started accepting radioactive material as collateral for credit lines. An empty container is put into the bank safe, and a certificate confirms the serious intentions of its presenter. It isn't that difficult to procure such a document. GIREMET employees make 35,000–40,000 rubles a month ($30–35). They will write anything on the institute's stationery and put the institute's stamp on it for $100.

Novice ventilators try to sell the sample to the client as a necessary condition of supplying the entire order of the merchandise. After they receive the money, they vanish. But the black market is tough on those who stray from the rules, and such deals are extremely dangerous. Four Moscow ventilators have died this past year under mysterious circumstances.

A Peaceful Atom for Every Home

In early June 1993, I got a call from one of our contacts. A dealer would be waiting for us at the entrance to the uranium enrichment plant in Elektrostal, near Moscow, from 3:00 to 4:00 p.m. every day that week.

Sure enough, when we showed up a few days later, a serious young man in a gym suit and hightops—the standard uniform of Russian racketeers—was indeed waiting.

"Decide—do you want the merchandise or not?" the man declared.

There are many factories in Elektrostal, a small, smog-filled town. This particular plant seemed to differ from the others only by the amount of barbed wire around it, a beaten sign announcing "radiation danger," and guards. But a militia battalion, 700 riflemen, and radiation-sensitive alarm systems guarded the entrances and exits. We simply did not believe it was possible to carry anything out of such a fortress.

"See for yourselves," the young man said, hurt.

He disappeared through the checkpoint of the plant. Half an hour later he reappeared with a lead box in the pocket of his gym pants. He said the box held three uranium tablets, the kind used as nuclear reactor fuel.

"Guards will turn off any alarm system for a few minutes for 1,000 rubles," he said. "But if you have to bring out a kilo, it will be much more expensive—and not in rubles. In any case, nobody really counts these tablets." When the young man learned that low-enriched uranium did not interest us, he was disappointed.

Rumors about the existence of a huge market for nuclear materials have played a cruel joke on the inhabitants of numerous secret cities, such as Arzamas-16 or Chelyabinsk-65, and on employees of facilities such as the Elektrostal plant. Employees of factories producing products ranging from irons to strollers in the former Soviet Union could sell these products on the black market during periods of economic reform. Thus they were able to maintain a modest standard of living.

Those employed by the nuclear complex, however, didn't have such opportunities. After carrying radioactive materials out of their workplaces, they had to keep them in garages or their own apartments. In the town of Glazov, 15 kilograms of commercial-grade uranium were found underneath the bathtub of a local plant employee. One of the patients in the Obninski Medical Institute of Radiology hospital ended up there because he carried a sample of plutonium in a homemade container in his breast pocket for two months while waiting for a buyer.

But Wait! There's More

Ultimately our investigation brought real results. The appearance of buyers interested in strategic materials got around the tight world of Moscow dealers and we started getting one offer after another, ranging from anti-radar shields for planes to a marine-based nuclear missile, the NAP-300. The brokers, whom we met through Nikolai, asked for $5,000 just for the opportunity to see the missile. Unfortunately, we didn't have that kind of money on us at the time.

Samples appeared from the most unpredictable places. One middleman produced a 5-liter iron vegetable can from the dark cellar of a respectable-looking office. He dropped the can on the floor with a loud thump and suggested that we come closer to measure the radiation level, which penetrated through the thick lead coating.

Later lab analysis showed that the highly radioactive vegetable can contained some uranium 235 and plutonium isotopes 239, 240, 241, and 242.

It was impossible to check the quality of the merchandise in most cases. Reliable middlemen usually agreed to give samples for analysis under the condition of "mirroring," the only true protection from ventilators: Both partners give several thousand dollars to a third party as collateral. The seller guarantees the quality of his merchandise. The buyer guarantees that the deal will take place. Any violation of deadlines or of any conditions of the agreement results in the loss of the deposit.

Our investigation led us to conclude that stories of nuclear materials crossing formerly Soviet borders by the ton are global myths.

We met 28 dealers. All of them traffic primarily in metals, a trade that has a real and stable market. They deal with radioactive elements only from time to time, when there is the possibility of a really profitable deal.

Only two of the 28 had succeeded in closing real deals. Of course, we did not take their word for it—we checked with their competitors. In December 1992, 10 kilograms of cesium 137 were sold to a German, and an Arabic-looking man bought half a kilogram of uranium 238 in March 1993. It is considered in bad taste to ask the first or last name of the buyers—or the purpose of the purchase—in these circles, so no further information is available.

The SS-20 ballistic missile warhead, which may or may not have been authentic, appeared only as we were ready to end our six-month investigation last August.

"If you take this one," Nikolai said, shoving the white, elongated cone with his foot, "then we will get another one. It's in Ukraine right now."

The warhead's exterior did check out; but the inside could have been fake, like the insides of warheads that serve as substitutes when the real ones are taken out and serviced. Needless to say, we didn't jump at Nikolai's offer—we could never manage to come up with $70,000.

At the conclusion of our investigation, we asked one of the top officials of the Atomic Energy Ministry of Russia for an official comment on our findings. He answered all our questions curtly: "We do not have such information."

For some reason we felt uneasy.

This is adapted from an article in the March/April 1994 *Bulletin*.

II.4 Potatoes Were Guarded Better

Oleg Bukharin and William Potter

On November 27, 1993, at about 1:00 a.m., Capt. Alexei Tikhomirov slipped through an unprotected gate and into the Sevmorput shipyard near Murmansk—one of the Russian navy's main storage facilities for nuclear fuel. The 35-year-old deputy chief engineer then climbed through one of many holes in the fence surrounding "Fuel Storage Area 3–30," sawed through the padlock on the back door, and pried open the door with a metal pole he found next to the building. Once inside, Tikhomirov located the containers of fresh submarine fuel, lifted the lid off container No. 23, and broke off parts of three assemblies for a VM-4-AM reactor core. Stuffing the pieces (containing 4.5 kilograms of enriched uranium) into a bag, he retraced his steps.

Outside the shipyard he was met by an accomplice, former naval officer Oleg Baranov. Baranov dropped Tikhomirov off at his home, and then drove to the nearby town of Polyarny, where he hid the nuclear material in his garage.

The third man behind this operation was Dmitry Tikhomirov, Alexei's younger brother, who at the time of the theft was chief of the refueling division at the shipyard. He had briefed his brother Alexei about security at the site, the holes in the fence, and the design of the fuel assembly.

None of the conspirators had a prior criminal record. They also lacked contacts for selling the stolen material, for which they hoped to receive $50,000. According to the official record of the investigation, they waited six months before they began to search for customers. But when Dmitry Tikhomirov told a fellow officer about the theft and asked for help in selling the stolen merchandise, the conversation was reported to a senior officer. In late June 1994, the three conspirators were arrested and the stolen fuel recovered.

The theft itself was discovered only 12 hours after it occurred. Carelessly, Alexei Tikhomirov had left the back door of the storage building open. Two guards on patrol noticed the discarded padlock and the broken door seal, and a prompt search revealed the broken fuel assemblies.

The theft at Murmansk is only one of many diversions of nuclear materials that have occurred in Russia since the collapse of the Soviet Union. But unlike most previously reported thefts, the operation at Murmansk involved stocks of highly enriched uranium. Enriched uranium is the standard fuel for propulsion reactors used in both Russian submarines and surface ships. The level of enrichment varies widely depending on the type of reactor—from approximately 20 percent like that found in the fuel assemblies stolen from the Sevmorput shipyard to "weapons grade," which is usually defined as containing 90 percent uranium 235.

The possible diversion of materials from these very large stocks of highly enriched naval fuel is worrisome, even if most of the stocks would be of little direct use in building nuclear weapons.

According to Mikhail Kulik, the special investigator for the Northern Fleet Military Procuracy—and the chief investigator of the Sevmorput diversion—potatoes were guarded better than radioactive materials at the time of the theft at Murmansk. "On the side [of the shipyard] facing Kola Bay, there is no fence at all. You could take a dinghy, sail right in—especially at night—and do whatever you wanted. On the side facing the Murmansk industrial zone there are . . . holes in the fences everywhere. And even in those places where there aren't holes, any child could knock over the half-rotten wooden fence boards."

Kulik reports that some security improvements were made after the theft. The number of guards was increased, and they were issued walkie-talkies. Planks from crates were torn off and nailed to the fence to cover some of the gaps, and barbed wire was added. Although more sophisticated alarm systems were proposed, they were not put in place because of cost. Reportedly, there still are no surveillance cameras around the perimeter, and the integrity of the fuel containers is checked by sight only. According to Kulik, the first and last time the contents of most of the containers was checked was at the fuel-fabrication plant. He believes the diversion at Sevmorput "could have been concealed for 10 years or longer," had the open door of the storage building not attracted the guards' attention. It is difficult to know if the security deficiencies at Sevmorput are typical for other facilities storing or handling highly enriched uranium and plutonium.

In contrast, the physical security system at a typical U.S. facility with weapon-grade material includes a perimeter enclosed by two razor-ribbon fences, with a cleared space between the fences controlled by intrusion-detection sensors and closed-circuit television cameras. Behind the fences is a vehicle barrier. The storage building itself is a structure with hardened walls and interior intrusion-detection sensors. The site is guarded by more than 60 armed security guards and has an on-site tactical response team.

Security at nuclear facilities in Russia is undermined by financial constraints and by shortfalls in design and implementation. According to Gosatomnadzor, the Russian nuclear regulatory body, physical security at nuclear facilities in both the civilian and defense sectors suffers from a design philosophy that attached low priority to protecting the storage building itself. Russian physical protection systems generally lack intrusion-detection devices and portal monitors that are operational. In the case of the Sevmorput theft, for example, the alarm connecting the storage building to the guard post did not work because its fixtures had rusted and it had never been repaired.

Gosatomnadzor has also criticized existing physical protection systems because they are not designed to address the threat of terrorist attack. Guards have inadequate protection (no bunkers or bulletproof guard posts); no vehicle barriers surround the facility; communications between on-site guards and off-site personnel is primitive at best; and the qualifications of many guards are suspect—a condition that is unfortunate but understandable, given the low wages and the irregular payment of salaries.

The absence of anti-terrorist nuclear protection measures in Russia may be explained by the rapid economic, political, and social transformation of Russia. Previously, the extraordinarily centralized state with pervasive internal security measures made the threat of nuclear terrorism virtually nonexistent. The lack of a domestic market value for nuclear material also eliminated the incentive for nuclear theft.

While one should not exaggerate the threat of nuclear diversion in Russia today, it should be recognized that the threat has arisen because of the general disintegration of central authority and the rise in ethnic tension and organized violence. Given the ease with which the Sevmorput storage building was penetrated, one must be concerned about the vulnerability of naval fuel sites to terrorist-minded groups.

The Sevmorput case also highlights the difficulty of guarding against the "insider threat," which represents the greatest security danger, according to Russian nuclear safeguards officials. The Soviet system of safeguards traditionally emphasized "personal responsibility," but the current crisis in Russia has eroded human reliability. A combination of factors—the end of the Cold War, the accident at Chernobyl, the contraction of the Russian defense and nuclear power sectors, and the inability of the state to subsidize previously privileged workers in the nuclear industry and the military—has resulted in tremendous economic and social upheaval. Moral standards have eroded. As a consequence, the primary threat to nuclear safeguards in Russia today is a knowledgeable and corrupt insider (or group of insiders) who have access to nuclear materials and may attempt to steal them for profit, for political reasons, or because they are coerced by a criminal organization.

In addition to the theft at Sevmorput, two other cases fit the insider profile: a 1992 diversion of 1.5 kilograms of weapon-grade uranium from the Luch plant at Podolsk, and the 1994 theft of 8 kilograms of low-enriched uranium fuel pellets from the Ignalina nuclear power plant in Lithuania—the same plant that was the target of a November 1994 bomb threat by organized crime.

This is adapted from the March/April 1995 *Bulletin*.

II.5 Nonproliferation: Jury-Rigged but Working

DAVID ALBRIGHT AND KEVIN O'NEILL

Not long after the first nuclear weapons were detonated in 1945, many expressed the fear that dozens of countries would eventually get "the bomb." Proliferation fears reached their height in the early 1960s when President John F. Kennedy said that more than 20 nations might have the bomb by the 1970s. Tom Lehrer, a satiric folk singer, captured the mood of the time in "Who's Next," a song that wondered, in the midst of the civil rights struggle, whether we would "stay serene and calm when Alabama gets the bomb."

But the truth is that, in 50 years, no more than nine countries have developed nuclear weapons or the ability to assemble them rapidly, although a few more are trying. Nine is an alarming number, to be sure, but it is far less than predicted.

Since 1945, about one nation has crossed the nuclear threshold every five years. But South Africa dismantled its nuclear arsenal as part of an effort to end apartheid and rejoin the international community, and North Korea may be in the process of trading away its nuclear program in exchange for the equivalent of $4 billion.

Why were early projections so wrong? In part they were flawed because their underlying assumption—that any country with the necessary industrial infrastructure would build a bomb regardless of its security needs—was wrong.

But the single most important reason why early fears have gone unrealized is the continuing development of national and international efforts to stop the spread of nuclear weapons. These efforts have increased the political and economic costs of proliferation and made countries think twice about seeking nuclear weapons. Many countries that started nuclear weapon programs have subsequently abandoned them.

Nonproliferation initiatives include the International Atomic Energy Agency (IAEA) and its international inspection or "safeguards" system, the Nuclear Non-Proliferation Treaty (NPT), the Nuclear Suppliers Group (NSG), bilateral arms control measures, diplomatic efforts to reduce regional rivalries, national regulations, bilateral discussions, and government policies.

Collectively, these efforts are often called the international nonproliferation regime.

This regime has largely succeeded in preventing the rise of what Albert Wohlstetter in the 1970s dubbed a "nuclear-armed crowd." But success should not obscure how tough the fight has been or how many problems remain. The extent of Iraq's clandestine nuclear weapon program, revealed after its defeat in the Gulf War, exposed the nonproliferation regime's overconfidence.

Although the regime is imperfect and in many ways fragile, it is nevertheless a dynamic and evolving system that can cope with future threats. But the system is only as strong as the support it gets. Complacency about the spread of nuclear weapons and weaknesses in the regime must be avoided, because the strategies used by those who seek nuclear weapons are also evolving—would-be proliferators have learned to respond creatively to efforts to halt proliferation.

The nonproliferation regime still needs to be strengthened, and the regime's discriminatory aspects need to be reduced or eliminated. Improving the regime, preventing proliferation, and rolling back nuclear arsenals will remain major national and international security challenges for the next half century.

The Nonproliferation Treaty

In the first two decades following the use of two U.S. nuclear weapons against Japan in August 1945, many countries decided to seek nuclear weapons. By the mid-1960s, five nations had conducted nuclear tests, and many more had tried to acquire weapons. After all, any nation would find it hard to resist the seductive appeal of the most powerful explosives ever developed, particularly since their possession also involved acquiring many other modern technologies.

Nevertheless, by the mid-1960s some nations had already abandoned the dream and others had been pressured to stop. Sweden is the best-known example of a country concluding that nuclear weapons were not in its national interest. When Sweden decided not to build nuclear weapons in the late 1950s and early 1960s, it was close to achieving the capability to produce a small plutonium-based nuclear arsenal. In other cases, the United States or the Soviet Union intervened to stop an ally's nascent program. In rare cases, however, they did nothing—or they actually aided an ally.

Collective concerns about the direction of the Nuclear Age were embodied in the NPT, which was negotiated during the 1960s to cap the number of proliferants, to promote civil nuclear energy, and to strive for total disarmament. Despite its weaknesses, it remains a successful arms control measure.

The NPT has fundamental inconsistencies that make it discriminatory. One in particular continues to provoke widespread debate and controversy. Under the NPT, a few states can legitimately possess nuclear weapons; the rest cannot. The five states that tested nuclear explosives before the NPT was signed were declared "legitimate" nuclear weapon states.

This condition is, however, tempered by Article VI, which commits the weapon states to reduce their nuclear arsenals and move toward eventual disarmament. Citing Article VI, the non-weapon states have repeatedly called for a halt to all nuclear testing, for cutoffs in the production of fissile material for weapons, and for a schedule for nuclear disarmament. In practice, the treaty review conferences, held every five years, have become acrimonious meetings where non-weapon states press the weapon states to meet these conditions.

The NPT was not universally accepted. Israel, India, Pakistan, Argentina, Brazil—and until recently, South Africa—decided to remain outside the treaty. Their refusal to join the treaty gradually stigmatized them and became the basis for other nations—most notably the United States—to deny them sensitive exports and to take other punitive measures.

Outside the NPT

During the 1970s, a few states began to modify their strategies for acquiring nuclear weapons. In 1974, India conducted a full-scale test of a "peaceful nuclear device." But the other states that joined the nuclear club after 1970—Pakistan, South Africa, and perhaps North Korea—have, like Israel, not announced their success with a nuclear explosion. Instead, they built nuclear weapons that did not require full-scale testing to be reliable.

The 1970s saw the rapid growth of nuclear energy, with attendant civilian plutonium separation or "reprocessing" programs. The idea behind these programs was that plutonium produced in conventional reactors would be separated and eventually used in a new generation of "breeder" reactors that would produce more plutonium than they consumed. However, civilian plutonium also can be used to make nuclear weapons.

In the 1970s, several countries, notably South Korea and Pakistan, tried unsuccessfully to obtain "commercial" reprocessing plants, ostensibly for nuclear power programs, although their real interest was in obtaining nuclear weapons. Taiwan tried to use a civil research reactor program with a small reprocessing capability to mask its weapons intentions. All these and others were thwarted, principally by the United States, which in the 1970s decided to stigmatize civilian plutonium separation programs as too dangerous despite their legitimacy under the NPT.

In the mid-1970s, Pakistan also tried another approach to obtaining fissile material. Pakistan defied the conventional wisdom at the time—that countries would pursue plutonium separation because it is easier than enriching uranium. Pakistan illicitly obtained designs and secret supplier lists for the gas centrifuges used to enrich uranium in Europe. Armed with this information, Pakistan managed to buy many components and materials from Western suppliers. By acquiring materials, components, and know-how from various sources, by the mid-1980s Pakistan had succeeded in completing an enrichment plant that was not subject to international safeguards.

Because the effort was successful, it alerted the world to another weakness in the nonproliferation regime. In response, supplier nations agreed to broaden nuclear export controls, in essence restricting business opportunities for their own industries. These actions made it harder for countries to acquire nuclear weapons, but they also stoked a continuing debate over how many items should be controlled.

If components are controlled, a nation seeking equipment may turn to acquiring subcomponents and equipment to make the components. Should these items also be controlled? This controversy was not settled satisfactorily, with the result that many countries, particularly Germany, remained important suppliers for threshold states until the late 1980s and early 1990s.

During the 1980s, Pakistan and possibly North Korea crossed the nuclear threshold, but several others retreated. The mid-1980s saw the restoration of democracy in Argentina and Brazil, and with it growing public opposition to the secret, unsafeguarded nuclear programs that had been accelerated under military dictatorships. As a result, in the early 1990s both countries abandoned their right to conduct "peaceful" nuclear explosions, ratified agreements accepting full-scope safeguards of all their nuclear activities, and cut back funding for some of the most proliferation-prone parts of their programs.

In 1989, newly elected South African President F. W. de Klerk decided to dismantle his country's nuclear weapon program and sign the NPT. This decision was tied to his determination to end apartheid and, with it, South Africa's isolation by the international community. His action remains unique; no other country has given up its nuclear weapons.

A Proliferation Crisis

The 1990s witnessed a resurgence in concern about proliferation. Following the end of the Gulf War in 1991, the world was shocked as IAEA inspectors, given broad powers by the U.N. Security Council, systematically uncovered Iraq's nuclear weapon program. In clear violation of the NPT and with great reliance on foreign suppliers, Iraq had come remarkably close to a nuclear weapon capability. Not since the 1960s had the nonproliferation regime faced such a challenge to its credibility.

In 1992, after seven years of negotiation, North Korea finally signed a safeguards agreement. The IAEA—conscious of its failure to detect Iraqi activities before the Gulf War—launched an aggressive inspection effort to verify North Korea's initial declaration.

North Korea had secretly built a small reactor and an associated plutonium separation plant, and it was building two larger reactors. It declared in its initial report to the IAEA that it had separated only a small quantity of plutonium. But, utilizing new inspection techniques developed during the intrusive post–Gulf War inspections in Iraq, the IAEA determined that the North had not declared all of the plutonium it had separated, although it could not be sure how large the discrepancy was. The North could have hidden enough plutonium for a bomb, and, based on IAEA evidence and its own analysis, the U.S. Central Intelligence Agency believed that the North had probably separated enough plutonium for one or two nuclear weapons.

Suspicions about North Korea's past activities were increased after member states gave the IAEA intelligence information showing two camouflaged sites that appear to be nuclear waste sites, one of which is near the plutonium separation plant—intelligence-sharing with the IAEA was one of the reforms that occurred after the Gulf War.

Because the North refused to answer IAEA concerns about the initial declaration or to give the agency access to the two suspected nuclear waste sites, the IAEA demanded "special inspections" of the sites. Although the inspection of undeclared nuclear facilities is provided for under NPT safeguards agreements, the IAEA had never before called for them. This initiative represented a new determination on the part of the IAEA and the Security Council to inspect undeclared sites. (Before the Gulf War, the IAEA had inspected declared buildings at the Tuwaitha Nuclear Research Center near Baghdad, while undeclared activities at nearby buildings went undetected.)

After months of uncertainty, North Korea and the United States negotiated an agreement in early 1995. The centerpiece of the "Agreed Framework" is the U.S. promise to lead an international consortium that will provide North Korea with modern light-water reactors in exchange for a freeze on its current activities at the reactors and reprocessing plant, and for the eventual dismantlement of these facilities and the removal of a stock of plutonium-laden spent fuel from North Korea.

The North also agreed to allow the IAEA to conduct special inspections and to finish verifying the North's initial declaration, but not before significant nuclear components for the light-water reactors are delivered. U.S. officials have said the process will take about five years. This long delay in carrying out special inspections and in finishing the verification of North Korea's initial plutonium declaration represents a setback for the IAEA's tough new inspection effort.

Nightmare Scenario

With the disintegration of the Soviet Union, the possibility of a frightening new shortcut to nuclear weapons has emerged—the "nightmare scenario." Although Russian nuclear weapons remain protected, stocks of plutonium and highly enriched uranium are significantly more vulnerable. Lack of adequate physical security and material control and accounting systems at many sites makes Russian facilities attractive targets for possible diversion of fissile materials.

Although the cases of smuggled plutonium discovered to date in Germany and Eastern Europe have involved relatively small quantities of fissile materials, the capture of this material should provide only a modicum of reassurance—the smugglers who have been apprehended may be the clumsiest or the most careless, or those most likely to fall for sting operations run by police and journalists.

So far, every country that has obtained nuclear weapons has built an indigenous industry to produce fissile material, either in the form of a uranium enrichment plant or a reactor and plutonium separation plant. Historically, building these facilities has been the hardest part of building a nuclear weapon. But poorly secured Russian materials could eliminate the need for these facilities. By exploiting poorly paid "insiders" at Russian facilities, countries or their agents could steal enough fissile material for a weapon or a small nuclear arsenal.

Production facilities are the most detectable part of a clandestine program. If fissile material is acquired abroad, nuclear weapons can be built in smaller installations with a significantly smaller "signature" than fissile material production facilities. Existing control and detection methods may not be able to sound a warning before a bomb is assembled.

The situation in Russia has also raised the specter of nuclear terrorism. It is now a more credible possibility that a terrorist group could fashion a crude nuclear explosive and hold a government hostage to its demands. Leakage of separated plutonium from the growing civilian nuclear power programs in Europe and Japan also raise this possibility, but these programs have significantly greater levels of physical protection. In any case, concern about the diversion of fissile material into the hands of terrorists or criminal elements has never been higher.

Taking Stock

The risky situation in Russia will continue well into the future, and correcting the inadequacies at Russian sites will be costly and time consuming. The U.S. nuclear weapons complex faced similar security weaknesses in the 1970s. Improving material controls and physical security at U.S. nuclear weapon sites required many years and billions of dollars. Until the Russian situation is fixed, quick international law-enforcement actions or Security Council intervention conceivably could be required against a country that had snatched significant quantities of fissile material in Russia.

Some countries, such as Iran, Libya, and probably Iraq, are determined to get nuclear weapons even though they have signed the NPT. In addition, if North Korea does not verifiably demonstrate that it has terminated its nuclear weapons program, South Korea and Japan might feel compelled to reconsider their decisions not to build nuclear weapons.

India and Pakistan appear to be stuck in a low-grade nuclear arms race, with neither side able to find a way out of the deadlock. Meanwhile, each side is gradually increasing its nuclear capabilities.

Israel remains the forgotten proliferator, seemingly protected by the United States and other countries from the embarrassment and pressure heaped on other threshold states. Its program can be expected to continue to stimulate other nuclear weapons programs in the Middle East.

The problems created when other former members of the Soviet Union inherited nuclear weapons and fissile materials appear to be well on the road to solution. Belarus and Kazakhstan have signed the NPT as non-nuclear weapon states and in November 1994 Ukraine ratified the NPT as a non-weapon state. Kazakhstan deserves credit for its recent sale to the United States of a poorly protected stock of about 600 kilograms of highly enriched uranium. Rounding up stray fissile material stocks needs to be a priority for the United States and the U.N. Security Council.

In the threshold states, however, the recent agreement between the United States and North Korea suggests that in the future the price of convincing them to give up nuclear weapons may be very high. An unintended consequence of the U.S.–North Korean agreement could be that no nation will follow South Africa, which gave up its nuclear arsenal as part of its effort to rejoin the international community. Some countries might even be encouraged to create confrontations in the hope of exacting a payoff for ending their programs or abiding by intrusive safeguards regimes.

Russia and the United States are making significant reductions in their nuclear arsenals, and they support a test ban and a cutoff in the production of fissile material for weapons. Although progress is slow, they appear, finally, to be living up to their NPT commitment to reduce their stockpiles. Once Ukraine joins the NPT, START I can enter into force and START II can move forward. This progress should ease the task of getting the NPT extended in April 1995, although the slow pace can be expected to be a point of contention.

Despite this progress, none of the original five nuclear weapon states appears willing to give up its arsenal, or even to discuss disarmament seriously. In some quarters disarmament is seen as dangerous because it might stimulate countries to seek nuclear weapons in the belief that they would be the only ones possessing them. Others believe that continued reductions in the U.S. arsenal could eliminate the nuclear umbrella still provided to many allies, stimulating them to revisit their own decisions not to build nuclear weapons.

This is adapted from the January/February 1995 *Bulletin*.

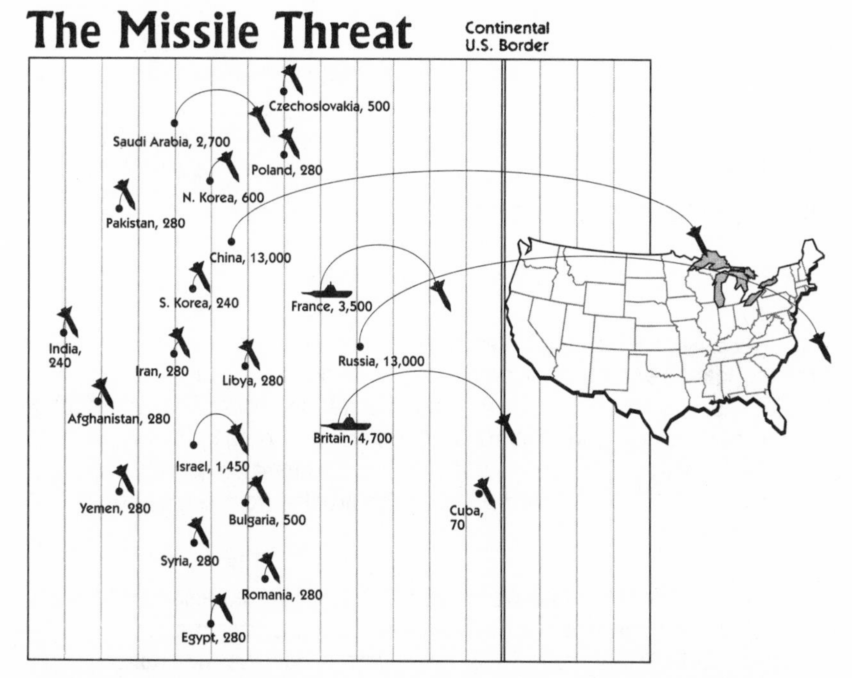

Distances in kilometers. Source: Lora Lumpe, Federation of American Scientists.
Graphics: Jandos Rothstein

Do any of the countries now possessing or seeking nuclear weapons pose a threat to the United States? Nuclear weapons are a major threat only if they can be "delivered" by bombers or missiles.

Despite scientists' warnings that defense against all-out missile attacks is technically impossible, missile defense remains popular with politicians. The Defense Department plans to spend more than $50 billion over the next 15 years to try to develop protection from ballistic missile attacks by "regional aggressors."

As this chart shows, the only countries who could reach the continental United States with any sort of missile are the known nuclear powers, none of which are our enemies. Iraq, which had the most developed missile program before the Gulf War, is now prohibited from purchasing or building any more missiles, and other countries the United States has identified as regional aggressors are decades away from intercontinental missile capability.

Chapter II
Discussion Questions

1. The president has appointed you coordinator of a new White House task force on dealing with nuclear proliferation. Before you come up with recommendations, she has asked you to testify before the Senate Foreign Relations Committee about the administration's understanding of the proliferation problem. Specifically, she wants you to make an opening presentation entitled, "Myths of Nuclear Proliferation." Using the articles from this chapter, write that presentation.

2. The authors of the last article of this chapter describe some of the central features and flaws of the nuclear nonproliferation regime. Which of the positive controls in the regime seem adequate to address the challenges presented in the other articles in the chapter? Which seem inadequate? How would you recommend improving the ability of nations to handle the problem of proliferation?

3. A frequent debate about nuclear proliferation is between those who argue that the flow of nuclear material is the problem, and those who argue that the greater problem is the movement of human, technological expertise about building nuclear weapons and delivery systems. Argue for one side or the other, or show how both sides are correct.

4. A frequent argument from would-be nuclear weapons nations is that they should not be asked to give up their quest for nuclear weapons unless major nuclear weapons states make a firm commitment to give up their own arsenals. How do you respond to this argument?

Chapter III

Legacies of Insecurity: Human Costs, Societal Impacts, and Environmental Disasters

Immediately after the demise of the Cold War, a debate began in the United States about why it had ended. Many believed that massive U.S. military spending and the nuclear arms race had brought the Soviet Union to its knees, and thus ended the Cold War; while others contended that these policies had actually prolonged the Cold War. Neither side doubts that the national price paid for the arms race was substantial. But views differ on how steep the costs actually were, and whether they were worth whatever results were achieved.

As time passes, the total effects of the arms race are becoming clearer in the United States and, increasingly, in the former Soviet Union as well. The impacts take many forms—economic, social, environmental, and even intellectual—as the articles in this chapter will illustrate.

One of the more troublesome questions over the years has been the extent to which massive arms spending has thwarted or distorted economic and technological development in the United States. The damaging economic effects of the arms race have been more obvious in the former Soviet Union. But many Americans are reluctant to say that their country is now less competitive economically and technologically because of years of—and continuing—large military budgets.

Among the strongest supporters of the prevailing U.S. defense strategies during the Cold War era were the defense workers themselves—from high-tech engineers commanding top salaries, to unionized machinists, to workers in plutonium-producing facilities. Now many of these workers find themselves in contracting industries that are coming under new investigation for health and safety reasons. If these workers enjoyed some of the obvious benefits of the arms race—including heavy government investment in certain geographic areas—they are also now paying some of its most trenchant costs. Jobs are rapidly disappearing, and many of the communities and individuals are left with serious environmental and health problems. These problems had become major issues in the United States by the 1980s, and, as these articles make clear, they will exert a toll for generations to come.

And then there was Chernobyl. Some would argue that what killed the Cold War was the world's worst nuclear accident, which occurred in the spring of 1986. That disaster may have marked the beginning of the end of the Soviet Union. Certainly it provided the most tragic demonstration since the Hiroshima and Nagasaki bombings of the poisonous effect of nuclear radiation. While many would argue that civilian nuclear energy and nuclear weapons should be considered as distinct policy arenas, the pattern throughout the Cold War was that they were dynamically related—politically, technically, and in public perception.

The articles excerpted in this chapter provide a panoramic view of various legacies of the nuclear arms race. The selections begin with the Nuclear Weapons Study Group assessment of areas of the U.S. economy and society that have been adversely affected by both the nuclear arms race and its demise. The specific dimensions of the environmental disasters generated by the work of nuclear weapons production facilities are the focus of the article by Linda Rothstein, which summarizes the U.S. government's own assessment of the damage. However terrible the messes, which are richly detailed in the article, the cost of cleaning them up is also horrific. The Energy Department's Office of Environmental Management has concluded that merely "stabilizing" the poisoned sites will cost more than $200 billion and take three-quarters of a century. Cleaning up the sites so they could be used for other purposes would double that cost.

The overall economic and environmental problems of the nuclear age are serious. But the societal impact involves individual human beings. Four selections in this chapter detail the diverse dimensions of the human toll—in life, health, quality of life, and sense of freedom—paid in different parts of the world.

Len Ackland examines the fate of nuclear weapons production workers in Colorado, recording not only their health problems but also their growing sense of abandonment in the early 1990s as their jobs were being phased out.

In the next article, Bengt Danielsson documents a familiar pattern of the nuclear arms race: the rush to develop and test weapons produces a wave of unforeseen environmental, health, and social problems, which are hidden, or at best ignored for as long as possible. In this case, the nuclear power is France, and the victims are the Pacific Ocean and Polynesian society.

Two articles discuss in detail the casualties of the 1986 Chernobyl disaster in Ukraine, then part of the Soviet Union. In the first, Alexander Sich surveys a wide range of issues associated with the reactions of the Soviet government and scientific communities to the accident in 1986. According to Sich, the accident and the response to it demonstrated and reinforced some of the worst Cold War thinking and practices in the Soviet Union: misinformation, poor leadership, secrecy, and questionable allocation of resources. Tragically, errors and mismanagement have increased the loss of lives and the health and environmental consequences that continue, even after a decade.

In the chaos that followed the accident and subsequent disintegration of the Soviet Union, documentation of the accident's effects was an early casualty. While no one knows for sure how many people have died as a result of the explosion, David Marples pieces together the most credible reports and estimates that Chernobyl has claimed at least 6,000 victims so far.

The final article by Carol Cohn pursues a theme that lies beneath many of the other articles in this chapter. Cohn analyzes how nuclear policy and procedures, especially as expressed in the language used by policymakers and defense intellectuals throughout the nuclear era, has altered our understanding of the fundamental ethical and human issues at stake in the arms race. Her argument, controversial to be sure, suggests that many of the environmental, social, and life-threatening impacts discussed in the other articles in the chapter were tolerated by government and society because we had developed a sanitized language for discussing them. The language made it easier to think abstractly rather than in real human terms, Cohn would claim, about the fate of workers, school children, or others suffering from the environmental effects of weapons production or nuclear accidents. And Cohn would say that the most damaging effect of "nuclear language" was that it made it possible for societies to build, and contemplate using, nuclear weapons.

The map at the end of the chapter reminds us that nuclear weapons were actually used on two August days in 1945. The serious environmental damage from nuclear weapons production, testing, and accidents still does not compare with the devastating loss of life and property in Hiroshima and Nagasaki. We recall with this map of Hiroshima the dreadful effects of one small atomic bomb—from the vaporization of life and substance at the epicenter to the increased cancer risk that pursues survivors to this day.

III.1 Victims of the Arms Race

U.S. Nuclear Weapons Cost Study Project
ARJUN MAKHIJANI AND
STEPHEN I. SCHWARTZ

Although nuclear weapons were not unleashed in anger during the Cold War, U.S. nuclear weapons and weapons production injured many people, principally in the United States and the Marshall Islands. While it is impossible to quantify the costs of lost wages, illness, medical care, and premature death, these costs are real and borne by society.

Workers in nuclear weapons production and testing facilities were among the most heavily exposed populations, along with military personnel and some "downwinders." Exposures varied significantly, depending on the specific nature of work and length of service. In general, workers employed from the war years until about the mid-1960s were the most heavily exposed.

Nuclear weapon workers were also exposed to a large number of non-radioactive toxic materials, including fluorine gas, hydrochloric acid, trichloroethylene, beryllium, mercury, and chromium. Radiation-exposure records are poor, and there are practically no records of worker exposures to other toxic materials. There are no studies of the effects of combined exposures to radiation and non-radioactive toxic materials.

Until 1994, the U.S. government's official position was that worker exposures were generally low and that there were no significant adverse health effects on the 600,000 people who have worked in the weapons complex since its inception. In March 1994, however, the Energy Department admitted that its records were incomplete, unreliable, and misleading.

Uranium miners were another highly exposed group of workers. Although it was well known during the 1950s that exposure to radon and its decay products in unventilated or poorly ventilated mines was a health hazard, the AEC stressed production over health and safety and did not require uranium mines to be adequately ventilated. Miners, many of them Navaho Indians, received an apology from the government in 1990 and are eligible for compensation under the Radiation Exposure Compensation Act. As of May 21, 1996, 1,170 miners had received nearly $123 million in compensation; another 1,095 claims were denied.

About 250,000 military personnel participated in the atmospheric nuclear testing program from the 1940s through the early 1960s. Some of their external dose records remain, but many were destroyed in a 1978 fire at a federal records repository in St. Louis, Missouri. Few measurements of internal doses were made, and the military has argued that armed forces personnel did not receive significant internal exposures. Congress has passed legislation compensating some of these "atomic veterans" or their widows.

Residents or downwinders who lived near nuclear weapons facilities comprise a third class of victims. In the case of exposure to fallout from above ground testing or large intentional or accidental releases of radioactivity, "nearby" can mean hundreds of miles downwind. Downwinders include U.S. citizens and Marshall Islanders. Under the Radiation Exposure Compensation Act, more than 1,200 downwinders had received nearly $72 million as of May 21, 1996.

The Marshallese have received two compensation packages, the first in the form of a $950,000 *ex gratia* (admitting no guilt) payment from Congress in 1964 ($5.4 million in 1996 dollars) for exposures resulting from the March 1, 1954, "Bravo" thermonuclear test, and a $150 million trust fund established by Congress in 1986.

In the 1980s residents near the Fernald Plant in Ohio sued the Energy Department for causing them to experience excessive and dangerous exposure from uranium processing. Although Energy claimed that only 135 metric tons (300,000 pounds) of uranium were released into the air during the life of the plant, an analysis performed by the Institute for Energy and Environmental Research suggested that the release was probably three times greater. An analysis done for the Centers for Disease Control and Prevention concluded that the releases were probably in the range of 370 to 600 metric tons, with a best estimate of 470 metric tons. Energy's estimates were based on flawed practices, poor record-keeping, and outright fabrications. For example, from 1969 to 1982, Fernald recorded zero uranium releases even though it made no actual measurements. In 1989, Energy settled for an unprecedented $78 million ($94 million in 1996 dollars).

Another category of victims includes the hundreds of unwitting subjects of radiation-related experiments. The October 1995 final report of the President's Advisory Commission on Human Radiation Experiments documented the range of experiments, and it suggested that a small number of victims of the most egregious experiments (or surviving members of their immediate families) be financially compensated. In November 1996 the government agreed to pay $4.8 million to the relatives of 12 victims—all but one now deceased—of plutonium and uranium injection experiments during the 1940s.

The project's final report, the work of a committee of 12, is forthcoming. This is adapted from the November/December 1995 *Bulletin*.

III.2 Nothing Clean about Cleanup

LINDA ROTHSTEIN

Over the past 50 years, the United States has spent hundreds of billions of dollars—at 1995 rates—to design and manufacture nuclear weapons. Now that the East–West arms race has finally ended, the nation may have to spend hundreds of billions more just to stabilize the poisonous mess left in the weapons complex.

Although her predecessors were all cut from the same secretive military cloth, Energy Secretary Hazel O'Leary has flung open the windows and doors, presenting the weapons complex's problems for public inspection. Two of the department's reports issued in 1995—*Closing the Circle on the Splitting of the Atom*, a generously illustrated survey designed for the general public, and *Estimating the Cold War Mortgage*, a massive study prepared for Congress—underline how difficult the mess will be to clean up.

In fact, both reports make it plain that "cleanup" is the wrong term. Most of the weapons complex is not going to be cleaned up in the foreseeable future. Merely stabilizing the wastes is an enormously sophisticated technical enterprise.

The Energy Department estimates that a comprehensive cleanup could cost in the range of $500 billion over 75 years. The more conservative $230 billion figure presented in *Cold War Mortgage* is a baseline cost (in 1995 dollars) that would be spread out over the next 75 years. That money would buy "stabilization" of the worst sites, not cleanup.

The creation of each gram of plutonium, reactor fuel element, and container of enriched uranium produced radioactive waste—virtually all of which remains with us today. The graphite bricks Enrico Fermi used for the first "atomic pile" at the University of Chicago were buried in a Cook County forest preserve. The acid used to extract plutonium for the first atomic test in the New Mexico desert is still stored at the Hanford Site in the State of Washington.

Not only do all the wastes remain, they pose a variety of hazards. Many are so toxic that they must be isolated for hundreds of centuries, and they need special treatment before they can be permanently disposed of.

During all of the nuclear weapons production period—and especially between 1943 and 1970—the nuclear weapons industry handled many wastes with little thought to the future. Billions of gallons of waste water were poured on the ground. Other liquid wastes were dumped into evaporation ponds, from which radioactive materials leaked, contaminating the soil and groundwater.

Weapons-complex wastes range from intensely radioactive acids used to separate plutonium to slightly radioactive items of clothing or chemical solvents used in purity tests. They differ in physical characteristics, chemical form, and radioactivity, and they need to be handled and stored in different ways. Among the great challenges to cleanup are the many deteriorating, unlabeled or unidentified waste containers whose precise contents are not known.

Waste has been the most abundant product of every step in the weapons production process: uranium mining and milling, uranium enrichment, handling spent fuel, spent fuel reprocessing, and plutonium production and plutonium parts manufacture. The following are some examples of the problems the Energy Department must solve.

Spent Fuel

The United States operated 14 nuclear reactors that produced plutonium and tritium for nuclear warheads. The last of these reactors was shut down in 1988. Most of the fuel rods and targets that were irradiated in the reactors were reprocessed to extract plutonium and leftover enriched uranium.

Although Energy has less spent fuel to contend with than does the commercial nuclear power industry, the two cannot be compared. Unlike commercial fuel, spent fuel from production reactors was not designed to be stored for any length of time. Its outer layer or "cladding" corrodes if it is stored in water. (But proper control of water chemistry can prevent or reduce corrosion.)

Eventually, the spent fuel will be placed in a deep geologic repository—when such a burial site becomes available. In the meantime, it must be stored above ground, and many of the existing storage facilities—some nearly 50 years old—do not meet safety standards. Some storage pools are unlined, with inadequate means for controlling water chemistry. Under some circumstances, both the rusted cladding and uranium will burn when exposed to air. A worst case scenario includes conditions that could lead to an inadvertent nuclear chain reaction or "criticality" event.

Reprocessing

Reprocessing of spent fuel produces the most chemical and radioactive wastes and is the most environmentally costly of all weapons-related work. Reprocessing wastes contain 99 percent of all the radioactivity produced in the weapons production process.

After spent fuel was irradiated in a production reactor, the plutonium and uranium had to be recovered—separated from the remaining material, which includes a variety of intensely radioactive fission products. The spent fuel was dissolved in acid and chemically separated, with the acids and chemicals used in the reprocessing retaining most of the radioactivity. The intense radioactivity is caused by the relatively rapid decay of fission products. This waste will generate only one-tenth as much heat and radiation after 100 years, and it will have decayed to one-thousandth of its original level in 300 years. Rapid decay may make its ultimate disposition easier, but high-level waste must still be isolated from the environment for a long time—essentially for as long as spent fuel.

Transuranic Waste

Plutonium production also created "transuranic" waste, which is a term used for any material that contains significant quantities of plutonium, americium, or other elements whose atomic weights exceed that of uranium. Transuranic waste includes everything from the chemicals used in crafting plutonium metal to the air filters, gloves, clothing, tools, and piping used in the plant.

Accidents have also generated transuranic waste. There were a number of fires at the Rocky Flats plant in Colorado that generated thousands of drums of transuranic waste, much of which was shipped to the Idaho Laboratory for storage.

The nuclear weapons complex has about 100,000 cubic meters—enough to fill half a million 55-gallon drums—of transuranic waste, much of which was put in "temporary storage." Some temporary containers have corroded and need to be repackaged and relocated.

Because of their long-lived radioactivity, transuranic wastes must be permanently isolated from the environment and from contact with people. The Waste Isolation Pilot Plant (WIPP) in New Mexico was built several years ago, and experiments are under way to study how waste materials would interact with the environment there. No wastes have yet been taken to the site, and there is local opposition to its use. If WIPP does become a permanent disposal site, much of the transuranic waste from the weapons complex will be stored there.

Plutonium

When the plants that manufactured plutonium parts for nuclear weapons were shut down, about 26 tons of plutonium were left in intermediate stages.

Frank Cotham

This stranded plutonium is in a wide variety of forms, from plutonium dissolved in acid to rough pieces of metal to nearly finished weapon parts.

Handling plutonium requires care, but the complex conditions at the weapons plants make for an even greater challenge. Radioactivity combined with corrosive acids is slowly destroying some of the plastic bags and bottles plutonium is packed in. Hydrogen gas is accumulating inside some of the sealed cans, drums, and bottles that clutter the aisles and fill the gloveboxes. Bulging and ruptured containers have been found. Both the hydrogen and some of the plutonium could ignite and burn. At Hanford and the Savannah River Site, plutonium is slowly collecting on the bottoms of tanks, where enough of it could produce a criticality event.

Because it can be used to make nuclear weapons, plutonium must be inspected, guarded, and accounted for, and the buildings that house it must be maintained, including ventilation systems, air filters, and fire and radiation alarms.

Plutonium "pucks" or "buttons" and other forms of plutonium metal are kept in storage vaults. These forms were stored in metal containers enclosed in plastic bags. In some cases, there are no records of what the packages contain. If it is exposed to air, plutonium can "rust," becoming a flammable powder.

The containers must be opened in sealed "gloveboxes" and the rust brushed off and treated. The metal and powder will then be repackaged separately, without plastic, to prevent this problem from recurring.

Plutonium parts not in operational warheads are stored at various facilities across the country. The supply increases steadily as weapons are dismantled at the Pantex Plant in Texas.

In December 1993, Energy Secretary Hazel O'Leary declassified the fact that the United States had produced more than 100 metric tons of plutonium. The ultimate fate of this material is now under discussion. Because it cost billions to produce, some argue that it should be used to fuel nuclear power plants. Others have suggested that some of it should be used to fuel a new tritium-production reactor. Others contend that neither plan is economical (it would require a new type of plant to fabricate fuel rods using a mixture of uranium and plutonium), and that we should find the safest, fastest, and cheapest way to spoil the plutonium's usefulness in weapons. One proposal is to vitrify it along with high-level waste. Other suggestions include storage in deep geologic repositories or deep boreholes, or disposal beneath the seabed.

Many Cold War weapon builders sincerely believed they were in an all-out struggle for national survival. Careful storage of waste products just didn't seem as important as "winning" the Cold War by building up the nuclear arsenal as rapidly as possible.

With the advantage of hindsight, it is both easy and popular to criticize the bomb-builders' mistakes and deplore their production practices. But, as the government focuses on cleaning up the weapons complex, it should be remembered that, if the present generation does not ask the right questions or press for carefully formulated decisions about environmental management, it will make its own set of mistakes.

This is adapted from a May/June article in the *Bulletin*, which in turn was based on *Closing the Circle on the Splitting of the Atom*, a report produced by the Energy Department's Office of Environmental Management.

III.3 Who the Hell Will Insure Us?

Len Ackland

A sliver of steel from a plutonium fabricating machine he was wiping off punctured Carlo Peper's glove and entered the thumb of his left hand. He rushed to a first aid station where a doctor yanked out the sliver with a pair of pliers. Today, after nearly three decades and three thumb operations to remove the plutonium, Peper's body is still contaminated.

Immediately after the December 1963 accident at the Rocky Flats nuclear weapons plant near Denver, Peper received medical treatment in an effort to flush the highly radioactive plutonium out of his system. A few months later, though, he recalls his boss telling him, "We've got bad news for you. You're too hot to stay in this building. We thought you'd cool off, but you're too hot."

So Peper was moved to a "cold" (or non-radioactive) building at the plant site and began working with a strong, lightweight metal called beryllium, also used in making nuclear bombs. "Here's the deal," he now explains, his voice filling with emotion. "They told me they were going to send me up there so I'd be safe. And they sent me up there and I got beryllium disease."

Peper, a deeply tanned 59-year-old outdoorsman, is one of 25 current or former Rocky Flats workers who so far have been diagnosed with berylliosis, an incurable lung disorder similar to "black lung" disease found in coal miners. And while an experimental screening program that began at the plant in 1987 is looking for beryllium disease, it has also found 12 cases of another lung disease called asbestosis, according to I. K. ("Ike") Roberts, the safety representative of United Steelworkers of America Local 8031.

These identifications of occupational diseases are probably just the beginning, adds Roberts, whose union represents the plant's 2,400 production workers. "There are a lot of things we just don't know yet. We're going to have to get into chemicals, solvents, all these other toxic materials," he says. "People talk about radiation exposures, but our problems are a hundred times greater for non-radioactive contamination."

Nobody knows the full extent of serious diseases incurred by workers at Rocky Flats and the dozen other major government-owned, contractor-operated facilities comprising the nation's nuclear weapons production complex. The U.S. Energy Department manages the complex, which at its peak in the mid-1960s employed some 133,000 people. It currently employs approximately 37,000 workers, of whom about 30,000 are blue collar and largely represented by unions. The total number of employees is expected to drop to 20,000 over the next 12 years, according to Energy Department officials.

Yet, hundreds of thousands of men and women have been employed by the weapons complex over the past 50 years and have potentially been exposed to radioactive and/or toxic substances. Unfortunately, poor record-keeping by contractors, long lapses between exposure to many hazardous materials and the diagnosis of disease, and scientific controversy about causal links to cancer and other diseases have created uncertainties about the health of U.S. nuclear workers.

The workers are, however, certain about one thing. They faithfully served their country, building the nuclear weapons deemed by president after president and Congress after Congress to be vital to "national security." Now the Cold War is over, nuclear weapons production has been halted, and environmental cleanup has begun. The workers want a fair shake.

"My fellow workers and I have served our country making components for nuclear weapons at the Mound, Ohio, facility," Shirley Lausten, an Oil, Chemical and Atomic Workers (OCAW) union member, told a Senate subcommittee in June 1992. "Some at Mound and many more at other defense nuclear facilities have paid a dear price for accepting this service. We have been exposed to life-threatening levels of radiation and toxic chemicals."

Lausten, 49, who has been a production employee at Mound for 23 years, made a strong pitch to the senators for government health insurance for nuclear workers. "The newspapers are filled with stories about the hazards of radiation. People are afraid of us. Employers don't want to assume the health insurance costs from hiring high-risk employees."

Such exposures set nuclear weapons workers apart from most other defense industry and armed services employees who also face job loss as the nation's military spending is reduced. In 1991, 5 million people had defense-related jobs. From 1991 to 1995 the total number of displaced defense workers could be as high as 1.1 million, or 275,000 a year, according to a study by the Office of Technology Assessment. (To put this figure in perspective, OTA notes that the "ordinary" annual displacement of American workers during the 1985–1989 period was 1.8 million.)

"Displacement is not a problem exclusive to workers at Energy Department facilities," acknowledges OCAW president Robert Wages, whose union represents about 6,000 employees at six Energy Department nuclear weapons facilities. But, says Wages, "Unique characteristics distinguish these workers from those laid off from private companies and conventional defense plants." He and others contend that broad problems in the economy shouldn't be used as an excuse to ignore the health plight of nuclear workers.

The workers' dual goals—keeping their health insurance and their jobs—are supported by many groups who opposed the nuclear arms race—groups the nuclear workers considered adversaries during the Cold War. The Natural Resources Defense Council (NRDC), the American Friends Service Committee, Greenpeace, and other organizations favor worker benefits.

"Who the hell's going to insure anyone with lung disease?" asks Peper, the Rocky Flats worker with berylliosis, who coughed throughout a recent discussion. He added that insurance coverage is one reason he is taking the early retirement offered by the plant's contractor, EG&G Inc.

The claims filed by workers (or in many cases their surviving spouses) who seek compensation for work-related disease through the courts are often denied as a result of the inadequate records Energy Department contractors have kept. Bruce DeBoskey, who has served as attorney for 11 widows of Rocky Flats workers in compensation cases, recently wrote that he has "consistently been disappointed with the inadequacy and inaccuracies of the Rocky Flats' radiation monitoring records, making it difficult, if not impossible, for workers, their widows, and their attorneys to demonstrate the true nature of exposure to radioactive and other hazardous substances during the course of their employment."

Marvin Thielsen, a good-natured 75-year-old retiree from Rocky Flats, says he would be in even deeper trouble if he had left his job at the plant without health insurance. Because the union's contract at the plant gives complete health insurance coverage, when Thielsen took regular retirement a few years ago the federal retirement law required the company to maintain his insurance.

So he was covered when a 1988 diagnosis showed that he has chronic beryllium disease, berylliosis. And, like his friend Peper, he also had been contaminated by plutonium (by a puncture wound in the index finger) decades ago and required to work in non-radioactive operations. Moreover, he already has been operated on for prostate cancer.

Whether his cancer, not uncommon among older men, was caused by the radiation can't be medically proven or disproven with today's technology. Not surprisingly, Thielsen has an opinion. "In my own mind, I think the exposure caused it." Today, though, he says he is more worried about the berylliosis than about a recurrence of the cancer. "I know I have it," says Thielsen, who is noticeably short of breath. "Day by day you get worse."

Unlike Thielsen, a retiree, workers who are laid off from their jobs at Rocky Flats won't automatically have health insurance coverage if occupational diseases show up later. Union official Roberts says that Congress's failure to provide health coverage is "devastating" to workers. And as he discusses the situation, the robust 64-year-old Roberts begins to boil. "We're literally victims of the Cold War. We've done their damn work, we took the chances, we got the radiation exposures, we got subjected to toxic hazardous materials, and now they want to throw our ass away."

This is adapted from the November 1992 *Bulletin*.

III.4 Poisoned Pacific

Bengt Danielsson

After three years of feverish preparations, on July 2, 1966, the French tried out their new atomic test site at the Moruroa atoll. The first bomb, a plutonium fission device, was placed on a barge anchored in the lagoon. When it was detonated, all the water in the shallow lagoon basin was sucked up into the air, and then rained down. The islets on the encircling reef were all covered with heaps of irradiated fish and clams, whose slowly rotting flesh continued to stink for weeks.

Trying a different tack, on July 19 the French dropped the next bomb from an airplane flying 45,000 feet above the empty ocean, 60 miles south of the atoll. Since no technicians or equipment were present to record the results, this exercise was uninformative. Two days later, an untriggered bomb on the ground was exposed to a "security test." While it did not explode, the bomb's case cracked and its plutonium contents spilled over the reef. The contaminated area was "sealed" by covering it with a layer of asphalt.

But these experiments were merely a prelude to the grand opening bang of the Centre d'Expérimentation du Pacifique (CEP), as the French called the Moruroa test site, in the presence of General de Gaulle himself.

For this blast, the technicians and troops were evacuated to another island, as they had been for the two preliminary tests. On the appointed day, September 10, de Gaulle embarked on a warship equipped with protective iron shields and sprinklers for washing away radioactive dust. This ship remained close enough to Moruroa to allow him to watch the test from the bridge. This time the "bomb," actually a box containing the 120-kiloton device, was suspended from a helium-filled balloon anchored to the reef and floating 600 meters above the lagoon.

Unfortunately, the sky was completely overcast and the wind easterly. There was nothing to do but postpone the test. On the following day, however, when the weather was even worse, so was the temper of de Gaulle, who was in a great hurry to return to Paris. So the box-like nuclear charge—the French technicians were still far from their goal of a sleek, operational bomb—was exploded. Monitoring stations set up by the New Zealand National Radiation Laboratory in the Cook Islands, Niue, Samoa, Tonga, Fiji, and Tuvalu—to the west of French Polynesia—immediately registered heavy radioactive fallout. In Apia, Western Samoa, the concentration of fission products in the rain water was 135,000 picocuries per liter.

During the next eight years another 44 French bombs, including five hydrogen bombs, were detonated in the Pacific skies above Moruroa and Fangataufa, another small atoll 40 kilometers further south. The monitoring stations New Zealand operated on other Polynesian islands regularly registered heavy fallout. But the French government each time claimed that the patriotic particles emanating from Moruroa managed to avoid all the islands of French Polynesia.

It was easy for the French government to brush aside local protests against atmospheric testing. But the vociferous opposition that continued to grow in

Australia, New Zealand, and the other Pacific islands was harder to ignore. The outcry culminated in 1973 in widespread boycotts of French goods, airlines, and shipping lines. That year Australia and New Zealand also instituted proceedings against France in the international Court of Justice at the Hague. As a result, in 1974 the new French president, Valéry Giscard d'Estaing, ordered the tests moved underground.

U.S. and British testing had long since moved out of the Pacific—the last British tests were conducted in 1958, as were the last U.S. tests on Bikini and Eniwetok. (The last U.S. tests in the Pacific were at Christmas and Johnson Islands in 1962.) No other nuclear weapon state had tried the technically difficult, costly, and dangerous task of conducting underground tests in the narrow base of a porous coral island. The French technicians sent out to Polynesia in 1962 had excluded this option in favor of atmospheric tests. Nevertheless, instead of moving the test program to France, where many suitable underground test sites existed, the CEP began in 1976 to detonate high-yield bombs in the narrow base of Moruroa atoll.

Sea Blasts

The only portion of Moruroa available for underground testing was a 23-kilometer strip of the southern half of the reef ring, since the rest of the island was covered with laboratories, warehouses, airstrips, and living quarters. Over the next five years, according to official statements, 46 shafts were drilled, 800–1,200 meters deep, depending on the size of the bomb to be tested. In other words, bomb blasts were spaced at 500-meter intervals along the available strip. Official documents reveal that the majority of the explosions hollowed out combustion chambers more than 100 meters in diameter and produced cracks 300–400 meters long, extending in all directions. In addition, accidents ripped gaping holes in the flank of the atoll. The volume of material torn out by the biggest of these accidents, which occurred on July 25, 1979, was estimated at one million cubic meters by the French commissioner for natural disasters, volcano expert Haroun Tazieff, who visited Moruroa in 1982. The full extent of the leakage of radionuclides into the ocean is unknown, mainly because technicians have been unwilling and unable to undertake studies at the depths where the explosions take place.

By 1980, the base of the atoll along the south coast was used up. Again, the most sensible solution would have been to transfer the testing apparatus to France. But President Giscard d'Estaing rejected this solution for political reasons, fearing that French voters would object to testing in their own backyards, despite official assurances that underground testing is harmless. Instead, barges and derricks were dispatched to Moruroa for drilling bomb shafts in the shallow lagoon in the center of the atoll, where most tests have been conducted since 1981.

When civilian and military authorities decided to keep testing at Moruroa, they did not take into account an additional risk that many critics mentioned at an early stage: the possible exposure of the atoll to severe storms. Up to 1980, typhoons were extremely rare in French Polynesia; the last one had occurred in 1906. French army engineers therefore completely disregarded the risk when they selected Moruroa in 1962, although like most atolls, Moruroa is only a few meters above sea level. However, before 1980 was out, a typhoon hit the island. The only reaction in Paris was to order the construction of huge refuge platforms for the 3,000 men and 12 women employed and living at Moruroa.

These were not completed when, against all odds, the island was hit by giant waves stirred up by an even bigger typhoon during the night of March 11–12, 1981. This time, the civilian technicians employed at Moruroa, fearing for their lives, leaked a secret report to the French press, revealing that the storm had washed out to sea the huge amounts of nuclear waste that had been allowed to accumulate on the north coast. As the technicians, who were members of the socialist CFTD trade union, told the story, this waste included 10–20 kilograms of plutonium which had been spilled out on the reef between 1966 and 1974 during the so-called "security tests," and later covered by asphalt. The 1981 storm tore off the asphalt and scattered the plutonium over the lagoon. These revelations, which were also reported in the foreign press, led to punitive action against the talkative technicians, and a bold promise by Defense Minister Charles Hernu to clean up the atoll. Nothing further has been heard about the cleanup in the last nine years; meanwhile, Moruroa has been hit by five more typhoons.

Keeping Secrets

The most common radiation-induced diseases are leukemia, brain tumors, and thyroid cancers. As could be expected, it is from the early 1980s that a sharp increase in the number of these three types of cancer has occurred in French Polynesia. The French government has not only continued to keep cancer statistics secret, it has also constantly brushed aside the numerous requests made by the Territorial Assembly and government for a health survey by impartial foreign doctors.

Nuclear testing has also been a political disaster for Polynesians. Above all, it has kept Polynesia under colonial rule long after French colonies in Africa gained independence. Despite the Polynesian political parties' determined efforts for more than 30 years to achieve self-government, all important decisions are still made by the French government and carried out by its local representative, the high commissioner, who is appointed by and responsible only to the French cabinet in Paris. Paris controls not only foreign affairs and defense, but also the police, justice, immigration, information, communications, foreign commerce, international air and sea traffic, currency, research, and higher education.

Local political parties and leaders are clamoring for more say in their own affairs, and pro-independence movements represent about two-thirds of the voters, but the colonial government is overpowering. About 8,000 troops and police maintain order. Bribes and subsidies are widely distributed. And the rapid development of a European-style money economy, based mostly on tourism, has made Polynesia more and more dependent on the "mother country."

French expenditures for the nuclear program far exceed monies for other Polynesian concerns. Up to 1974, when nuclear tests moved underground, the CEP spent more than twice the amount allocated for the territorial budget. Meanwhile the local economic base has eroded. As a result of the French nuclear testing program, agricultural production has sagged: exports of coffee and vanilla have ceased, and exports of copra and coconut oil have fallen substantially. Once nearly self-sufficient, French Polynesia now imports 80 percent of its food.

This is adapted from the March 1990 *Bulletin*.

III.5 Chernobyl: The Decade of Despair

David R. Marples

The Chernobyl accident on April 26, 1986, was the world's worst disaster at a civilian nuclear power plant. It is also one of the most widely known and controversial industrial disasters of all time. Wildly exaggerated claims have been made about the accident's impact; equally wild assertions have been made in dismissing its effects. Objective assessments are few. The truth about Chernobyl has been bent from the start—the Soviet Union wanted to protect the reputation of its ambitious nuclear power program, and the nuclear industry everywhere wanted the public to believe that a similar disaster "could not happen here."

In the Soviet Union, "Chernobyl" became a battle cry for anti-Moscow protest, and for an assault on an industry with a poor record. (Ironically, its record was no poorer than that of other Soviet energy industries; both the coal and oil industries had suffered higher casualty rates, and the coal industry had caused terrible air pollution for years.)

Scientists have attempted definitive studies of the effects of Chernobyl, but they have invariably fallen short of the mark, mainly because of the lack of adequate or reliable data.

In August 1986, when the Soviet delegation to the International Atomic Energy Agency (IAEA) in Vienna reported its findings on the accident, there was a widespread tendency to praise the new openness of Mikhail Gorbachev's presidency. The Soviets emphasized that the disaster was caused by "human error," and a show trial was staged the following July in the contaminated town. The hapless plant director, absent at the time of the experiment that caused the accident, received a ten-year sentence. His colleagues got lesser penalties (two to five years). Repudiating this staged nonsense, Valery Legasov, the leader of the Soviet delegation to the IAEA, hanged himself nine months later, on the second anniversary of the accident. By all accounts, Legasov was plagued with guilt about the design faults and technical shortcomings of the Soviet-made reactor.

Ten years later, there is no consensus on the number of victims or the overall health impact of Chernobyl, nor has the accident engendered a new safety consciousness at the nuclear plants in the newly independent states.

Direct Casualties

One of the most controversial arguments about the accident concerns the number of direct casualties. The official Soviet toll rose from 2 to 31 during the summer of 1986, where it remained thereafter. Several Western scientists have adhered to that number, and it is a staple of Chernobyl stories in the Western press. The "official" casualty report has developed into something of a truism—if something is repeated often enough, people begin to accept it.

But the figure of 31 direct fatalities at Chernobyl is as mythic today as it was in 1986. During the early cleanup phase, it was clear there would be many more victims, particularly among the crews decontaminating the plant, those flying helicopter sorties over the roof of the gaping reactor in a flawed attempt to stop radiation from leaking into the atmosphere, and those working at the reactor scene at a variety of other hazardous tasks.

By 1990, at least 5,000 decontamination workers had died, although not all their deaths can be attributed to Chernobyl.

Nina Adamovna Franko is one of the many residents who refused to leave the "exclusion zone" established by authorities around Chernobyl after the explosion. *Impact Visuals/Fabienne Bouville*

For the most part, these people were not volunteers. They were military reservists, brought in from various parts of the Soviet Union. Most were in their 20s and 30s, but some were older. One of their missions was to fill in the great hole in the reactor roof—workers on the roof flung shovelfuls of radioactive graphite into the hole and, wearing heavy shielding, made their way as quickly as possible to safety. Radiation levels were so high that geiger counters, which were in inadequate supply, went off the scale.

Contrary to regulations, some of the workers remained in the "Exclusion Zone," an area around the damaged reactor with a 30-kilometer radius, for six months or longer, accumulating potentially fatal doses of radiation. Many were cavalier about safety. When I traveled by car to the Chernobyl plant in the summer of 1989, I saw reservists sitting in ditches above which had been posted signs declaring, "Danger! Radiation!" Wearing only overalls, they were evidently taking a smoke break. A friend at the German magazine *Stern* showed me one of his prize photographs: it was of cleanup crews taking a lunch break at the site of the damaged reactor. They wore no protective headgear or clothing as they sat on the ground eating their sandwiches, with the roofless reactor looming behind them.

Is it possible to make a reasonable estimate of the number of direct casualties of Chernobyl? The National Committee for Radiation Protection of the Ukrainian Population recently issued what appear to be reliable figures, indicating that 5,722 cleanup workers, or "liquidators" have died. To this total must be added approximately 100 plant personnel, Pripyat residents, local farmers, coal miners, and officials who died in the immediate aftermath of the disaster. This number may be low, because it is very difficult to obtain accurate information about those who were evacuated. Still, total deaths directly related to the Chernobyl accident must be in the region of 6,000. To say more is to enter the realm of the unknown. Nevertheless, I believe that 6,000 represents the *minimum* possible number.

Fallout

The Chernobyl reactor spewed highly radioactive fallout over a vast area, but only in the spring of 1989 was detailed information about fallout made available to the public. The accident contaminated an area of more than 100,000 square kilometers (about the size of the state of Kentucky), and lower levels of contamination affected many parts of Europe, particularly eastern Poland, southern Germany, and Scandinavia. The worst hit regions were in the then-Soviet republics of Belarus, Ukraine, and Russia.

An estimated four million people live in areas where the soil is [signifi-

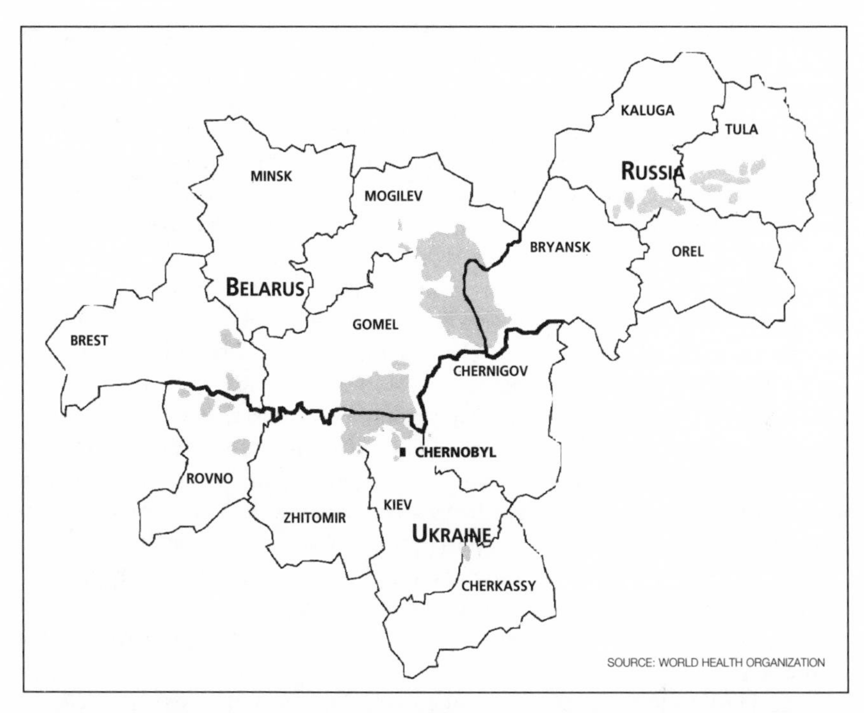

The explosion spread varying degrees of radioactive contamination over much of Europe; the most heavily contaminated areas (in gray) are in Ukraine, Belarus, and eastern Russia.

cantly] contaminated. Approximately 60 percent of this territory is in Belarus, 30 percent in Ukraine, and 10 percent in Russia. Because the region is predominantly agricultural, most families continue to rely on the food they produce on their private plots. Most of the local population has been consuming contaminated food for nearly a decade.

I visited the Chausy district in Belarus in spring 1995. This region, which is 250 miles north of Chernobyl, has not received much public attention. Contaminated wells have been boarded up and local factories have closed down. The local economy is depressed and the local stores stock little food. Families must provide for themselves. In one house, an elderly man was even raising pigs in his kitchen.

Is the health of the local population at risk? The opinion of the villagers was mixed, but most were fatalistic. Children from local villages were being sent by a Minsk charitable organization to Europe and North America for summer vacations, in the hope that it might improve their generally poor health.

Evacuation is a controversial and much debated affair. About 116,000 people were evacuated immediately after the accident, all from the Exclusion Zone. In addition, both the Soviet and post-Soviet authorities have had a policy of immediately evacuating residents in other areas with the highest levels of cesium contamination. Less urgent evacuation has been based on the degree of contamination in a given area and whether residents—especially families with children—can obtain uncontaminated supplies of food and water. A much wider area than the original 30-kilometer zone was evacuated in 1989. There was a great clamor for evacuation between 1986 and 1990, but this sentiment has been less in evidence since then.

The declining interest in evacuation may be a reflection of the plight of evacuees in their new surroundings. The Belarusian press is filled with evacuee complaints—they are often unable to find employment and their new housing is shoddy, often lacking hot water (or just water). Sewerage is often inadequate. Many would-be evacuees prefer to wait in the zone, hoping to be moved to Kiev or Minsk. In some cases, though, the authorities have simply failed to act: A recent Ukrainian report noted that 2,000 families had been waiting to be evacuated from the Poliske district, just west of Chernobyl, for more than five years.

One family moved from the contaminated zone in Belarus to a "clean" area in Ukraine. At their new destination they were shunned by their neighbors, who feared the newcomers would contaminate them. Their children were ostracized at school for the same reason. The situation became so intolerable that the family decided to return to Belarus.

In Minsk, a group of newly constructed apartment blocks at the far north of the city is occupied almost exclusively by evacuees, who sit outside the apartments in rural style, conversing, smoking, and drinking. It has been difficult for the evacuees to adjust suddenly to their new environment. As one reporter said, "There is a lot of drinking there," and people are nostalgic for their native villages.

Many elderly people chose to remain in the zone. A 1991 study commissioned by the International Atomic Energy Association notes the strains caused by evacuation, but my visits to the zone suggest that staying behind is also a strain—few of those who remained receive an adequate or nutritious food supply.

Both Ukraine and Belarus have had to make deep cuts in spending for post-Chernobyl problems. Neither republic can afford to provide adequate funding on a long-term basis. Both have depended on international aid, and on charitable assistance in particular. In Minsk Hospital No. 3, I saw testing equipment for diabetes and other items that had been sent from Germany to the Belarusian Charitable Fund's "For the Children of Chernobyl." At one time, 38 charitable organizations were devoted to assisting children in Belarus who were affected by Chernobyl. But it would be a mistake to think that these organizations are generously supported. Most are struggling for survival. As time passes, it becomes more difficult to raise funds.

Long-term Health Consequences

Few questions have been debated more heatedly than the effect of Chernobyl on the long-term health of the population. At one end of the spectrum is Anatoli Romanenko, the Ukrainian health minister, who announced in June 1986: "Medical services are keeping a close eye on health protection of everyone involved in relief work at Chernobyl. . . . The main thing is to preserve people's health. There is no cause for alarm whatsoever in the rest of Ukraine's territory [outside the 30-kilometer zone]. . . . Doctors have checked tens of thousands of people, and thousands of tests have been carried out in the laboratories. Their results give us grounds to say that there is no danger to people's health."

At the other end of the spectrum is the current Ukrainian health ministry, which issues statements that require careful analysis. One communiqué noted that the health of those in the contaminated zones was deteriorating. By 1991, only 28–32 percent of adults and 27–31 percent of children were said to be in good health. Such astonishing figures reflect mainly heightened rates of respiratory diseases and diseases of the blood and nervous system.

These conflicting statements show how variable a single institution has been throughout the course of the disaster. The later claim—surely exaggerated—is the antithesis of the attempt to cover up in the first months after the accident.

Health information was classified during the Soviet period, and apart from a single and nearly unreadable volume issued by the Soviet Academy of Medical Sciences in 1989, little was forthcoming other than the proceedings of scientific conferences. Before Chernobyl, little research was conducted on the kinds of problems a Chernobyl-type accident would produce.

We do know that in general, health and health care are problematic in both Belarus and Ukraine, and that in recent years, health statistics have taken an alarming turn. (In part, that may reflect a notable improvement in disease detection.) The infant mortality rate is more than double that for Europe as a whole, and cases of infectious diseases have risen markedly over the past four years. Both Ukraine and Belarus have experienced negative population growth in recent years. Diseases like tuberculosis and diptheria, once thought to be under control, are back; vaccination rates have dropped. In southern Ukraine, 400 cases of cholera occurred in the summer of 1995 as a result of polluted water.

U.S. bone marrow specialist Robert Gale, speaking at a conference in Kiev in 1991, remarked that although Kiev's hospital beds were full, he doubted that the occupancy rate was specifically related to Chernobyl. More recently, the deputy chief of Minsk's Children's Hospital No. 3 told me that there has been a dramatic increase in congenital diabetes. "Before Chernobyl," he added, "we had no such problems." By 1995, according to the Belarusian State Information Agency, the lung cancer rate among the 32,000 evacuees was four times the average of the rest of the capital's population.

These reports present the observer with a predicament: Which current health problems are related specifically to fallout? There is no known or previously suggested link between congenital diabetes and radiation or the consumption of irradiated products. Yet the largest number of cases of childhood diabetes emanate from Gomel province, the most heavily contaminated region.

As a group, the cleanup crews, or liquidators, have clearly been affected the most. They suffer from a variety of diseases, particularly skin ailments. But not all liquidators have been monitored on a regular basis, and information from official Ukrainian sources is unreliable.

Has Chernobyl had adverse genetic consequences for the human population? Of the three republics most affected, only Belarus has a program that monitors the incidence of congenital deformities. Using the period 1982 to 1985 as a baseline, the overall rate of congenital defects rose 24 percent from 1987 to 1992; in areas where the cesium contamination of the soil was highest, the increase was 83 percent. On February 1, 1991, the Belarusian parliament established the "National Preventive Program of Genetic Consequences of the Chernobyl Accident." Unfortunately, this study, like many others, has been plagued by a shortage of funds.

After the atomic bomb was dropped on Hiroshima in 1945, the rate of leukemia increased within 18 months, and the number of cases peaked within four to five years. Given the Japanese experience, it was anticipated that an increase in the rate of leukemia would be a major consequence of the Chernobyl accident.

Although it may take as long as 15 years after exposure to develop the disorder, there has not been a significant increase in leukemia in the affected areas so far. Levels have risen somewhat in Ukraine and Belarus generally, and the leukemia rate is at the upper end of the European average. But the rate of leukemia seems to be lower than it was in the 1970s. It may be premature to say that the Chernobyl accident has not resulted in increased cases of leukemia, but one can say that original predictions have not materialized.

In contrast, the rate of thyroid cancers in children has increased dramatically, and the increases appear to correlate closely with the areas that received the most radioactive fallout. These cancers may be attributed to the radioactive iodine in the atmosphere in the first days after the accident, or to the consumption of contaminated milk, which affects infants far more than adults.

Evgeni Demidchik, head of the Minsk Thyroid Tumor Clinic, has monitored the incidence of the disease in Belarusian children since 1966. Before the Chernobyl disaster, he saw an average of one case per year. "Excess" cases began to appear in 1990, and from 1993 to 1995, the number of new cases rose from 79 to 91 per year. By 1994, Belarus alone had reported that 424 children had thyroid cancer. Contrary to expectations, the number of cases has continued to rise each year.

Almost all of the afflicted children were born or conceived before the Chernobyl accident. Because of the close correlation of cases with the pattern of fallout and the ingestion of radioactive iodine, it seems probable that, of the 91 cases of thyroid cancer in Belarusian children in 1994, some 90 percent were radiation-induced.

Belarus also reports an increase in the rate of non-cancerous tumors in children. Before the Chernobyl accident, the average rate was one a year; now the annual rate exceeds 60.

The increased incidence of both benign and cancerous tumors is a discernible and disturbing consequence of the Chernobyl accident. It is reasonable to conclude that Ukraine and Belarus had serious pre-existing health problems and that those problems have been exacerbated by the accident.

Facing the Future

Daunting problems await. The roof over the destroyed reactor is cracked and its longevity is doubted. The situation has been aptly described by a Ukrainian expert who stated that virtually all the problems engendered by Chernobyl still remain, including the destroyed reactor and over 100 radioactive burial sites nearby. In spite of their financial and safety problems, both Ukraine and Russia have decided to continue to commission new nuclear power plants. Ukraine cannot afford to finance the building of a new iron and concrete shell to cover the now-decaying sarcophagus in which Chernobyl's Unit 4 is now encased.

Few long-term safety lessons appear to have been learned. If anything, the chance of a major nuclear accident in the region is greater today than in 1986.

Several recent nuclear incidents could, potentially, have been serious, and one resulted in the loss of life. Of most immediate concern is the giant nuclear edifice on the Dnieper River at Enerhodar, near the industrial city of Zaporozhe, where there were two incidents in the first week of December 1995.

Meanwhile, the Ukrainian nuclear industry has lost a number of specialists to Russia, where wages are higher and economic conditions are somewhat better. Over 8,000 nuclear workers left Ukraine between 1993 and 1995 alone, and the economic crisis has meant that many employees in the industry have worked for extensive periods without receiving wages. Small wonder that nuclear workers are described as "demoralized."

Ukraine's situation is not unique. The collapse of the Soviet Union created an energy-rich Russia and Turkmenistan, and energy-hungry countries everywhere else. With an urgent need for energy, the basic rules of safety have been pushed into the background. On one occasion I heard a Ukrainian nuclear official being lectured by a U.S. specialist about this sorry state of affairs. The response was angry, and can be paraphrased as follows: "It's all very well for you energy-rich capitalists to sit in your armchairs and lecture our people, who shiver in frozen apartments. But if you were in our position, what would you do?"

This is adapted from the May/June 1996 *Bulletin*.

III.6 Nuclear Language and How I Learned to Pat the Bomb

CAROL COHN

My first encounter with nuclear strategic analysis started in the summer of 1984. I was one of 48 college teachers attending a summer workshop on nuclear weapons, strategic doctrine, and arms control that was held at a university containing one of the nation's foremost centers of nuclear strategic studies, and that was co-sponsored by another institution. It was taught by some of the most distinguished experts in the field, who have spent decades moving back and forth between academia and governmental positions in Washington. When at the end of the program I was afforded the chance to be a visiting scholar at one of the universities' defense studies center, I jumped at the opportunity.

I spent the next year immersed in the world of defense intellectuals—men (and indeed, they are virtually all men) who, in Thomas Powers's words, "use the concept of deterrence to explain why it is safe to have weapons of a kind and number it is not safe to use." Moving in and out of government, working sometimes as administrative officials or consultants, sometimes in universities and think tanks, they create the theory that underlies U.S. nuclear strategic practice.

This article is the beginning of an analysis of the nature of nuclear strategic thinking, with emphasis on the role of a specialized language that I call "technostrategic." I have come to believe that this language both reflects and shapes the American nuclear strategic project, and that all who are concerned about nuclear weaponry and nuclear war must give careful attention to language—with whom it allows us to communicate and what it allows us to think as well as say.

Clean Bombs

I had previously encountered in my reading the extraordinary language used to discuss nuclear war, but somehow it was different to hear it spoken. What hits first is the elaborate use of abstraction and euphemism, which allows infinite talk about nuclear holocaust without ever forcing the speaker or enabling the listener to touch the reality behind the words.

Anyone who has seen pictures of Hiroshima burn victims may find it perverse to hear a class of nuclear devices matter-of-factly referred to as "clean bombs." (These are weapons which are largely fusion rather than fission. They therefore release a somewhat higher proportion of their energy as prompt radiation but produce less radioactive fallout than fission bombs of the same yield.) Clean bombs may provide the perfect metaphor for the language of defense analysts and arms controllers. This language has enormous destructive power, but without the emotional fallout that would result if it were clear one was talking about plans for mass murder, mangled bodies, human suffering. Defense analysts talk about "countervalue attacks" rather than about incinerating cities. Human death, in nuclear parlance, is most often referred to as "collateral damage." While Reagan's renaming the MX missile "the Peacekeeper" was the object of considerable scorn in the community of defense analysts, the same analysts refer to the missile as a "damage limitation weapon."

These phrases, only a few of the hundreds that could be chosen, exemplify the astounding chasm between image and reality that characterizes technostrategic language. They also hint at the terrifying way the existence of nuclear devices has distorted our perceptions and redefined the world. "Clean bombs" as a phrase tells us that radioactivity is the only "dirty" part of killing people.

It is hard not to feel that one function of this sanitized abstraction is to deny the uncontrolled messiness of the situations one contemplates creating. So that we not only have clean bombs but also "surgically clean strikes": "counterforce" attacks that can purportedly "take out"—that is, accurately destroy—an opponent's weapons or command centers, without causing significant injury to anything else. The image is unspeakably ludicrous when the surgical tool is not a delicately controlled scalpel but a nuclear warhead.

Sex in the Silos

Feminists have often suggested that an important aspect of the arms race is phallic worship; that "missile envy," to borrow Helen Caldicott's phrase, is a significant motivating force in the nuclear buildup. I have always found this an uncomfortably reductionist explanation and hoped that observing at the center would yield a more complex analysis. Still, I was curious about the extent to which I might find a sexual subtext in the defense professionals' discourse. I was not prepared for what I found.

I think I had naively imagined that I would need to sneak around and eavesdrop on what men said in unguarded moments, using all my cunning to unearth sexual imagery. I had believed that these men would have cleaned up their acts, or that at least at some point in a long talk about "penetration aids," someone would suddenly look up, slightly embarrassed to be caught in such blatant confirmation of feminist analyses.

I was wrong. There was no evidence that such critiques had ever reached the ears, much less the minds, of these men. American military dependence on nuclear weapons was explained as "irresistible, because you get more bang for the buck." Another lecturer solemnly and scientifically announced, "To disarm is to get rid of all your stuff." A professor's explanation of why the MX missile is to be placed in the silos of the newest Minuteman missiles, instead of replacing the older, less accurate missiles, was "because they're in the nicest hole—you're not going to take the nicest missile you have and put it in a crummy hole." Other lectures were filled with discussion of vertical erector launchers, thrust-to-weight ratios, soft lay downs, deep penetration, and the comparative advantages of protracted versus spasm attacks—or what one military adviser to the National Security Council has called "releasing 70 to 80 percent of our megatonnage in one orgasmic whump."

But if the imagery is transparent, its significance may be less so. I do not want to assert that it somehow reveals what defense intellectuals are really talking about, or their motivations; individual motives cannot necessarily be read directly from imagery, which originates in a broader cultural context.

The interesting issue is not so much the imagery's possible psychodynamic origins as how it functions—its role in making the work world of defense intellectuals feel tenable. Several stories illustrate the complexity.

At one point a group of us took a field trip to the New London Navy base where nuclear submarines are homeported, and to the General Dynamics Electric boat yards where a new Trident submarine was being constructed. The high point of the trip was a tour of a nuclear-powered submarine. A few at a time, we descended into the long, dark, sleek tube in which men and a nuclear reactor are encased underwater for months at a time. We squeezed through hatches, along neon-lit passages so narrow that we had to turn and press our backs to the walls for anyone to get by. We passed the cramped racks where men sleep, and the red and white signs warning of radioactive materials. When we finally reached the part of the sub where the missiles are housed, the officer accompanying us turned with a grin and asked if we wanted to stick our hands through a hole to "pat the missile." Pat the missile?

The image reappeared the next week, when a lecturer scornfully declared

Tom Herzberg

that the only real reason for deploying cruise and Pershing II missiles in Western Europe was "so that our allies can pat them." Some months later, another group of us went to be briefed at NORAD (the North American Aerospace Defense Command). On the way back, the Air National Guard plane we were on went to refuel at Offut Air Force Base, the Strategic Air Command headquarters near Omaha, Nebraska. When word leaked out that our landing would be delayed because the new B-1 bomber was in the area, the plane became charged with a tangible excitement that built as we flew in our holding pattern, people craning their necks to try to catch a glimpse of the B-1 in the skies, and climaxed as we touched down on the runway and hurtled past it. Later, when I returned to the center I encountered a man who, unable to go on the trip, said to me enviously, "I hear you got to pat a B-1."

What is all this patting? Patting is an assertion of intimacy, sexual possession, affectionate domination. The thrill and pleasure of "patting the missile" is the proximity of all that phallic power, the possibility of vicariously appropriating it as one's own. But patting is not only an act of sexual intimacy. It is also what one does to babies, small children, the pet dog. The creatures one pats are small, cute, harmless—not terrifyingly destructive. Pat it, and its lethality disappears.

Much of the sexual imagery I heard was rife with the sort of ambiguity suggested by "patting the missiles." The imagery can be construed as a deadly serious display of the connections between masculine sexuality and the arms race. But at the same time, it can also be heard as a way of minimizing the seriousness of militarist endeavors, of denying their deadly consequences. A former Pentagon target analyst, in telling me why he thought plans for "limited nuclear war" were ridiculous, said, "Look, you gotta understand that it's a pissing contest—you gotta expect them to use everything they've got." This image says, most obviously, that this is about competition for manhood, and thus there is tremendous danger. But at the same time it says that the whole thing is not very serious—it is just what little boys or drunk men do.

Cookie Cutters

Sanitized abstraction and sexual imagery, even if disturbing, seemed to fit easily into the masculine world of nuclear war planning. What did not fit was another set of words that evoked images that can only be called domestic.

Nuclear missiles are based in "silos." In the friendly, romantic world of nuclear weaponry, enemies "exchange" warheads; weapons systems can "marry up." "Coupling" is sometimes used to refer to the wiring between mechanisms of warning and response, or to the psychopolitical links between strategic and theater weapons.

The images evoked by these words may also be a way to tame the uncontrollable forces of nuclear destruction. Take the fire-breathing dragon under the bed, the one who threatens to incinerate your family, your town, your planet, and turn it into a pet you can pat. Or domestic imagery may simply serve to make everyone more comfortable with what they're doing. "PAL" (permissive action links) is the carefully constructed, friendly acronym for the electronic system designed to prevent the unauthorized firing of nuclear warheads. The president's annual nuclear weapons stockpile memorandum, which outlines both short- and long-range plans for production of new nuclear weapons, is benignly referred to as "the shopping list." The "cookie cutter" is a phrase used to describe a particular model of nuclear attack.

The imagery that domesticates, that humanizes insentient weapons, may also serve, paradoxically, to make it all right to spend one's time dreaming up scenarios for the use of massively destructive technology, and to exclude human beings from that technological world, because that world itself now includes the domestic, the human, the warm and playful, the things one pats affectionately. It is a world that is in some sense complete in itself; it even includes death and loss. The problem is that all things that get "killed" happen to be weapons, not humans. If one of your warheads "kills" another of your warheads, it is "fratricide." There is much concern about "vulnerability" and "survivability," but it is about the vulnerability and survival of weapons systems, rather than people.

The Abstraction Trap

Although I was startled by the combination of dry abstraction and odd imagery that characterizes the language of defense intellectuals, my attention was quickly focused on decoding and learning to speak it.

What I learned at the program is that talking about nuclear weapons is fun. The words are quick, clean, light; they trip off the tongue. You can reel off dozens of them in seconds, forgetting about how one might interfere with the next, not to mention with the lives beneath them. Nearly everyone I observed—lecturers, students, hawks, doves, men, and women—took pleasure in using the words; some of us spoke with a self-consciously ironic edge, but the pleasure was there nonetheless. Part of the appeal was the thrill of being able to manipulate an arcane language, the power of entering the secret kingdom. But perhaps more important, learning the language gives a sense of control, a feeling of mastery over technology that is finally not controllable but powerful beyond human comprehension. The longer I stayed, the more conversations I participated in, the less I was frightened of nuclear war.

How can learning to speak a language have such a powerful effect? One answer, discussed earlier, is that the language is abstract and sanitized, never giving access to the images of war. But there is more to it than that. The learning process itself removed me from the reality of nuclear war. My energy was focused on the challenge of decoding acronyms, learning new terms, developing competence in the language—not on the weapons and wars behind the words. By the time I was through, I had learned far more than an alternate, if abstract, set of words. The content of what I could talk about was monumentally different.

It is tempting to attribute this problem to the words themselves—the abstractness, the euphemisms, the sanitized, friendly, sexy acronyms. Then one would only need to change the words: get the military planners to say "mass murder" instead of "collateral damage," and their thinking would change. The problem, however, is not simply that defense intellectuals use abstract terminology that removes them from the realities of which they speak. There *is* no reality behind the words. Or, rather, the "reality" they speak of is in itself a world of abstractions. Deterrence theory, and much of strategic doctrine, was invented to hold together abstractly, its validity judged by internal logic. These abstract systems were developed as a way to make it possible to, in Herman Kahn's phrase, "think about the unthinkable"—not as a way to describe or codify relations on the ground.

So the problem with the idea of "limited nuclear war," for example, is not only that it is a travesty to refer to the death and suffering caused by any use of nuclear weapons as "limited," or that "limited nuclear war" is an abstraction that obfuscates the human reality beneath any use of nuclear weapons. It is also that limited nuclear war is itself an abstract conceptual system, designed, embodied, and achieved by computer modeling. In this abstract world, hypothetical, calm, rational actors have sufficient information to know exactly what size nuclear weapon the opponent has used against which targets, and adequate command and control to make sure that their response is precisely equilibrated to the attack. No field commander would use the tactical nuclear weapons at his disposal at the height of a losing battle. Our rational actors would have absolute freedom from emotional response to being attacked, from political pressures from the populace. They would act solely on the basis of a perfectly informed mathematical calculus of megatonnage. To refer to limited nuclear war is to enter a system that is de facto abstract and grotesquely removed from reality. The abstractness of the entire conceptual system makes descriptive language utterly beside the point.

This realization helped make sense of my difficulty in staying connected to concrete lives as well as of some of the bizarre and surreal quality of what people said. But there was still a piece missing. How is it possible, for example, to make sense of the following (from the January 21, 1985, *New Republic*):

"Since it takes roughly two warheads to destroy one enemy silo, an attacker must expend two of his missiles to destroy one of the enemy's. A first strike disarms the attacker. The aggressor ends up worse off than the aggressed."

The homeland of "the aggressed" has just been devastated by the explosions of, say, a thousand nuclear bombs, and the aggressor, whose homeland is still untouched, "ends up worse off"?

I was only able to make sense of this kind of thinking when I finally asked myself: Who—or what—is the subject? In technostrategic discourse, the reference point is not human beings but the weapons themselves. The aggressor ends up worse off than the aggressed because he has fewer weapons left; any other factors, such as what happened where the weapons landed, are irrelevant to the calculus of gain and loss.

The fact that the subjects of strategic paradigms are weapons has several important implications. First, and perhaps most critically, there is no real way to talk about human death or human societies when you are using a language designed to talk about weapons. Human death simply is collateral damage—collateral to the real subject, which is the weapons themselves.

Understanding this also helps explain what was at first so surprising to me: most people who do this work are on the whole nice, even good, men, many with liberal inclinations. While they often identify their motivations as being concern about humans, in their work they enter a language and paradigm that precludes people. Thus, the nature and outcome of their work can utterly contradict their genuine motives for doing it.

In addition, if weapons are the reference point, it becomes in some sense illegitimate to ask the paradigm to reflect human concerns. Questions that break through the numbing language of strategic analysis and raise issues in human terms can be easily dismissed. No one will claim that they are unimportant. But they are inexpert, unprofessional, irrelevant to the business at hand. The discourse among the experts remains hermetically sealed. One can talk about the weapons that are supposed to protect particular peoples and their way of life without actually asking if they are able to do it, or if they are the best way to do it, or whether they may even damage the entities they are supposedly protecting. These are separate questions.

This discourse has become virtually the only response to the question of how to achieve security that is recognized as legitimate. If the discussion of weapons was one competing voice in the discussion, or one that was integrated with others, the fact that the referents of strategic paradigms are only weapons might be of less note. But when we realize that the only language and expertise offered to those interested in pursuing peace refers to nothing but weapons, its limits become staggering. And its entrapping qualities—the way it becomes so hard, once you adopt the language, to stay connected to human concerns—become more comprehensible.

A-bomb Damage to Hiroshima, August 6, 1945

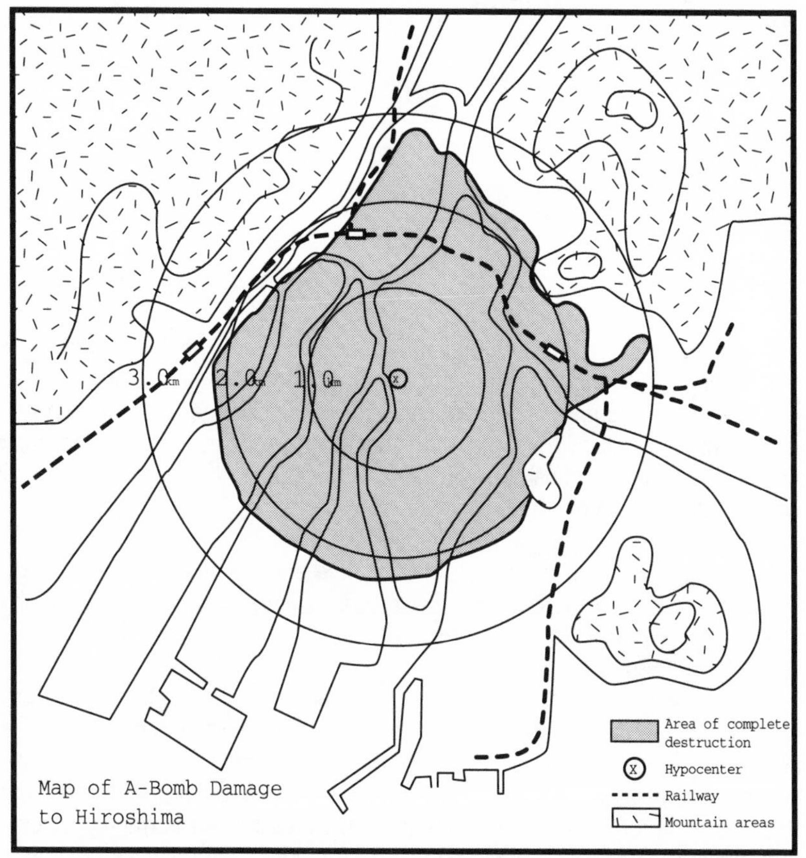

The temperature in the hypocenter is believed to have reached 3,000–4,000 degrees centigrade. (Iron melts at 1,536 degrees.) Within two kilometers of the hypocenter, ruins melted together like lava and people's clothes spontaneously combusted. Most people in this area at the time of the blast died immediately or within a few days. Buildings toppled throughout the city, trapping thousands more in the sea of fire ignited by the bomb. Workers who had removed their shirts were burned noticeably as far away as 3.5 kilometers.

Even today, it is difficult to know how many people died. The city of Hiroshima estimates that 140,000 out of 350,000 living in the city died immediately or within several months. Hundreds who were exposed to radiation died later of cancer. Survivors today still face a higher than normal risk of cancer.

A single warhead on a typical U.S. missile now has a yield about 20 times greater than the Hiroshima bomb. Current missiles carry as many as 10 warheads. *Courtesy Hiroshima Peace Memorial Museum*

Chapter III
Discussion Questions

1. A number of the authors indicate, directly or indirectly, that in addition to the economic, environmental, and health costs of the arms race, "democracy" may be a casualty of the policies of the nuclear age. In what ways do the various legacies of the Cold War and the nuclear arms race jeopardize democracy? What reasons can you provide to suggest that democracy is not endangered by these events?

2. Articles in this chapter examine negative environmental impacts of the nuclear age in quite different locales. Compare the various environmental impacts of the building of the U.S. arsenal with the explosion at Chernobyl and the effects of French nuclear testing.

3. Taking the issues discussed in the articles in this chapter as a guide, and using the data about environmental and community impacts as your baseline information, outline a policy speech for a U.S. presidential candidate titled, "Making a Commitment to Cleaning Up after the Arms Race." Discuss the scope of the problems to be addressed, and note what policies, resources, and actions need to be developed to correct these problems.

4. Using the Cohn article as a guide, analyze five current news stories that discuss either weapons development or defense policy, *or* that describe the fighting in a current war. In the descriptions of policies or actions, do you detect patterns that dehumanize the participants or victims? Do the news reports tend to sanitize accounts of destruction or de-emphasize the destructive effects of weapons? Are there differences between the language used in reporting the story and the quoted words of officials or participants?

Chapter IV

From Foe to Friends? The Soviet Successor States

In the early 1980s, U.S. President Ronald Reagan set in motion foreign and military policies aimed at winning the Cold War with the Soviet Union. These included

- large increases in U.S. military expenditures, including major new weapons programs and the funding of research for the Strategic Defense Initiative (SDI—often called Star Wars);
- active use of U.S. military sales to aid groups fighting communist regimes in various Third World countries—with Nicaragua and Afghanistan heading the list;
- verbal salvos aimed at what Reagan considered the moral, political, and economic bankruptcy of the Soviet system. In answer to criticism, Reagan and his supporters often claimed that they had no animosity toward the people of the Soviet Union. Rather, U.S. policies were said to be directed against the communist government of that nation.

Anti-Soviet rhetoric reached a level in the Reagan administration unmatched since the McCarthy era of the early 1950s. But Reagan's rationale for the U.S. posture in the arms race was not substantially different from that of all previous American Cold War presidents. Ironically, President Reagan and his successor, President George Bush, encountered the ultimate test of their claims to be sympathetic to the Soviet people but against the Soviet form of government. That test came in a process of governmental and social reform generated by, of all people, the leader of the Soviet Union himself, Mikhail Gorbachev.

Soon after coming to power as general secretary of the Communist Party in 1985, Gorbachev introduced sweeping new policies:

- "Glasnost," or openness, unblocked the flow of information in this long-closed society, lifted the lid on past and present secrets, and introduced press freedoms. Voices opposing and criticizing the government and the Communist Party were heard openly for the first time in decades.
- "Perestroika" was an attempt to restructure the empire economically, with a gradual introduction of privatization and free-market reforms.
- As part of his "new thinking" about a more cooperative and peaceful foreign policy, Gorbachev asserted that his goal was mutual security based on "reasonable sufficiency" for defense. He declared that the bulging nuclear arsenals of the two superpowers threatened security. And he assured East European leaders that Soviet troops would no longer be used to force communist orthodoxy on their people. This set the stage for the "revolutions" of 1989 in which these nations broke from the Soviet sphere of control.

The forces of change unleashed by Gorbachev soon spun out of his control. He understood the dissatisfaction generated by local nationalisms and by the overburdened centrally controlled economy. He hoped that giving greater autonomy to groups clamoring for independence would improve the economic condition for all and thus hold the ailing political system together. In the summer of 1991 he tried to negotiate a "union treaty" providing greater autonomy for the 15 republics of the Soviet system. But by August, only eight were prepared to sign. In the middle of these negotiations, a group of old-guard party officials, KGB members, and army officers, angry at Gorbachev for giving away the empire, launched a coup in Moscow. Boris Yeltsin, president of the Russian Republic, marshaled citizens and military personnel to resist the attempt, and the coup failed.

Nevertheless, the attempted coup accelerated the dissolution of the Soviet system. By the end of 1991, Latvia, Estonia, Lithuania, and Ukraine had declared or actually achieved independence from the Soviet Union. Yeltsin, whose power had increased dramatically, forged a treaty with Ukraine and Belarus and sought to draw other republics into a new "Commonwealth of Independent States." Gorbachev resigned, the Soviet system was retired, and the Cold War was over.

Despite these chaotic changes, the United States and its fragmenting former enemy moved rapidly through various arms control agreements, set in motion major reductions in nuclear weapons stockpiles (as evidenced by the chart at the end of Chapter I), and began to forge a kind of friendship. Various programs of Western financial and technological assistance helped to dismantle and move to Russian soil weapons systems inherited by Ukraine, Belarus, and Kazakhstan. Western governments, corporations, and citizens began to deal with the reality of 15 nations where, for decades, there had been only one.

The situation was most complex for the new nations themselves. The fragmentation continued as the new entities strove for greater economic and political distance from Russia. The newly formed commonwealth of Independent States was soon hardly more than a formality. Ethnic nationalism and political conflict led to fighting in Georgia, Azerbaijan and Armenia (over the disputed territory of Nagorno-Karabakh), Tajikistan, Chechnya (still part of Russia), and elsewhere. Corruption, inflation, and shortages plagued most of the struggling economies.

The new nations also had to deal with legacies of the Soviet system and the Cold War, such as unsafe but much-needed nuclear reactors, the weakness of democratic institutions such as a free press, and still-powerful former leaders and bureaucrats. The articles in this chapter were written by journalists who lived through these changes and who understood the poignant choices facing the former Soviet states in the 1990s.

Writing just before the June 1996 Russian elections, Viktoria Tripolskaya-Mitlyng predicts that Russia's political attention will continue to turn inward. The author provides a rich historical perspective on how times of crisis have led Russia to rediscover its national character and take its own unique path.

Russian journalist Nina Chugunova writes movingly about the courage and tension that marked the separation of the Baltic states from Russia in 1990–91. Her article reminds us of the fragility of independence and democracy and the power of events to forge the identities of people, both historically and politically.

The next two articles describe two stages of change and adaptation in Kazakhstan. Leonid Zagalsky provides a panoramic view of post-Soviet life in this country less than two years after it became an independent nation. Mikhail Ustiugov writes about the dynamics of nuclear politics in Kazakhstan several years later: lingering regret about the nation's relinquishing of its nuclear weapons, controversy over plans for a nuclear power plant, and struggles with Russia's continuing influence.

Astghik Vardanian also writes about nuclear power in the Armenian quest for energy independence from Russia and other neighbors. In Armenia, the difficult choice to reopen a precariously situated nuclear plant was made after six years of social chaos brought on by war, an earthquake, and economic coercion from the outside. In this case, a lively environmental movement—a mark of the emerging civil society so important to democracy—was silenced by the severe hardships of daily life in an energy-short, war-torn nation.

We end the Chapter with a map of the new republics and a summary of the new trends and groupings that have begun to emerge among them.

IV.1 Russia Will Turn Inward

VIKTORIA TRIPOLSKAYA-MITLYNG

There are times I am overwhelmed with a sense of well-being as a new citizen of the United States; I feel that my interests are protected and my future relatively secure. Then I think of my homeland, and I know that the vast majority of Russians have not experienced such feelings since the victory of World War II.

There are 105,870,000 people registered to vote in Russia and 400,000 Russian citizens living abroad who are registered to vote. To many the choice between Boris Yeltsin and Gennadi Zyuganov is equivalent to jumping out of the frying pan into the fire. As I write this in early June 1996, they must decide who they will vote for two weeks from now.

The majority of Russian voters are not ideological democrats, staunch communists, or ultranationalists. They are ordinary people tired of strong and historically misleading political ideologies. However, Russian voters have strong ideals and beliefs that do translate into political will.

It is well known that the majority of Russians have not experienced significant improvements in their lives since the collapse of the Soviet Union. For many, everyday life has become more difficult if not simply worse. The present and the future are unstable and unpredictable—a condition human beings find profoundly uncomfortable, no matter where they live. Though the shelves of private stores are lined with merchandise today, most cannot afford to buy what they want; sometimes they can't even buy what they need.

The disparity in the lifestyles of the small wealthy elite and ordinary Russians is growing wider. The resentment toward the super-wealthy is so widespread, it has become a social phenomenon. Many of the new rich come from the Soviet *nomenklatura*, or they were Soviet industrial bosses, or they were—and still are—criminals. Russians do not see or recognize legitimate success stories yet; they don't see the new class of people who have "made it" on their hard work, ingenuity, and business sense. What they see are people who had power in the Soviet times turning that power into money in the new market economy, leaving ordinary people in the cold, as always.

Clues from the Past

For centuries the Russian people have felt that they had a special fate, a particular destiny in the world. The Soviet system capitalized on these feelings, using them to ask people for sacrifices, obedience, and patience. The people were rewarded with displays of military might, parades and celebrations, and a powerful program that sent the first man into space. Today, after the conflict in Chechnya, the military is disgraced. The parades are not believable; public celebrations are only a shadow of what they used to be; and the space program cannot subsist on its own. Survival of the space program, once the Soviet crown jewel, now depends on cooperative projects with Americans, Western Europeans, and Japanese.

When the Soviet Union expressed its political will on the international arena, its word was considered with equal respect by friend and foe. The word of the Soviet Empire could make the United States and its citizens tremble, as it did during the Cuban missile crisis. Soviet political leaders, even when their conduct was clownish, like that of Nikita Khrushchev, commanded attention from world leaders. Today Russia has to struggle for its wishes to be considered on the international arena, be it on the war in the Balkans or NATO expansion. The post-Soviet government has made itself accountable to Western countries, especially the United States.

All these changes have taken place within the past seven years, too short a time to radically change the life of a country and allow it to find and express its new identity.

Four earlier eras in Russian history stand out as pivotal in the development of Russian culture and political institutions: the rule of Ivan the Terrible (1533–84), who made the Russian state powerful through bloody and terrible means; the rule of Peter the Great (1682–1725), who brought Western culture to Russia by force and made the monarch's power absolute, even stronger than that of the Orthodox Church; the Russian Revolution (1917), which created an entirely different political system, the first of its kind in the world; and the rule of Josef Stalin (1927–1953), the first Soviet monarch, who made the will of the Soviet state supreme for its citizens, and who made the nation a superpower.

These four historical epochs were marked by great social and political changes, by unrest, cruelty, and suffering. All four led to powerful brooding in many aspects of Russian life and society. This brooding, followed by great productivity, was pivotal in Russia's development as a country. These were the times when Russia redefined and recreated itself. Even Russians who condemn the excessive cruelty particular to times of upheaval in Russian society—Ivan the Terrible's psychotic cruelty to the aristocracy, Peter the Great's mockeries of ancient Russian customs and religious rituals in favor of Western culture, the bloodshed and destruction of the revolution, and the harsh fate of Stalin's innumerable victims whose faces history will never know—have to recognize the fecundity that followed these periods.

Russia today is living through yet another time of doubt, sacrifice, and redefinition. The choice the country faces during this summer's presidential elections is not simply the choice between Zyuganov and Yeltsin, between the Soviet past and a democratic future, or between more or less chauvinism. It is the old choice formulated for modern times.

It is the old argument brought about by Peter's imposition of Western Renaissance culture on medieval Russia. It is an argument between Slavophiles and Westernizers formulated in the 1830s. Slavophiles believed that Russia had a unique destiny, that it would play a major role in the world, and that Russian culture and religion would eventually save the world. This particularly Russian self-definition was formulated in response to the belief of Westernizers that the only difference between other European nations and Russia was that Russia was less advanced on its path toward civilization and that it just needed to catch up.

Peter the Great, the first Westernizer, was also the first to reveal the fact that every Westernizer in Russia conceals the Slavophile at his core. He said that Russia's goal was not only to catch up to the West, but also to go farther than the West. Even Russians who see themselves as belonging to a greater European culture today believe that Russia's contribution to it has been great and that this fact is not recognized widely enough.

The West is concerned about choices Russians have to make this summer between the democratic Russian government represented by Yeltsin and the new brand of communism—a mixture of communist ideology, nationalist rhetoric, and whatever else the disillusioned and the disheartened of Russia might want to hear—represented by Zyuganov.

The West is convinced that democracy and a market economy are in Russia's best interest, and it has tried to secure this choice by political and economic means: with a new $10.2 billion loan from the International Monetary Fund and a seven-year delay for repaying the $40 billion debt to Western governments, and President Bill Clinton's skirting around the most sensitive issues between Russia and the United States during the G7 meeting in Moscow last April. Western leaders say they will accept the choice Russia makes during summer elections, but their lack of confidence in Russia's ability to choose wisely for itself is obvious.

Choosing Its Own Way

In reality, Russia made its choice long before the elections. Yeltsin and Zyuganov, both astute politicians, hear and understand this choice and the policy direction it implies.

In the past seven years, as during other times in its national history, Russia opened its doors and its heart to the "Other"—to the West. It has looked, learned, and imported the best—and the worst—of this other culture.

Now the country is in the process of rediscovering its difference. Russia does not imitate; it never has. Russia does not follow in the footsteps of others. Russia always reinterprets what it has learned from the other, always makes what was foreign specifically Russian. Russia adapted Chinese tea and Western enlightenment; it translated Persian onion domes into the golden domes of Orthodox churches and transformed Versailles into the Peterhof Palace, a Russian architectural jewel.

Now Russia is entering a new phase of reprocessing what it has been exposed to and what it has learned. Russia is undoubtedly turning away from the West and what is Western in its search to make what is Western its own. It is not a rejection of democracy or the market economy, nor a rejection of human rights or political freedom. It is a country's search for its own political, social, and cultural identity.

It is difficult to predict what form this process will take; it is hard to predict how the Communists will act if they come to power or what the democrats will do if they stay in the Kremlin. What is absolutely clear, however, is that Russia will become more strongly nationalistic and concentrate on its specific agenda.

Its foreign policy will be more strongly expressed and articulated. Russia will continue to speak out against NATO expansion. It will look for allies outside the United States, as is already apparent in its rapprochement with China and South Korea. It will attempt to forge closer ties with its former allies in Eastern Europe. Russia will probably go through some redefinition of its disarmament goals and international treaties. Basically it will continue to search for its own interests, which will often not coincide with Western interests or wishes.

Domestically the rate of reform will slow even more. The economy could get a lot worse, whether Yeltsin or Zyuganov is in power. They are both making promises they will not be able to pay for without further endangering the slow recovery the economy has seen this year. As people become more restless, the government becomes more autocratic, more tyrannical. Russia will have to go through this phase because people's lives will simply not get better quickly enough. The prospect of a Western-style democracy in Russia is, in my opinion, dubious.

David Johnson, research director at the Washington-based Center for Defense Information, wrote recently in an electronic newsletter that what's good for the West is not necessarily good for Russia. Influencing Russia by putting economic and political pressure on it will no longer produce positive results. Senator Sam Nunn said in one of his speeches that if it weren't for U.S. Nunn-Lugar funds, Russia would not have disarmed as quickly as it did. He was probably right. At that time, U.S. pressure through assistance, gifts, and loans, had certain benefits for Russians and Americans.

However, there is a reason why Zyuganov's claims that Russia was brought to its knees by a Western capitalist plot, and that the West is still out to destroy Russia, hit home for so many ordinary Russians. Like an over-eager parent, America does not know when to let go of its child, the new and fragile Russian democracy and its shaky market economy. There is a danger that the United States may continue to push too hard.

Russia will look for its unique path no matter what anyone says or does, as it always has. We can try to let go and understand this process, or we can resist it. But by resisting we could destroy the new ties we have formed after the Soviet era.

This appeared in the July/August 1996 *Bulletin*.

IV.2 Baltic Pride, Russian Tears

Nina Chugunova

During my university years in Moscow it was a treat to take a trip to our West—the Baltics. They weren't like Russia. They were clean and green. Their cities were pockets of European culture, where Soviet film-makers shot their Paris and London scenes.

To Russian students, the Baltics represented Europe and freedom. We, who had no opportunity to see the world, reveled in the experience of being foreigners—unwanted foreigners. The natives didn't like Russians or the Russian language. And they didn't like us in a special kind of way: they avoided us.

We enjoyed being ignored. We liked being the untouchables. It was such a relief from the way we were treated at home. There, from the earliest days of childhood, we were never let alone. There we could be scolded for our outfits on the street. There people with flashlights could walk into our dormitories in the middle of the night to conduct passport checks. It was a relief to escape temporarily to the cold sea.

It was even more remarkable when Balts spoke in anger: "Russians will never be able to learn our language!" my college roommate said, even before we had settled in the dormitory. The bitter hatred in her voice stunned me. An Uzbek would not have spoken that way, nor a Kirghiz, nor a Ukrainian.

No one else would have dared to say that in the 1970s—not after the Tashkent Conference had made Russian the official language throughout the Soviet Union.

Still the Balts spoke their own languages. A Russian felt flattered if an Estonian or a Lithuanian spoke to him without resorting to the Russian language. It meant he had been taken for a native, for a civilized person! In all the other corners of the boundless Soviet Union, the Russians were the bosses, the smart ones, the civilized ones. In the Baltics a Russian could never, ever feel that way.

The Giant Dies in the West

For more than four decades the "Soviet Baltics" separated Russia from Europe. Europeans paid little attention to political events in Latvia, Lithuania, and Estonia because they were of no significance to European politics.

When the West did cast its eyes on the Soviet Union, Moscow was the object of its scrutiny; Moscow, where the action was; Moscow, which could inspire fear or offer hope. The three little Baltic nations were merely a spot on the map.

We, the Russian Soviets, had an equally vague but different idea about Baltic politics. We knew something of the "brothers of the forest," the Baltic partisans ("bandits" in Soviet history books). These were the Lithuanian patriots who fled to the forests in the 1940s, from which they attacked Soviet organizations and killed Soviet administrators.

We knew it took a long time to get rid of these brothers of the forest—the unrest continued into the early 1960s. But what did their persistent resistance mean? Unfortunately, we rarely looked beyond university textbooks, where, instead of answers, it was dutifully reported that Lenin's office had been guarded by "faithful Lithuanian riflemen," a fact repeatedly stressed by Soviet historians.

In 1988, the giant "Baltic Path" demonstration jolted Europe. Europeans suddenly saw a stream of blue-eyed people illuminated by candlelight, wearing white garments, crying and holding hands in a human chain that went unbroken for hundreds of kilometers along the Baltic Sea. It was an elegant way of signaling to the outside—or perhaps it was meant only as an internal affirmation of Baltic pride.

A year and a half later, the Baltic republics, one after another, declared their independence from the Soviet Union. (The other republics' swift "parade of sovereignties" followed immediately.)

I think it is no coincidence that the disintegration of the Soviet Union began at its Western borders, and no coincidence that the greatest armed response to disintegration that the dying giant mustered was a foray into Lithuania.

From the moment Soviet Russia was born, it built internal and external barricades. The barricades inside were the camps for workers created by the giant Soviet industries; the collective farms were camps for peasants. The annexed European nations formed a protective shield against the West.

According to Soviet historians and Soviet propaganda, new Soviet republics always resulted from age-old friendships and the irresistible inclination of nations to unite. A nation's entry into "the family of Soviet peoples" was invariably said to be accompanied by a flourishing of its economy and culture. But "age-old friendship" covered a multitude of motivations and means of expansion.

The Baltics were seized openly, in full view of Europe. Still, "age-old friendship" was trotted out to cover over centuries of animosity. A 1970s Russian textbook, *A Short Course of Soviet History*, makes for ironic reading: "The working class and the working peasantry of the Baltics remembered that their government was overthrown in 1918–19 with the military aid of imperialistic countries. Conscientious and brave representatives of the working class and peasantry, united into communist parties, led a struggle against the bourgeoisie for the restoration of Soviet power for over 20 years."

And on the Soviet arrival: "In June of 1940 the streets of large proletarian centers: Riga, Tallinn, Kaunas, and Vilnius were filled with thousands of demonstrating workers. They were liberating political prisoners, creating armed detachments, occupying government buildings. People were fraternizing passionately with Red Army soldiers who were here on agreement between the Soviet Union and the governments of these countries."

It is true that in 1939 communist movements did exist in the Baltic countries (as they did in much of Europe). But the secret pact with Hitler that allowed Soviet troops to enter these countries had nothing to do with this movement. "Fraternization" meant nothing but occupation.

The hated Soviet takeover remains a painful memory in the Baltics because it took place without a single shot being fired in defense. It's no surprise that from the first moment they declared independence in 1990, each Baltic country began to assemble its own small army. Lithuania's army was designed "to meet possible occupation by an act of resistance."

Born Dissident

During the Soviet years, the Baltics—the Soviet "West"—worked hard and put out products that helped Moscow maintain its habits and its desire to live

Lithuania has brought bodies of deportees back from Siberia for reburial at home. At a spring 1994 memorial service, a young girl holds a picture of one of those who died. *Yevgeny Stetsko*

better then the rest of the Soviet Union. Petersburg (Leningrad), another city that enjoyed living off the efforts of others, was also drawn to the Baltics.

In turn, the Baltics made themselves indispensable to Moscow and Petersburg. (It helped that Baltic farmers failed to adopt the habits of Russian collective farm workers, who stole and drank with a passion for self-destruction.)

The bureaucrats knew how to take advantage of the situation. During the Brezhnev years, party bureaucrats from the Baltics carried suitcases filled with meat and vodka when they traveled to Moscow on business. As a result, local ministries had more rubles than they knew what to do with and did practically anything they wanted at home.

In the meantime, the Baltics' natural resources were pushed to their limits. Lithuanians had always been proud of how well they tended their land, how much they made it produce. But under Soviet occupation, Baltic farmers used so much fertilizer that the land started falling apart.

The dissident movement in the Soviet Union began in the 1960s. But no such movement could be identified in the Baltics.

Why couldn't we see a dissident movement in the Baltics? Because we couldn't see the forest for the trees. The Balts were already *the* Soviet dissidents. Ordinary people, intellectuals—who fed their spirituality with emigrant literature and Catholic underground chronicles—even party bureaucrats who collaborated but never believed, were all united in opposition to the Soviets. No one needed to be a dissident; the nations were undivided.

The consciousness of being under occupation helped save these nations from the worst effects of the Soviet life-style and ways of thinking. The Balts lived under an imposed regime but never accepted it. Their struggle was never within themselves the way it was for Russians. They were consistently and solidly opposed to the Soviet regime.

Did Gorbachev's coming to power change Moscow's attitude toward the Baltics? Not at all. Gorbachev moved Soviet thinking forward in other areas, but with regard to the Baltic republics, he shared the limits of Soviet thought.

In the end, the Baltics were liberated by pure chance—their independence served a purpose in the power struggle in the Kremlin. Russia gave them up in order to become the free successor to the Soviet Union. Russia had to be "the liberator"—or it would simply have been liberated along with everyone else. Russia needed to hand out the flowers of liberty to prove it was still an empire.

Boris Yeltsin's chance came during the events of January 13, 1991, when Russian troops tried to retake control in Vilnius. Yeltsin condemned Mikhail Gorbachev and the armed attack on the Lithuanian people so eloquently that even his speech from the top of a tank during the August coup in Moscow did not overshadow it.

People gathered around the parliament building in Vilnius and cheered: "Yeltsin! Lithuania! Russia! Landsberghis!" There was really no need for the August coup; Gorbachev's political career was finished in January.

"I Am the Boss!"

The first time I visited the Baltics after my university years was in 1988. I was surprised by the abundance of national flags, an even greater coldness toward us Russians, and the nervous expectation of Soviet tanks. A friendly Lithuanian was one who was willing to recite the history of Russian aggression, occupation, and their nation's suffering.

In the fall of that year, Lithuania was preparing a number of expeditions to Siberia to bring back the bodies of countrymen who had been deported in the 1950s. Everyone complained about all the obstacles Soviet bureaucrats were putting in the way.

Lithuania seemed enlivened and inspired. When I returned to Moscow I tried to keep up on what was happening, but for almost an entire year the Central Committee of the Lithuanian Communist Party censored all publications about Lithuania. When I wrote a biographical article about Romualdas Ozolos, an independent politician I had interviewed there, the censor described him as an "undesirable figure."

On March 11, 1990, I was on a train, headed in another direction. The radio was on. I heard the news that Lithuania had announced its independence. I changed the destination of my trip to be able to report Ozolos's understated message to the Lithuanian Parliament: "Everything is going well."

I remember the rejoicing in the streets. Everyone was saying that tomorrow they would be happy. "We will live as they do in Finland!" they shouted.

But on the train back to Moscow I heard an angry Russian yelling: "I am the boss in Lithuania! I am the boss!" From the radio came the words of a Russian commentator, reporting that one of the Soviet leaders said he could not accept Lithuanian independence. Gorbachev, on the other hand, was still deliberating. But it didn't take him long to make a decision. Less than a year later, in January 1991, Soviet troops spilled Lithuanian blood.

Russia could not accept the loss of Lithuania—but Lithuania was only the first in line. Careful Estonia was the next to declare independence, then half-Russian Latvia. Finally, Gorbachev made the choice that ultimately sealed his political fate. He declared the Baltic declarations of independence to be illegal, and initiated an economic blockade of Lithuania. (Russia also set up "defense committees," tried to provoke violence in Lithuania, and manipulated Russian public opinion.)

In turn, Lithuanians were torn between their need to remain rational and a sense of revolutionary zeal. At the end of 1990, Ozolos told me that bloodshed was inevitable. "It will occur simply," he said. "Soviet paratroopers will enter the Soviet of Ministers." He was right. Later I was to see Russian soldiers march through the streets of Vilnius under a banner that read: "No to extremism."

In the official Russian press, "extremism" means the desire for national independence. To the newly "independent" press in Russia, the Baltics were suddenly a very dangerous topic, more dangerous than Joseph Stalin. Articles about the Baltics "being even farther away from independence than they were before" appeared on the pages of these publications with alarming frequency.

Waiting for the Tanks

On January 12, 1991, photojournalist Yevgeny Stetsko—my husband—and I heard alarming reports about events in Vilnius. We wanted to cover the story, but the roads were already closed. Trains were no longer going to Vilnius. So we went to Belarus, and from there managed to cross the border into Lithuania to catch a train. At the train station in Vilnius, Ozolos's aide, a young university student, ran up to me and exclaimed, "It's possible everything is already finished."

We drove quickly on the empty highway. The radio was broadcasting an announcement by the just-appointed commander of Vilnius, a Soviet officer. He said that authority in Lithuania was being transferred to a special defense committee. We didn't know what this meant to the independent Lithuanian government, which had been "dismissed" a few days earlier, allegedly because the population was "indignant at the rise in prices."

The "dismissed" parliament was, of course, still meeting. Huge concrete blocks had been placed around the parliament building to protect it from Soviet tanks. Using our press passes, we got in and made our way to the press box. Parliament was already in session. I saw the pale face of Ozolos, whose son had been killed on New Year's two weeks earlier.

As evening turned into night, the names of journalists who remained in the building were recorded. We were given gas masks. People were sleeping on the floor or roaming through the corridors. The air was thick with cigarette smoke.

The members of the parliament seemed cool. Prime Minister Kazimiera Prunskene wore a dress adorned with a crisp white lace collar. "We will be able to die with dignity because we've always been ready for that." I had heard these words before, in 1988 and 1989, when Lithuanians were waiting for Soviet tanks that we Russians believed existed only in their imaginations.

Although a handful of demonstrators had been killed in Tbilisi in Georgia in 1990, we still thought: Not in the Baltics. They wouldn't dare.

In spite of the curfew, during the night people gathered around the parliament building and encircled it tightly with their bodies. We didn't bother to wear our gas masks—if the tanks came, a gas mask would be nothing but a toy defense. I remember my fear. It resembled a sudden migraine attack against which you can't fight. The only thing you can do is try to save face.

Today it's commonly believed that it was the presence of more than 200 news correspondents in Lithuania that prevented the Soviets from storming parliament. The world had already seen enough bloodshed on New Year's night, when Lithuanians had tried to prevent the Soviet takeover of the television station.

Every one of us former Soviets said good-bye to the Soviet Union at our own specific moment. For me, it was during those frozen January days, when I looked at the tops of the iron spikes of the man-made barrier around the parliament building. There, a multitude of abandoned party membership cards had been pinned like dead butterflies.

This article was translated by Viktoria Tripolskaya-Mitlyng and adapted from the September/October 1994 *Bulletin*.

IV.3 Kazakhstan Finds Its Own Way

LEONID ZAGALSKY

From the very beginning of its emergence as a state in the aftermath of the disintegration of the Soviet Union, there has been something special about Kazakhstan: it has been peaceful. People in Kazakhstan are not killing each other in the kind of senseless ethnic battles for the lost identity of nations demolished during all those dark years of communism. Elsewhere in the former Soviet Union people are dying for being Armenian, Azeri, or Chechen. The conflicts seem endless. Kazakhstan, on the contrary, has barely experienced demonstrations, let alone riots.

Its transition to independence—that is, separation from the Soviet Union—has been without fanfare. Contrast this to Ukraine's loud proclamation of its independence all over the universe, or to the Baltic states, which immediately issued their own money and set up customs stations on their borders.

Kazakhstan's borders are still imaginary. You do not need to fill out any forms to enter this country from any other former Soviet republic, or open your bags for customs inspectors. Regular air service connects Moscow and Almaty (yes, the Kazakh capital, formerly Alma-Ata, has been renamed).

Unlike Ukraine, which has already sold its oil and gas abroad and can hardly refuel its planes, or Armenia, which is at war with Azerbaijan, Kazakhstan still has oil—plenty of it. It contains some of the world's largest reserves, most of which remain to be developed. Kazakhstan now has a new national minority—American corporate people who spend hot summer evenings in Almaty hotels drinking soda or warm beer while waiting to have endless discussions with government bureaucrats about oil deals.

A recent cover of the country's most popular new magazine, published in English, proclaims Kazakhstan the "bridge between Europe and Asia." President Nursultan Nazarbaev keeps himself in a kind of golden mean between the forces of Islamic fundamentalism and the world of his technical education. Like Prime Minister Sergey Tereshenko, a Russian, Nazarbaev is bilingual.

Contrasts and incongruities are everywhere. The huge Soviet nuclear test site occupies the middle of the Kazakh steppes. It was run by Russians; Kazakhs were not involved and few of them understood what nuclear power and nuclear weapons were. The Kazakh people were supposed to sit in their yurts and watch indifferently while underground nuclear explosions ruthlessly destroyed the environment.

Kazakhstan's natural environment is beautiful and nearly untouched in places. But the huge Aral Sea, which straddles the border between Kazakhstan and Uzbekistan, is dying, and there are no decent projects to prevent this from happening.

The routine mode of transportation is still the horse. The nation's favorite food is horse sausage.

On the other hand, a Mercedes dealership recently opened in Almaty and business is booming. Foreign advertising is everywhere, nearly obliterating the signs reminding everyone of the era when the Communist Party was "mind, conscience, and honor of the epoch."

The commercial bank in Kazakhstan recently established a joint venture with Visa. I was the first to get a cash advance using my Visa card in this bank. Unfortunately, the free gifts customers were supposed to get had not arrived yet.

Of course, only a fraction of a percentage of the population can afford to buy things sold for hard currency. Most must satisfy their taste for Western culture by watching American movies on VCRs or on TV. There are a couple of so-called commercial channels on Kazakh TV that alternate American movies with commercials.

Kazakhstan is one of the few Soviet republics to make a peaceful transition to independence. Other regions have been less fortunate, especially the Transcaucasus, which includes the troubled province of Chechnya as well as the independent states of Georgia, Armenia, and Azerbaijan. Here refugees flee fighting in the Georgian city of Sukhumi, fall of 1993. *Mark Shteinbock*

Even Coca-Cola is still an exotic product and very expensive, a treat for honored guests. At dinner, the cans of Coke will be placed on one side of the table, the *kumis* (horse's milk) on the other.

For all the peculiarities of life in Kazakhstan, the important thing to remember about this newly independent state of the former Soviet Union is that it will play an important role in the Asian community, if not in the whole world.

What meal is cooking in this huge pot "the size of four Frances," as Kazakhs love to say? One image reflects Kazakhstan's status of the moment. In the most beautiful park in the middle of Almaty, an attentive tourist will notice the bust of Dinmuhammed Kunayev, former first secretary of the Communist Party of Kazakhstan. According to a Brezhnev-era tradition, one who was twice awarded the gold star as a hero of socialist labor—as was Kunayev—would be immortalized in bronze and fixed in the central square of his home city. Perhaps Kunayev is the only member of Brezhnev's Politburo who still stares severely from his pedestal.

Kunayev died in late August. In his eighties, he was still highly respected. Kazakh culture bestows respect on old people, regardless of their intelligence. Nazarbaev reportedly asked Kunayev for advice on how to proceed on what Nazarbaev described as his "complicated way of restructuring Kazakh society." This may have been a joke, but if so, there was probably some truth in it, as there is in most jokes. At any rate, the former leader of the Communist Party of Kazakhstan had also organized a foundation, supported by his own money and that of other donors, to "maintain and develop the spiritual and cultural heritage of Kazakhstan and its people."

Adidas and Tubiteykas

But the pervasive influence these days is the invasion of material goods from both East and West, because it is new to this part of the world. As part of the Soviet Union, Kazakhstan was not on a main trade route with the outside world. All economic as well as political decisions were made in Moscow. When foreign goods arrived in the Soviet Union, Kazakhstan could only hope to receive scraps, and these would be distributed to top-level party leaders. Now the curbsides of Almaty and the other cities are occupied by hordes of kiosks selling American cigarettes and foreign liquors, clothes, watches, and electronics.

Chinese goods are all over the place, traded on every corner. China and Kazakhstan have agreed to make a small stretch of their mutual border free for trade and visiting. Hundreds of Kazakhs cross into China to shop for a day, then sell the Chinese goods in the flea markets of Kazakhstan. Chinese also bring goods themselves and sell them. This trade is not regulated by law, but there are certain requirements. The chief of the Almaty city police complains that every day the police must arrest and fine dozens of Chinese vendors trading in Almaty markets without licenses and visas.

Big Chinese business ventures, on the other hand, have not been very successful in the republic. Perhaps the Kazakhs and Chinese have too much in common: both nations are very cautious and afraid of being ripped off.

Koreans are doing somewhat better. A Korean businessman recently opened a casino, "Olympos," in the biggest hotel in Almaty. On a June evening when I visited, about 10 Kazakhs and Russians and five foreigners, mostly Koreans, were gambling without much success. The casino has been struggling, probably because of the huge gap between the dollar and the ruble. The owner decided to park a limousine in front of the Olympos to make his establishment look more Western and attractive. The limousine is never driven; it is part of the decor. Besides, it would be impossible to drive a limo on the rutted roads in the area.

Americans in Almaty—they are mainly oil people and Christian evangelists—avoid the casino, but it is a place for German and Dutch businessmen to kill their evenings. Michael Stalenhoef, 24, a partner with the Dutch S&P Trading Company, complained as he was placing a $10 bet that he had spent most of his profits from selling beer "gambling in this boring place." In fact, he was happy with the business he was doing in Kazakhstan and said that he was going to sign a permanent agreement with the Kazakh government to sell other products besides beer.

Igor Meltser, 42, vice-president of Karavan Company, said that business has been going well since he started three years ago. Karavan publishes, in Russian, the most popular newspaper in Kazakhstan, with a circulation of 200,000. It publishes two weekly supplements for the business community, one in Russian and one in English.

"We are three Jews at the top of the company," said Meltser, "and this is the first time that Jews have been allowed to have their own private businesses." He expressed doubt about the future, however. "Anti-semitism can always come back," he said.

Not all ventures are so successful. One businessman from Almaty decided to make some quick money and bought 10,000 T-shirts from the Moscow Prosper Company. He should have looked at the shirts before he bought them. They had come to the Moscow company from Hamburg, Germany, and were leftovers from the European Gay and Lesbian Festival. It will be a long time before Kazakhs wear T-shirts proclaiming sexual preferences. The shirts are still wandering through Kazakhstan and may end up in some remote province where people cannot read or may not know about all the varieties of human sexual experience.

Kazakhstan is not yet on the main road of the drug business but it may be approaching it. The marijuana growing wild in the Chuisky Valley in the Altai Mountains could be harvested, 5,000 tons in a year. The Kazakh police do not have a drug investigation department. The few investigators assigned to control drug dealers also have other tasks. There are few cars to patrol the area, and renting a helicopter is merely a dream for Kazakh cops, considering the price of gas.

Nevertheless, even with these obstacles, the police managed to uncover more than 2,000 drug-related crimes in 1992. Recently, Kazakhstan joined Interpol, which may help incorporate the republic in the worldwide fight against drugs.

True Believers

Religion is blooming in Kazakhstan. During the years of communism, the authorities tried to substitute propaganda for religion, Lenin's writings for the Bible and the Koran, Party meetings for religious rites. That is over. People are free to practice religion without hampering their careers. The president of the republic says: "I am asked very often who Kazakhs are. I answer, Kazakhs are Muslims first and foremost."

There are now 24 religious confessions practicing in Kazakhstan, including 581 mosques, Christian Orthodox churches, and synagogues. Ninety-five more are under construction.

It is hard to forecast whether Kazakhstan will become part of worldwide Muslim fundamentalism. It hardly seems likely that Kazakh women will wear veils and sit at home; this tradition is gone. Nor will Kazakhs become totally Europeanized and drink coffee in the morning. They will resurrect old traditions destroyed during communist rule.

A Russian friend told me that even though the Kazakh government says that all ethnic groups in the republic are equal under the law, the majority of Kazakhs consider the land to be theirs. "We will have to leave soon," he said bitterly. "I have been living here for more than 24 years but still cannot fit myself into this culture. It was all right, and it might be all right if the issue of nationalism does not prevail over common sense. If it does, we must leave."

Time passes quickly. It will be possible to know the answer to this and the other enigmas of Kazakhstan before long. One can only hope that Kazakhstan will retain its unique status as a peaceful new outgrowth of the dead giant named the Soviet Union.

This is adapted from the October 1993 *Bulletin*.

IV.4 Power Play in Central Asia

Mikhail Ustiugov

Kazakhstan expects eventually to benefit from the exploitation of its vast reserves of oil and gas in the Caspian region. Meanwhile, this largest republic in Central Asia is making plans to build three to 10 nuclear power reactors over the next 10 to 12 years.

The government of Kazakhstan intends to announce an international tender for the construction of the first of these nuclear power plants in the fall. The first plant, to be built at the former Soviet nuclear-weapons testing site at Semipalatinsk—one of the most contaminated regions of the former Soviet Union—is opposed by environmental groups. At the same time, the promise of a cure for Kazakhstan's energy shortage and its high rate of unemployment is likely to dampen the opposition.

After the collapse of the Soviet Union, the nuclear weapons that were deployed in Ukraine, Belarus, and Kazakhstan were considered to be the property of those republics. The newly independent republics had the option—theoretically—of retaining the weapons or transferring them to Russia in exchange for compensation.

In Kazakhstan—as in Ukraine—not everyone believed the country should relinquish its weapons. Kazakhstan lives under Russia's "nuclear umbrella." If ultranationalists come to power in Russia, and if they are willing to use force to rebuild the old Soviet empire, that same umbrella would be a threat.

Kazakhstan shares a 1,000-mile border with another restless and powerful neighbor, China. Thus it is squeezed between two superpowers whose political systems could undergo a number of complicated and dangerous changes in the near future.

This situation motivated some Kazakh officials—including the president, Nursultan Nazerbaev—to argue in favor of remaining a nuclear-weapon state, at least temporarily, after the Soviet Union collapsed. Eventually though, under pressure from the West—primarily from the United States—Kazakhstan relented. It renounced its nuclear ambitions in May 1992, and the last of Kazakhstan's nuclear warheads were shipped to Russia in 1995.

Today, Mikhail Isinaliev, the former minister of foreign affairs, says Kazakhstan should reacquire nuclear weapons, which he sees as the only reliable national security guarantee. Others think that the Nazarbaev government has yet to abandon its nuclear weapon ambitions, and that a pro-nuclear policy will eventually emerge. Tulegen Askarov, a former member of the president's cabinet, thinks that the government's decision to build a series of nuclear power plants is part of a larger nuclear strategy: "The hawks have triumphed in the republic. They believe in the power of the atom and of weapons and [they] understand the real value of the republic's nuclear complex. . . . [They] have support from foreign countries with nuclear ambitions."

Askarov believes the completion of a trans-Asian complex of highways and the just-opened rail line to Iran will provide many opportunities for smuggling. "Iran, Pakistan, and India will receive direct access to the nearby uranium complex of Central Asia."

Kazakh officials reply that such predictions are alarmist. Instead, they say, the development of nuclear power will help the country "step into the twenty-first century with confidence."

Public Reaction

I happened to learn about the decision to go ahead with the plant at Semipalatinsk the day after it was agreed to by Vice Premier Akezhan Kazhegeldin, a Semipalatinsk native and former head of the Semipalatinsk administration. Most citizens of the republic learned about it two weeks later—and then they didn't find out from the local press. They got the news from a Russian newspaper, *Izvestia*.

The immediate response of the populations of Semipalatinsk and Karaganda, a large industrial center near Semipalatinsk, was negative. Local deputies issued an appeal to the government, asking: "How long will we turn our long-suffering land into a nuclear dump? What will we do with waste from the nuclear power station?"

Activists, including those from the Nevada-Semipalatinsk environmental movement, joined the deputies in protesting the plan. Nevada-Semipalatinsk is perhaps the best known social movement in the republic, having waged a successful, internationally celebrated struggle to get the test site shut down. During one meeting, members of the movement expressed anger that a government that had no funds to clean up contaminated land or to pay restitution to local inhabitants was contemplating spending $1.5 billion to build a nuclear power station.

But a sharp division in local sentiment about nuclear power became apparent late last December when the results of a poll conducted in the Semipalatinsk region were released. Forty-four percent of those polled were opposed to building a nuclear power station, but 40 percent favored it.

The Kazakh nuclear establishment sees the polling results as assuring victory. That 40 percent of the inhabitants of Semipalatinsk, a community that is well aware of the potential health and environmental risks connected with nuclear testing, voted in favor of a nuclear power plant is astonishing. It is even more surprising given the level of radiophobia after the Chernobyl accident—and the fact that the local leader who conducted the poll opposes the construction of the nuclear power station.

Kazakhstan has always depended on outside supplies for its energy needs. It receives nearly 20 percent of its energy from three neighboring republics, Russia, Kirgizia, and Uzbekistan. After the collapse of the Soviet Union, energy prices soared.

In 1995 Kazakhstan spent the equivalent of $630 million to import energy; the bill will be higher in 1996. And the International Monetary Fund has predicted that the growth of Kazakhstan's economy will depend on its ability to purchase the energy it requires to develop its oil and gas industries.

Kazakhstan cannot afford to continue importing energy, and it is now involved in a series of complex negotiations with its neighbors regarding the repayment of their enterprises' debts to Kazakhstan. Some of these debts date back to Soviet times.

Ordinary citizens worry less about the debt than the energy shortage, which is especially severe in the countryside. Even in the capital of Almaty, it is common to have no electricity for two to three hours a day. Meanwhile, in the villages, many have gone back to using candles and oil lamps, as their ancestors did in the last century. But candle power cannot run a milking machine, and a number of collective farms, privatized or not, are impoverished today. Building a nuclear power plant would alleviate these problems.

Secret Negotiations

After Chernobyl, Russian nuclear scientists are not popular in Kazakhstan. Kazakh officials say Canadian and French companies, and a U.S. firm, General Atomics, will be the leading contenders in the bidding for the Semipalatinsk reactor project.

Russia's nuclear establishment therefore decided to try another route to obtain reactor business in Kazakhstan. Early this year, Russia made a proposal to the Kazakh government to build a second reactor in one of the southern parts of the republic where energy shortages are most acute.

Kazakhstan apparently accepted the Russian proposal because of its economic advantages. Although the last of the nuclear warheads on Kazakh soil were returned to Russia in April 1995, Russia has yet to pay for them. Instead, it offered to use the money it owes as a down payment on the nuclear power plant.

Another major source of funding could come from Kazakhstan's share of the money the United States will pay for the uranium fuel it is purchasing from the former Soviet Union. Kazakhstan's share has not been agreed on yet. Almaty claims that it should receive between $400 and $500 million, but how and when it would actually get the money is unclear.

Russia also agreed to loan Kazakhstan the remaining $800 million. Russia's intentions are not altruistic: Its reactors use only enriched uranium for fuel, which means that the Kazakh nuclear complex would be even more dependent on Russian supplies. Russia is also counting on getting at least some of the construction business at Semipalatinsk, even if a foreign firm wins the bidding, because it will be most practical to bring the heaviest reactor parts from Russia.

Has the Kazakh government explored all its energy options? Perhaps the republic could develop less expensive energy sources. But an influential government advisor dismisses all other possibilities: "It is better not to burn oil and gas, but to process them in advanced technology enterprises. Thermal power stations that work on coal cause great ecological damage. A number of international environmental organizations have already complained that the largest power station in Ekibastuz caused great damage to the environment. No alternatives to nuclear power exist for the republic."

This article is adapted from the July/August 1996 *Bulletin*.

IV.5 Armenia's Energy Choice

Astghik Vardanian

For six years Armenians lived in the semi-darkness of the Middle Ages. Beginning in 1989, these 3.7 million people in the southern Caucasus survived without adequate heat, transportation, or medical care. There were only endless candlelit evenings with no television or music. "You lived in the Sabbath all year long," a Jewish friend commented.

The crisis was precipitated by a devastating earthquake and the closure of Armenia's only nuclear power plant. It was compounded by the breakup of the Soviet Union and an economic blockade that cut the country off from other energy sources. The power shortage left the post-Soviet government with a stark choice: nuclear power or continued crisis.

For those living through the dark years, the risks associated with nuclear power were overshadowed by the hardship of this period. The reopening of the power plant, which occurred last fall, could never be merely a technical question.

The earthquake of December 7, 1988, measured 6.7 on the Richter scale. It took the lives of 30,000 people, leveled two cities and 55 villages, and destroyed one-tenth of the country's industry. It also shook faith in the safety of Armenia's only nuclear power plant, Medzamor, which sits in an unsafe seismic zone 30 miles south of the capital of Yerevan and 60 miles from where the quake hit.

The plant, which consists of two VVER 440/270 reactors (modified from VVER 440/230s), had one of the best safety records of Soviet-style reactors. Unit 1 came on line in 1976, and Unit 2 in 1980. They provided Armenia with a surplus of energy, which was exported to other parts of the Soviet Union and Turkey.

Even though the plant experienced no damage and was designed to withstand earthquakes of up to 8.0, a large movement led by the country's Green

Union called for its closure amid safety concerns and anti-Soviet sentiment. Armenia's growing self-determination movement focused on the potentially risky power plant as a symbol of Soviet domination and exploitation.

After heated disputes among politicians, scientists, and the Greens, the Supreme Soviet, the highest government body in the then-Soviet republic of Armenia, agreed to shut it down. Between January and March 1989, the two reactors went off line. Nearly 40 percent of the country's total energy supply was no longer available.

The breakup of the Soviet Union, following closely on the heels of the plant closure, further destabilized the country. While many problems were common to all former Soviet republics, the era of independence began particularly unfavorably for Armenia, the smallest among the newly independent nations. Since 1989 Armenia has been locked in a bloody dispute with neighboring Azerbaijan over the territory of Nagorno-Karabakh, an enclave of Armenia deemed part of Azerbaijan by Josef Stalin in 1922. The ongoing war monopolized the human and financial resources necessary to build an independent post-Soviet infrastructure.

This once scientifically and culturally advanced country also was subjected to a total blockade related to the war by Azerbaijan and Turkey. Armenia's only remaining connection to the outside world was through its northern neighbor, Georgia. But during the fighting, the railway lines and gas pipelines that pass through Georgia were permanently destroyed by Azeris living in that country. Georgia, which did not investigate this terrorism, was believed to be pilfering the Armenian share of gas sent from Turkmenistan. With barricades on all sides, even the delivery of humanitarian aid, now completely dependent on air shipment, was slowed.

The Woodcutters

And so the crisis began. Industry slowed, factories shut down, and office workers were laid off. Even ambulance service was halted because of a lack of gasoline. People passed the winters in their apartments, where room temperatures hovered close to freezing. Deprived of their jobs, they had only two reasons to go out—to get fuel and food.

Under the blockade, Armenia could provide for only one-fourth of its daily bread. This brought long and excruciating bread lines, and often the military was required to keep order. Eventually a voucher rationing system was enforced, providing a daily ration of 8.8 ounces per person. "Every day pupils in the school are fainting," said Hasmik Sargissyan, the director of studies at a secondary school in Yerevan. "The teachers used to keep sandwiches in their bags for emergency cases."

During this period people received only one to two hours of electricity a day, and their lives were defined by it. "We had to manage to do everything in two hours—to cook, to bathe, to wash, to watch TV," said Theresa Arazian, a professor of musicology at the Yerevan Conservatory. The rest of the time was spent planning how to get candles and the fuel to fire wood stoves and kerosene lamps.

After the first two years, the government became more efficient in its use of energy and more became available for necessities including hospitals and factories. But people rigged up cables known as "left lines" to siphon off electricity from these high-priority users to augment their two-hours-a-day allowance. Some even attached the left lines to unused metal bed frames, heating them like giant radiators. According to Armenergo, the government's electricity agency, 40 percent of the electricity generated was used illegally. People joked that Armenia's President Levon Ter-Petrosian promised to provide the whole nation with "left lines."

The only outside help with heat came from a U.S. humanitarian program

With temperatures below freezing in schoolrooms, Armenian children stood for hand-warming exercises every 15 minutes. *Jerry Berndt*

called "Winter Warmth," which provided kerosene to Armenia from 1992 to 1995. Some people, however, were reluctant to use this fuel, as Armenian doctors warned that the fumes could be harmful to children.

Many people left the country. "I couldn't survive another winter in Armenia. This was sheer hell," said David Babayan, a writer and actor who immigrated to Moscow. According to the U.N. Development Program, 676,000 people—or about one fifth of the population—left during this period, many settling in Russia, the United States, or Israel. Much of the country's professional and artistic elite were part of this exodus.

But millions of others remained.

At first chopping down city trees for fuel was considered shameful, and the main concern of woodcutters was to go unnoticed. At night, armed with axes and saws, they chopped the trees they had targeted during the day.

Very soon it was commonplace and no longer considered a dishonorable deed. The soot billowing from round holes in apartment windows was a sign of success. "I can plant trees in the spring, but I can't bring back my kids," said my neighbor, the father of five children.

People started with the trees in their gardens and ended up with those decorating the House of Parliament. The Ministry of Ecology estimates that 800,000 trees were chopped down throughout the country in the first two winters. After intensive woodcutting the cities seemed bald. "Good bye, and good luck in wood cutting," a television showman would say at the end of his program, as wood became harder and harder to find. Today there is a memorial in Yerevan, a sculpture of a tree, erected as a reminder of the "Genocide of Nature."

Concentration Camp for Animals

The streets of Yerevan were filled with pedestrians. People walked and drove by instinct, without the aid of street or traffic lights, which were turned on for only two days a year at Christmas time.

The energy shortage also paralyzed public transportation. Often trolleys would be stalled on hills when the electricity was cut off. At these times male passengers would get out and push the trolley to the top, and then, like kids on a roller coaster, jump back in to enjoy the ride. When the rare trolley did get electricity, it carried many times more people than it could comfortably hold. And trolley doors never closed as dozens of people hung out of them in acrobatic positions. Teenagers took to hanging from the emergency staircases.

Others chose to walk rather than stand in claustrophobic trolleys. With many extra pedestrians came extra falls on icy sidewalks. A common joke in Yerevan was that Armenians had become better at falling than Charlie Chaplin or Buster Keaton.

It was a sad day at the Yerevan Zoo when its only elephant, Vova, died in 1993. "The specialists failed to give a precise cause—cold, malnutrition, bad living conditions," said Hripsime Brutian of the zoo's publicity department.

The inhabitants of the zoo were kept in their winter houses, without electricity. "The animals have been in complete darkness for five months and will live [this way] another month until the winter is over," Karo Mandalyan, the zoo's manager, explained. Members of the zoo's staff did what they could. Many brought food from their homes. The snake keeper even took the snakes in their glass containers to his apartment where he could keep them warm with a wood heater. When the elephant died, it was used to feed the other animals.

"Only this winter, we lost 64 big and small animals: zebras, tigers, birds, wolves, and sheep—all from cold and hunger," said the manager. "Every morning I come to the zoo with the fear in my heart to see another dead animal." A visiting journalist filming the zoo for Germany's Stern Television said, "Damn, it was a concentration camp for animals."

A Decision

As the energy crisis lingered with no end in sight, the Armenian government announced in April 1993 that it would restart one of the two units at Medzamor as the only viable short-term solution.

Armenian citizens were fully behind the decision, but they were alone in this view. All of the country's neighbors held protests, questioning the safety of the reactor. Turkey, which supported Azerbaijan in its war with Armenia, even offered at one point to lift its blockade if Armenia would keep the reactor off line.

The West also opposed Armenia's decision, and from the start refused to provide technical assistance or guidance for the plant's reactivation, arguing that because the plant was in a zone of high seismic activity, it could never meet safety standards. "We wanted to do all we could to prevent its restart," said a representative of the European Bank for Reconstruction and Development's Nuclear Safety Account (International Herald Tribune, October 25, 1995).

Armenian officials attributed Western objections to their interest in securing contracts for new power plants for Western businesses. "This is a struggle for the market," Vanik Nersisyan, deputy head of Armenia's Department of

Atomic Energy, told the International Herald Tribune. "This is an issue of the employment of the Western population." Compared to building new plants, little money could be made in assisting in the upgrade of Medzamor. Armenia was not eligible for the aid provided by the Nuclear Safety Account, which was designated for the 11 other VVERs currently operating in Bulgaria and Russia.

Spurned by Western authorities, the Armenian government turned to Russia for help. Russia provided Armenia with loans to upgrade the plant, including the addition of reinforcements against seismic activity and the construction of a new cooling-water lake.

When it became clear that Armenia would go ahead with or without Western assistance, equipment also was provided by France, Germany, Bulgaria, and other European countries. According to the April 6, 1996, *New Scientist*, some countries were changing their stand on even the more dangerous RBMK reactors like those at Chernobyl. Again, some interpreted the change as a means of helping Western businesses benefit in the post-Soviet marketplace. "The closure of the reactors would mean that Western nuclear corporations would lose potentially valuable contracts for fitting safety equipment," said German Environment Minister Angela Merkel.

Between 1994 and 1995, more than 500 tons of equipment was airlifted to Medzamor, and 800 upgrades were performed to improve the reactor's safety. After frequently sending World Association of Nuclear Operators and International Atomic Energy Agency (IAEA) inspectors to Medzamor, the IAEA concluded in 1994 that "the plant is safe and there are no principal obstacles for the restart."

Ironically, when Medzamor's Unit 2 was turned on November 5, 1995, it was greeted with the same euphoria that attended the decision to turn it off in 1989. The plant ran at 92 percent capacity during the winter, according to the government's nuclear regulatory agency. It produces enough electricity to satisfy 25 percent of the needs of the country's population and industry.

Armenians are gradually recovering from the dark experience of the past years. They are coming round from the absurdity under which they lived, and getting back to a normal life—or as normal as life can be in the midst of war and a blockade. Today in Armenia we no longer hear children's hoorays when electricity is turned on. It is an accepted part of life, and these cheers are once again reserved for fireworks and Christmas trees.

But the recovery was built on nuclear energy—a necessary short-term compromise for a country that has no other reliable source of power available. The country's government and scientists continue to look into alternatives including natural gas, oil, solar, and hydroelectric energy, but nuclear power remains most viable. The government is even considering restarting the older Unit 1 at Medzamor and commissioning a new plant. But to implement these more ambitious nuclear alternatives safely will require Western technical help—and political will.

This article appeared in the July/August 1996 *Bulletin*.

New Nations of the Former Soviet Union

The *Central Asian* republics have large Muslim populations. Civil war continues in Tajikistan and repression prevails in Uzbekistan. But Kirgizia is a democracy, and Kazakhstan and Turkmenistan are gaining prosperity.

The *Caucasus* or *Transcaucasus* is the mountainous region between the Black Sea and the Caspian Sea. Georgia, Armenia, and Azerbaijan and the bordering areas of Russia, especially Chechnya, have been troubled by bloody conflicts—partly because ethnic divisions do not always correspond with old Soviet and new national borders.

The *Baltic* states—Lithuania, Latvia, and Estonia—were the last republics to be annexed by Moscow after World War II and the first to leave the Union. The Russian "exclave" of Kaliningrad nestles between Lithuania and Poland.

Moldova suffers from internal divisions. It has strong ties to Romania, which it was part of until 1940. Ukrainian nationalists have not fully succeeded in cutting relations with Russia and making their nation part of Europe. The government of Belarus, on the other hand, is renewing ties with Russia.

Chapter IV
Discussion Questions

1. During the Cold War, "Soviet watchers" often debated whether the Union of Soviet Socialist Republics was actually a single nation. What evidence do you see in these articles that the USSR was or was not one nation?

2. Although Russia and the United States are no longer major threats to each other, both countries still have particular sets of security concerns. Based on your reading of the articles in this chapter, what issues would you say Russia considers most threatening in the late 1990s?

3. Nuclear affairs are still prominent in the politics of a number of former Soviet states. Detail how the holding of nuclear weapons, nuclear disarmament, and nuclear energy have intertwined with politics and democratization in particular nations of the former Soviet Union.

4. Describe the new manifestations of national and ethnic consciousness in several former Soviet states. How do you account for the fact that in some cases these new expressions lead to conflict and in other cases they do not?

Part Two

Building Peace and Security

Chapter V

Promoting Global Cooperation: Multilateral Peacekeeping and Sanctions

When the Cold War ended unexpectedly, the United Nations was faced with unprecedented opportunities and burdens as the major international guarantor of peace and security. Because the United States and Russia were no longer ideological enemies, the U.N. Security Council might, for the first time since the organization's creation in 1945, approve actions that would fulfill its mandate to keep peace and promote humanitarian concerns around the globe. In the past, most proposed actions of this sort faced a nearly automatic veto from one superpower or the other.

The challenges came quickly. Iraq invaded Kuwait in 1990, and the Security Council imposed its harshest economic sanctions ever. Nevertheless, a variety of political pressures—and Saddam Hussein's unwillingness to withdraw from Kuwait—led to the U.N.-sponsored and U.S.-led Gulf War of January 15 to February 26, 1991.

In late 1992, internal warfare raging in Somalia was threatening mass starvation. In this case, the United Nations departed from its tradition of interpositionary peacekeeping, that is, of imposing its forces between warring factions in order to allow the factions to seek diplomatic solutions. Instead, the U.N. deployed troops to stabilize the situation so that its agencies and others could provide emergency food relief.

These cases illustrate two new trends in U.N. actions since the Cold War: an increase in the use of multilateral economic sanctions against nations that violate norms of the U.N. Charter; and the use of armed intervention in a variety of humanitarian emergencies.

From 1945 to 1990, sanctions were imposed about 60 times in some form, by one or more nations against another. Three-quarters of these cases were initiated by the United States—and two-thirds of those actions involved unilateral U.S. action. During this period the U.N. Security Council imposed multilateral sanctions only twice: against Rhodesia in 1966 and against South Africa in 1977.

In the 1990s, by contrast, the Security Council has imposed partial or comprehensive sanctions against Iraq (since 1990), the government of the former Yugoslavia (1991–95), Libya (since 1992), Liberia (intermittently since 1992), Somalia (1992–95), Haiti (1993–94), and Rwanda (1994–95). In unprecedented actions, the Council also imposed sanctions on two subnational groups which were interfering with U.N.-sponsored reconciliation efforts: the Khmer Rouge in Cambodia/Kampuchea and UNITA in Angola. Sanctions have been imposed for a wide range of purposes—for example, to stop aggression, restore democracy, condemn human rights abuses, or punish those who harbor terrorists.

Despite these changes in the use of sanctions, the operating principle behind them remains unchanged: that economic suffering will cause citizens in targeted nations to either replace their rulers or force those rulers to change their behavior. Although some analysts have called this way of understanding or using sanctions naive, it remains a harsh reality. However, another claim is implied and now being debated: that economic sanctions are less damaging than war.

The changes, both in quantity and character, in the U.N. use of armed intervention since the end of the Cold War are equally striking. The United Nations was involved in 11 multilateral operations, including five peacekeeping missions, in 1988. By 1994, it was involved in 28 conflicts, including 17 peacekeeping missions. Multinational troops supporting such missions increased from just under 10,000 to nearly 75,000. The budget for these operations exploded from $230 million to more than $3.5 billion.

These actions have increasingly focused on internal humanitarian crises previously regarded as matters of national sovereignty: anarchy, refugee crises, and human rights abuses associated with internal war. The most notable success among U.N. ventures may have been the creation of safe havens for Iraqi Kurds in 1991 and, with U.S. assistance, the subsequent protection of these territories. By contrast, the U.N. humanitarian intervention in Somalia in 1992–93, dominated by the United States, was perceived as a debacle, as warring Somali groups made a mockery of the mission. This humiliation was repeated by Serb forces in the former Yugoslavia as they attacked U.N. "safe havens," disrupted the delivery of humanitarian relief, and even took U.N. personnel hostage.

Both "new" policy realities—economic sanctions and expanded roles for peacekeeping—have raised agonizing questions, many of which U.N. Secretary General Boutros Boutros-Ghali captured in his 1995 report, *Supplement to an Agenda for Peace*. Boutros-Ghali noted that sanctions are a blunt instrument that inflicts suffering on vulnerable groups, complicates the work of humanitarian agencies, damages the productive capacity of nations, and imposes hardships on neighboring countries. He did not reject the use of sanctions but pleaded for reform in their implementation, calling for a new mechanism to monitor sanctions and maximize their political impact while minimizing the damage they impose, especially on the most vulnerable. At the same time, he noted that humanitarian crises would continue to take high priority in thinking about the development and deployment of U.N. peacekeeping missions.

Implicit in these issues, and in the organization of the selections, is the reality that economic sanctions and the deployment of United Nations forces are two sides of the same coin which has come to be called by different names: U.N. enforcement actions, peace enforcement, or multilateral engagement. Both sanctions and peacekeeping are important components of the U.N. Charter and, as the chart at the end of the chapter illustrates, they have often been used in tandem in the past decade.

Readings in this chapter address some of the most difficult and controversial dimensions of U.N. peacekeeping and economic sanctions. Richard Longworth discusses the mix of policy and practical problems facing U.N. peacekeeping missions, especially the tension between the role of assuring humanitarian assistance and any role that calls for more aggressive combat. This is followed by a Bosnian journalist's sharp criticism of the behavior of U.N. peacekeeping troops toward citizens they were assigned to protect.

The third and fourth articles challenge the critique of the United Nations often heard in the United States. First, Jonathan Dean argues that a strong United Nations serves U.S. national security interests. Then Steven Kull presents evidence that U.S. citizens are less opposed to U.S. participation in peacekeeping operations than media reports and government assertions might indicate.

Finally, two articles address economic sanctions. Ivan Eland concludes that sanctions have been most successful when they have been comprehensive and have been imposed swiftly and with maximum force. But Drew Christiansen and Gerard Powers ask, at what cost to innocent citizens? They argue that sanctions, like other coercive measures, must be governed by ethical criteria.

The concluding map locates the most important U.N. sanctions and peacekeeping operations of the 1990s.

V.1 Phantom Forces, Diminished Dreams

Richard C. Longworth

The sharpest weapon in the United Nations' arsenal—the ability to make peace by waging war—has been sheathed for the foreseeable future. It may, in fact, be the one weapon which is beyond the world body's ability to wield and control. Two years after it was first used, it already has become widely discredited. It's doubtful that any amount of reform will make it work the way the framers of the U.N. Charter meant it to work.

This weapon is Chapter VII of the charter, which empowers the Security Council to order forces from the U.N. member nations to "take such action . . . as may be necessary to maintain or restore international peace and security."

Chapter VII was meant to be the iron fist inside the velvet glove of U.N. peacemaking and peacekeeping. In principle, as embodied in the charter, this power is unlimited. In practice, it has only been used once in its truest sense—in Somalia, where it failed. Because of that failure, it may never be used again. And because of this restriction, a debate is going on at U.N. headquarters and among member nations: What can the United Nations do instead to cope with the crises—all the Rwandas, Somalias, Angolas, and Tajikistans—that challenge it almost continuously these days?

Chapter VII was meant to be used when all else has failed. The preceding chapter provides for the "pacific settlement of disputes" through "negotiation, enquiry, mediation, conciliation, arbitration, judicial settlement, resort to regional agencies . . . or other peaceful means." If this sweet reason falls short, Chapter VII provides for sterner action to deal with "threats to the peace, breaches of the peace, and acts of aggression." First, it says, U.N. members could use economic embargoes, block transportation lines, cut off mail delivery or break diplomatic relations. If that still doesn't do it, the chapter authorizes "such action by air, sea, or land forces as may be necessary. . . . Such an action may include demonstrations, blockades, and other operations by air, sea, or land forces of member states."

Chapter VII has been used several times to wrap the cloak of international respectability around national—usually American—missions. This was the case with Security Council resolutions authorizing the Korean War, the Gulf War, and the current U.S. incursion into Haiti. This approach is likely to be used again, either by the United States or by some other nation—a Russian mission into one of the former Soviet states like Georgia, for instance.

But as one U.N. official said, "The lesson of Somalia may have been that you can't impose peace." Considering that the imposition of peace was the stated purpose of Chapter VII, this means that the dream of what the United Nations can do in the world—a dream that animated the framers of the charter, and more recently underlay the hope of a new world order—has been severely deflated. In 1992, Secretary-General Boutros Boutros-Ghali, in his *An Agenda for Peace*, argued that while action under Chapter VII should be taken only when all else has failed, "the option of taking it is essential to the credibility of the United Nations as a guarantor of international security." Since Boutros-Ghali wrote those words, the U.N.'s credibility, by his own standard, has diminished.

Chapter VII envisaged the member nations, armed both with modern weapons and the conscience of humanity, marching behind the blue-and-white U.N. flag into the world's trouble spots to crack heads for peace. In the place of this shrunken dream is a search for new ideas, most of them stopgaps.

An Army of Its Own

One casualty has been any hope for a standing U.N. army, a sort of international foreign legion recruited by the United Nations itself, directly under U.N. command, and not attached to any national forces. Such a force would be permanently on call, ready to go the moment the Security Council gave the word. Among other things, it would be able to take casualties in a way that the present multinational forces could not. Presumably, the idea of a dead U.N. legionnaire, even one from Iowa or Oregon, would be more acceptable to American public opinion than the sight of a dead soldier from the U.S. Army serving temporarily under U.N. command. The United States is particularly sensitive to casualties among its peacekeepers, but other nations have similar qualms. France and Britain effectively blocked heavy NATO bombing of Serb positions in Bosnia out of fear for their soldiers serving with the United Nations there.

The idea of a standing U.N. army has been a hardy perennial. According to Sir Brian Urquhart, former director of peacekeeping for the United Nations, the idea was backed by John Foster Dulles when he was U.S. secretary of state. The then secretary-general, Dag Hammarskjold, shot the idea down as politically unrealistic, because of the "legal restrictions imposed on the [United Nations] by national sovereignty."

But with the end of the Cold War, the burdens being placed on the United Nations generated new demands for a standing army. Urquhart himself proposed a permanent but limited force that could go quickly to any crisis, where it would hold the fort until larger forces arrived. A similar force, with 5,000 to 10,000 volunteer troops, was endorsed in 1993 by a U.S. commission on the United Nations led by Cong. James Leach "to contain conflicts before they escalate out of control or deter them altogether."

But a standing U.N. army is now a dead issue, even though Boutros-Ghali said in January 1995 the United Nations must give "serious thought" to it. The secretary-general would like to see a "rapid reaction force" composed of "battalion-sized units from a number of countries," and under the direction of the Security Council.

Boutros-Ghali is whistling into the wind. In the wake of U.N. debacles in Somalia and Yugoslavia, virtually no one believes that member nations would agree to set up such a legion or pay for it—and no one believes that the United Nations would be competent to manage it.

As recently as January 1995, in a supplement to *An Agenda for Peace*, the secretary-general plaintively noted that the United Nations lacked the capacity to "deploy, direct, command and control operations" for peace enforcement, "except perhaps on a very limited scale." Boutros-Ghali also said he would like a larger U.N. force, under his command, that could take on "enforcement actions," presumably like the Gulf War, "but it would be folly to attempt to do so at the present time when the organization is resource-starved and hard pressed to handle the less demanding peacemaking and peacekeeping responsibilities entrusted to it."

In its place is a plan, more realistic but still shaky, for standby troops that the United Nations could call up in case of crisis. Member states would designate certain units to be trained in peacekeeping that could be called up to serve in a U.N. force in an emergency. Such a force could be on the scene within two to four weeks after a crisis breaks—lightning speed compared to the three to six months it took to get troops to Somalia or Rwanda.

This idea is more than a gleam in the U.N. eye. For the past year or so, U.N. officials have been negotiating contributions with member nations. As of this writing, 62 countries have said they would participate, and five have signed memos of understanding. According to U.N. statistics, this commitment amounts to about 75,000 troops, plus ships, planes, and other materiel. It is, in short, a formidable international force ready to move out at the Security Council's call.

There's just one hitch—and it's a big one. These troops are committed, but that commitment is subject to confirmation on a case-by-case basis. In other words, a country may have committed its troops, but it can still veto this contribution when the United Nations asks it to live up to its promise.

This is precisely what happened in 1994 in Rwanda. Nineteen nations had joined the standby force when the Rwanda crisis broke out, but after hearing that U.N. troops from Belgium were being macheted on the streets of Kigali, all 19 reneged.

"The problem is that these commitments are like American Express travelers' cheques," said Hedi Annabi, the U.N.'s director of peacekeeping operations in Africa. "They can be signed once, but they're no good unless they're signed again."

In truth, the "standby force" is misnamed, because there is no real force and it's not standing by ready to go. Instead it's more of a data bank than an army, a catalogue that lets the United Nations know that X member nations have Y troops with Z equipment that theoretically might be available in a crisis.

In practice in Rwanda, Annabi said, "We just got a quicker 'no' than we would have before, so we could start looking elsewhere."

If Somalia was the test of Chapter VII, Rwanda was the test of the standby force, and the failure was just as dramatic. According to Annabi, Boutros-Ghali asked the member nations for 5,500 troops on May 16, six weeks after the crisis began and 100,000 people had already been killed. "The silence that followed was deafening." It was the end of July, 10 weeks later, before 550 soldiers were on the ground in Rwanda: by that time, a half million people were dead.

Of the five permanent members of the U.N. Security Council, only France acted with any speed at all, and it did that on its own, not within the U.N. framework. This is not because those five had balked at joining the standby force—quite the contrary. The nations that promised to join the standby force included most of the heavy hitters, among them France, Britain, and the United States. Their promise still holds—but apparently, not in the case of Rwanda. What about the next crisis? Maybe yes, but probably no.

States' Rights v. Human Rights

There is an overriding philosophical issue in the exercise of Chapter VII that has received much less attention than it deserves. This is the question of sovereignty—whether other nations, using U.N. authority, have the right to intervene in the internal affairs of sovereign nations, no matter how good the cause.

For 350 years, the world has run itself on the guidelines laid down at the Peace of Westphalia in 1648. This established the principle of sovereignty, first to the principalities within the Holy Roman Empire and then, by extension, to all nations. The Cold War tended to reinforce this principle because the Soviet Union treated any criticism of its system as interference in its internal affairs. Both the Soviet Union and the United States, of course, violated the sovereignty of other nations at will—Hungary, Czechoslovakia, Guatemala, Grenada, Vietnam. But no one pretended that these violations were based on anything but pure national interest.

The new interventionism under Chapter VII is more disturbing because the reasons for it are so unassailable. This theory holds that human rights override sovereignty: when a government abuses its people, the sovereignty of the government can be ignored in favor of the superior sovereignty of the people themselves. The Kurds are said to have sovereignty as a nation and if that sovereignty is abused by Saddam Hussein, then the United Nations has the right—which it exercised in Security Council Resolution 688—to intervene, in violation of Iraqi sovereignty.

Boutros-Ghali has written, in *Agenda* and elsewhere, that "the time of absolute and exclusive sovereignty . . . has passed. It is undeniable that the centuries-old doctrine of absolute and exclusive sovereignty no longer stands. . . . Underlying the rights of the individual and the rights of peoples is a dimension of universal sovereignty that resides in all humanity."

The sentiment is impeccable, but its implementation, as we have learned in places like Yugoslavia and Somalia, is uncertain. Moreover, the United Nations is not likely to intervene to help the oppressed blacks of the West Side of Chicago or the abused Catholics of Londonderry: this reduces this new intervention, based on a higher devotion to human rights, to a new colonialism, a morality imposed by the strong on the weak.

The world, of course, has changed in the last five years. The way that governments treat their citizens has become a legitimate concern for the world's conscience. There is no geopolitical reason, as there was during the Cold War, to turn a blind eye to the misdeeds of dictators. But quite clearly, the world has not decided how to express this concern. At one point, a more active use of Chapter VII seemed a useful weapon. Today, two years after Somalia, that seems unlikely.

As Robert T. Grey, Jr., an American diplomat who is now a senior fellow at the Council on Foreign Relations in New York, has pointed out, the United Nations and Chapter VII have their uses. But, he adds, they are likely to be no more than an adjunct to national policies, a tool that individual nations can use when it suits their national interests.

As Grey notes, while Chapter VII authorizes multilateral U.N. action, it reaffirms "the inherent right of individual or collective self-defense" by each member nation. This right, he says, "will remain the bedrock of the international security system and the guarantee that, when our vital national interests are at stake, we retain the right to act alone if necessary."

The United Nations has proved in Namibia, El Salvador, and Cambodia that it can use its powers to build or rebuild nations. It has also proved in Somalia and the former Yugoslavia that those powers are limited and, if misused, can do more harm than good. Neither the United Nations nor its member nations have clearly defined how far those powers should reach, or whether Chapter VII can be used under any circumstances. Now that the first euphoric blush of interventionism is past, the time for that definition has come.

This is adapted from the March/April 1995 *Bulletin*.

V.2 We Are Dying of Your Protection

Dzenita Mehic

In January 1993, Bosnian Deputy Prime Minister Hakija Turajlic was assassinated by a Serb soldier while under U.N. protection. At least seven shots were fired at Turajlic as he was returning from the Sarajevo airport in a French armored carrier on a road that the Serbs had guaranteed in writing would be controlled by the United Nations. U.N. Gen. Philippe Morillon cited U.N. errors, but dodged questions about who had committed them and failed to clarify conflicting accounts from his officers on the scene.

Sarajevans, unable to comprehend such a crime and another Serb humiliation of the United Nations, delivered a message: We are dying of your protection.

We didn't think it would be this way in the beginning.

At first the citizens of Sarajevo naively welcomed the U.N. Protection Force—"UNPROFOR"—sent in in the spring of 1992 to support the humanitarian relief effort. Sarajevans believed that the authority of the United Nations would help restore some of the city's dignity and stability. As a local radio news reporter, I covered the U.N. mission at close hand.

The first 350 peacekeepers who arrived in Sarajevo in March 1992 were almost immediately trapped by the heavy shelling of the city. Their mission quickly turned to self-preservation, and their presence in the town had little effect. Lacking the force or determination to deal with the villains who were besieging the city, or even to implement decisions made at U.N. headquarters in New York, the mission became one of simple survival, even if it meant forsaking the principles that might have given it credibility.

The U.N. officials' lack of preparation for a mission in the heart of Europe was stunning. One U.N. officer new to Sarajevo was astonished to see that there were as many TV satellite dishes in Sarajevo "as in Madrid," that there were special recycling containers for newspapers and glass, and that Muslim women wore miniskirts and spoke English. U.N. officials (especially the French) were amazed to see sleek-looking women in a city under heavy shelling, as if it would have been different in a besieged Rome or Paris.

Idle amid the chaos of war, the U.N. forces' contribution to the decadent moment was their unique incompetence, further polluting an already war-polluted environment and arousing the residents' contempt.

The UNPROFOR forces in Sarajevo fell prey to the corruption and abusive power of any occupying army. The failure of this international force in Sarajevo was reflected in every aspect of the mission, from the behavior of the troops to the decisions of the leadership. In a way, the situation was worse than with an ordinary occupying army, because this army had to pretend to the world that it was engaged in a purely humanitarian mission. Therefore, its first concern was for its own image.

The discovery of civility and culture in the midst of the "wild Balkan tribes" revealed a path the U.N. forces could follow to improve that image, which had been seriously harmed by the first U.N. general in Bosnia, Louis McKenzie. He had made a ruinous start by describing the Serbian attacks on the city and efforts in its defense as equally reprehensible.

Although cultural sensitivity was one of the rare things that U.N. commanders were able to improve, some of their activities led to surreal images which, after a time, left Sarajevans feeling bitter and deceived. One such image was the result of an attempt by one of the U.N. commanders, Gen. Michael Rose, to promote the idea that life had returned to normal. In March 1994, he arranged to hold a soccer match, complete with a brass band—Coldstream Guards in full ceremonial uniforms—just a few yards from the front line.

In the winter of 1993, his predecessor, General Morillon, attempted to reach out to the town's cultural elite by asking a few hungry and desperate intellectuals to his residence for a dinner of lobster soup. The intellectuals felt like traitors feebly protesting UNPROFOR politics as they sat in the only place in town that night that was warm and bright, eating food from which they would get diarrhea. The hospitable general gave a speech about his appreciation of Bosnian tradition and culture, and then the hapless intellectuals were loaded into armored personnel carriers and sent back to their cold and gloomy homes.

Morillon's aptitude for handling the media, however, helped him last through his tour of duty. Gen. Francis Briquemon, who was more interested in implementing U.N. resolutions than in "marginal" activities like communicating with the local residents, declared at a farewell press conference after his resignation: "I do not need the Security Council resolutions any more

Like these Namibian women in 1978, residents of Sarajevo welcomed the U.N. Protection Force sent in the spring of 1992 to support the humanitarian relief effort. But many were soon disillusioned. *United Nations*

because they do not help me. The resolutions contain beautiful words but it [the Security Council's general approach] was a bit of hypocrisy."

At his own farewell address, Morillon said that during his term in Sarajevo he had been cheered by the sight of all the elegant, smiling women he saw from his passing car. As long as Sarajevo streets offered such sights, he said, he believed in Bosnia's future. Back home in France, he told another story: Bosnia's only hope was military intervention, he said.

French officers and soldiers gained a reputation for supporting Sarajevo's cultural community, which, in the undivided Bosnia, had been known for its affirmation of multiculturalism and multi-ethnicism. The French appreciation of Bosnian culture was nice, but ironic, given the French government's declaration that "Bosnia has never existed and will never exist." And occasionally a Gallic sneer showed through their "sensitive and empathic" smiles.

A Kidnapping

Near the end of summer 1993, a radio colleague of mine, a 19-year-old girl, was kidnapped from the street by three French officers, two men and a woman. They said they were lost, and asked if she would be kind enough to show them the way back to their barracks.

Once there, she was held in an office and forced to look through pornographic magazines and to watch pornographic films. Perhaps her torturers thought this would prepare her for the orgy they anticipated. At first the officers tried to persuade her to cooperate by arguing that it was her duty because they were helping Bosnia—saving her people by bringing in food. Finally, after hours of trying to "soften up" the girl, who remained frozen in fear, they lost their tempers and changed their tactics, telling her that other Bosnian girls "make good money," and that selling herself was "your destiny anyway."

Her ordeal lasted from late afternoon until the next morning, when another French officer appeared. After a brief but angry discussion with the young woman's captors, he warned them "not to do that again." Then he released her, saying "Run away now, nothing has happened to you. . . . You have been lucky."

Before the war came to Sarajevo, Goran Milic, a popular journalist and commentator on a frequently watched news program, remarked, "When our wives and daughters start to sell their bodies for chewing gum and stockings, it will be a sign that we have hit rock bottom." Today their bodies are sold for cigarettes and cans of food from UNPROFOR.

Sometimes the payment is a job. Another friend of mine, a professor of piano, was hired to work as a waitress in the bar at the U.N. office building. After 20 days she was fired. When I asked the reason, she said, "I did not want to sleep with my Egyptian boss."

The U.N.'s reputation also became a joke because so many U.N. workers, civilian and military, quickly joined in illegal activities at all levels. A city under siege provides endless opportunities for the criminally inclined. Soldiers can smuggle fuel and food; commanders and administrators can sell more sophisticated services: they can get someone out of town.

A U.N. investigation of UNPROFOR corruption in January 1994 reported "evidence of some abuses," but suggested that the worst charges were unfounded or had been corrected. But as a practical matter, the investigation was doomed from the start. When U.N. officers are paid $3,000 for smuggling someone out on a plane or in a U.N. vehicle, the one who pays for the service—often to save his life—is not about to testify against his savior. Even the smuggler has a sense of righteousness—he has saved another life. The "victims" are simply desperate people, struggling to survive.

UNPROFOR's dynamic structure—soldiers' tours of duty last from four to six months, depending on their country of origin—means that a quick getaway is possible. Their replacements, and the bureaucrats and volunteers, all fall prey to the same tempting opportunities. The considerable differences in the soldiers' salaries also inspire some to seek a little extra on the side (the Ukrainians' salaries are miserable).

Locals lucky enough to work for the U.N. forces can also make a little extra by selling food and fuel—or by assisting other locals in getting UNPROFOR jobs (the "placement fee" is $1,300).

Each new mission commander brings his own set of rules. The forces' discipline and firmness of purpose—as well as other elements that determine U.N. credibility—depend on each commander's character and cultural background—and the views of his government.

Prostitution

On a talk show that I hosted in fall 1993 the theme was the problem of prostitution and U.N. soldiers. The subject was provoked by assertions by local doctors that the post-war period would bring a disastrous AIDS epidemic, because protection against the disease was merely symbolic. The show included an interview with a 15-year-old girl who had turned to prostitution to survive. Her customers, she said, included members from every U.N. battalion stationed in Sarajevo.

The commander of the Egyptian battalion was extremely upset because the girl included Egyptians in her list of customers. This, to his mind, challenged the quality of his leadership and dishonored the entire Egyptian mission.

He demanded, in an authoritarian manner, that I deliver the girl to him so that he could "find the sinner[s]." My reward would have been his cooperation in another show devoted to the U.N. force—cooperation I had received as a matter of course from his more open and friendlier predecessor. "The girl, if she accepts, will get food," he added.

This was just one more example of the different attitudes of U.N. personnel and the local population. I was trying to consider how to deal with the rapid rise of prostitution in the city, particularly around U.N. barracks, and what measures might be applied to protect peoples' lives, especially those of young, sexually uneducated people. The U.N. representative was concerned only with his own image.

UNPROFOR was often slow to react to sometimes very urgent and desperate needs. I remember when a truck with several tons of food was pinned down by Serbian sniper fire at the intersection in front of the Holiday Inn. Four foreign journalists saved the driver of the truck and the food—a job that was supposed to be UNPROFOR's. The U.N. people, stationed next door to the Holiday Inn, appeared at the site after the operation was over, when their help was no longer needed. Scornful Sarajevans welcomed them by whistling.

The communication between members of the multinational force is another problem. I remember that the French ambassador was kept waiting for a very long time to enter a U.N. general's Sarajevo residence, which was guarded at the main door by Egyptian soldiers. They spoke only Arabic and were unable to understand who the visitor was.

The public relations staff at general headquarters in Sarajevo is supposed to speak English, be equipped to deal with foreign journalists, and be able to write military reports. In reality there was usually only one man skilled at his job, who acted as spokesman. The others tried to follow the instructions they kept on their desks on how to talk to someone over the phone in English, or they spent their time writing reports suggesting that Sarajevans had been killed by too much sunny weather. When asked about the "new world order" and their mission within it, they talked about ecology, the green movement, and feminism.

Playing God

It was not just the money—which was very good—that kept U.N. people attached to their jobs. Or even career-building—promotions, awards, and higher ranks were usual after an assignment in Sarajevo. It was the sense of excitement (under the relative safety of the U.N. banner), the flak jackets, the armored cars, mingling with the social elite, the beautiful women—the feeling of great significance. Playing God made U.N. officials, who lived in the best area in town, in apartments packed with a generous supply of food and assorted antique Sarajevan "souvenirs," so committed to the organization.

In October 1993 Jose-Maria Mendiluce, special envoy of the U.N. High Commissioner for Refugees in the former Yugoslavia for 20 months, told an audience at Princeton University that the UNHCR and UNPROFOR humanitarian mission could not counteract the logic of the Balkan war. The disaster could only have been prevented and could only be stopped by other means.

The deceptive U.N. mission, trying to stay in an imaginary world of neutrality and impartiality—not admitting that just by ignoring the differences between victims and aggressors you are taking sides—can operate only as a decoration, deciding whether to increase its public affairs activities, whether to deliver toys to the children, organizing receptions, and deciding on the design of its signs.

After almost a year of war, I was sitting and chatting with a prominent UNPROFOR official. We were discussing the mission. "This is an impossible mission. It is hopeless," he said—something everyone else in Bosnia had known long ago, but which I had never heard from any of the U.N. people.

"It must be very frustrating for you not to accomplish anything. Why don't you simply leave?" I asked.

He answered: "Yes, it is frustrating. But if I go back to New York, even though I will have a nice office and a very good position, I will be just another insignificant bureaucrat. Staying here is exciting, and it makes me feel important."

This was published in the March/April 1995 *Bulletin*.

V.3 A Stronger U.N. Strengthens America

JONATHAN DEAN

In 1994, an increasingly cautious Clinton administration adopted a national security strategy that makes multilateral peacekeeping operations acts of charity to be indulged in from time to time when humanitarian considerations are overwhelming—and risks minimal. Peacekeeping per se has been omitted from the administration's definition of the primary national security interests of the United States. This continues to be the case despite the administration's belated 1995 decision to back NATO involvement in Bosnia, and a late 1996 decision to participate in peacekeeping in Zaïre and Rwanda.

This omission is a mistake, and a serious one. U.S. support for an increasingly capable global peacekeeping system, with direct U.S. participation when it is needed for the effectiveness of the operation, is a priority U.S. national security interest, and should be so defined in national policy. That peacekeeping priority should then be reflected in the budget, the structure, and the mission of the U.S. armed forces.

At one level, the debate is about the nature and conduct of peacekeeping operations. But it is also about three larger issues: One is the role of the United States in the post–Cold War world. And, because the U.S. position may be decisive in both cases, the debate is also about the nature of the United Nations and about the nature of the international system in the first part of the coming century. No matter what our own views on peacekeeping may be, what is done or not done in this field will, together with the state of relations between the world's major powers, be the main determinant of war and peace in the coming decades.

America's National Security Interests

The concept of "national security interest" is traditionally used by governments to justify committing military forces to potential combat in situations other than straightforward defense of national territory. When the United States cites these interests, the arena is often very distant, but the outcome is deemed by U.S. leaders to affect its extended security environment. Historically, definitions of U.S. national security interests have shifted, reflecting changing circumstances. Defeating Germany was the primary U.S. national security interest during World War II; defending Germany became a primary interest after the war.

In democracies the public must share leaders' perceptions to a significant degree; democratic governments are engaged in a continuous dialogue with their publics over defining national security interests. "Political will"—the determination to act even when action may cost in lives and money—flows from the conviction that certain issues do affect national security interests.

Subjecting citizen-soldiers to possible injury and death through the deliberate decision to use military force is possibly the state's most serious responsibility, and it must be exercised with great restraint. The problem is most acute in democracies. Democratic governments are accountable to legislatures, to the media, and to the public.

Friendly blue-helmeted Napalese soldiers, part of the U.N. Interim Force in Lebanon in 1978, chat with Lebanese boys. *United Nations*

The Cold War, which threatened the physical existence of many countries, provided a persuasive rationale for making such decisions, even if that rationale was sometimes overused. With the Cold War's end, it became far more difficult for Western governments to justify the commitment of armed forces to combat. Today, all Western governments face commendable resistance from their publics to committing their own armed forces to combat—intensified in the case of the United States by the widespread conviction that earlier administrations erred tragically in making this decision in Vietnam. When public resistance is amplified by televised, shockingly accurate glimpses of combat—increasingly the case since the Vietnam War—the decision to commit forces is even more difficult.

When peacekeeping is presented, as the administration has done, in a context of humanitarian altruism rather than in a context of pursuing national security interests, it is understandable if the public rebels at the prospect of troop casualties. The American electorate is usually prepared to contribute money, resources and logistics, and even individual acts of heroism, to save the lives of others, but not widespread casualties in its own forces. The main argument of this article is that reducing the incidence of armed conflict in the regions of the world is a national security interest of the United States. If this argument is accepted, it follows that, under stringently selected conditions, a decision to participate in a peacekeeping operation can justify committing U.S. forces to combat conditions.

What the Administration Says

In its report on national strategy, the Clinton administration has identified nuclear nonproliferation, support of allies, the spread of free-market democracy, and countering the activities of rogue states as post–Cold War national security interests. This list is acceptable as far as it goes. Enlarging the area of free-market democracy, in particular, is a long-term goal that can make a realistic contribution to national security; functioning democracies do not often fight each other.

But the administration says that peacekeeping lies outside the scope of this definition of national security interests—therefore it is not an activity that justifies putting at risk the lives of American soldiers. "The United States views peace operations as a means to support our national security strategy, not as a strategy unto itself. The primary mission of our Armed Forces is not peace operations; it is to deter and, if necessary, to fight and win conflicts in which our most important interests are involved."

Instead of urging the United Nations to broaden its peacekeeping capabilities and pledging U.S. aid to that end, President Clinton retreated in the face of domestic criticism after the death of 18 U.S. peacekeepers in Somalia. In September 1993, even before that tragic incident, he told the United Nations that it should learn "when to say no" and should undertake fewer peacekeeping operations. This was a turn in the wrong direction. Instead of urging the United Nations to do less, President Clinton should have urged member states to do more, especially in conflict prevention.

In May 1994, the United States persuaded the Security Council to adopt restrictive criteria limiting future U.N. peacekeeping activities. These criteria resembled the just-issued standards the administration developed in Presidential Decision Directive 25 (PDD 25) to evaluate potential peacekeeping operations. The U.S. standard included: whether U.N. involvement advances U.S. interests; whether there are clear objectives, multilateral support, and adequate financial means for the potential operations; and whether there are realistic criteria for ending them. Taken individually, these criteria are reasonable. They would be desirable restrictions to accompany a previously articulated positive objective for multilateral peacekeeping.

Both the administration's statement of national security policy and PDD 25 emphasize that the chief mission of the U.S. armed forces is to be prepared to fight two major regional wars at the same time. That concept, developed under Presidents Bush and Clinton, has become the sizing requirement and the mission for the nation's armed forces. As a result, military commanders without standing orders about peacekeeping operations justifiably complain that such operations drain personnel, resources, and money intended for assigned missions. Their public complaints reinforce the impression that peacekeeping is a kind of charity, a luxury that detracts from national defense.

Something Is Missing

Something important is missing from the administration's list of national security objectives and from the policy the administration has articulated to support its objectives. What is missing is a high-priority U.S. security interest: the gradual reduction, in cooperation with other countries, of the level of conflict and large-scale armed violence throughout the world. Put another way, the U.S. goal should be to enlarge the world's "zones of no-conflict." Zones of no-conflict are regions like North America and Western Europe, where resorting to war to resolve interstate differences has become highly improbable.

Conflict prevention and peacekeeping are the major tools for achieving this objective. In the broader sense of the term, "peacekeeping" includes the whole spectrum of measures to prevent or curtail regional conflict: identification of conflicts in the making, negotiation of interstate differences, third-party mediation, preventive peacekeeping, and also large-scale military intervention to prevent war. Peacekeeping in this sense represents America's first line of defense abroad, preventing developments that could ultimately threaten its own people and territory.

The goal of reducing global violence should be incorporated with a high priority in the hierarchy of national security interests. Individual peacekeeping operations may have a humanitarian motivation; but for the United States, peacekeeping activities aimed at reducing the incidence of conflict should not be considered altruistic acts of charity but far-sighted self-interest. (The repeated contributions of the Scandinavian countries to U.N. peacekeeping are not motivated by heedless idealism, but by the patient hope that these actions will ultimately have a positive cumulative effect on the world in which these countries have to live.)

Lowering the Level of Organized Violence

The end of the Cold War has created uniquely favorable conditions for moving toward a more peaceful world. But neither the Cold War nor its end has meant the end of war. To the contrary, as many as 50 million people have died in more than 100 conflicts since the end of World War II. Nonetheless, the statement remains true: never in history has there been a better opportunity to reduce armed violence. In the past decade, epochal political change occurred virtually without bloodshed, thanks to gifted leadership and cooperation between the West and the Soviet Union. There has been revolutionary political and economic change in the entire area once covered by the Warsaw Treaty—the liberation of Eastern Europe from Soviet domination, German unification with membership in NATO, and the peaceful collapse of the Soviet Union itself. True, these changes produced misery as well as joy, and they were followed by the outbreak of fighting in the former Yugoslavia, in several of the republics bordering Russia, and in Russia itself. But the changes themselves were almost nonviolent.

Even if these measures are applied more widely and systematically than ever before, we cannot hope to end armed conflict everywhere for all time. Total world peace will remain a dream, although a powerful one. But it has become quite feasible to think in a hard-headed way about preventing specific disputes from erupting into war, or curtailing wars when they do occur. As a consequence, it is also feasible to imagine that the incidence of organized armed violence throughout the world can be gradually reduced, and existing zones of no-conflict expanded.

Even if it becomes broadly accepted, the goal of reducing the level of conflict has clear limits: Peacekeeping will remain selective. Intervention will often have to be guided by mere feasibility rather than by broader criteria. This is so because of limited resources, the frequency of conflict, the great obstacles to effective intervention—especially if an incipient conflict has become a full-scale war—and the tenacious obstacle of non-intervention in the domestic affairs of sovereign states. Successes will not be easy and almost certainly there will be failures. Even if a lower level of violence is achieved for a time, it may not endure. But at least there will be a rational answer to the basic question on peacekeeping—"Why are we doing this?"

Implications for U.S. Defense Posture

If there is no comprehensive rationale for peacekeeping as part of an overall policy, U.S. participation in peacekeeping operations will remain a random reflex largely dependent on the amount of media coverage a crisis receives. Public confusion about the aim of individual peacekeeping operations will continue, with negative public reaction to operations that bring casualties. As a result, the U.S. government (and other democratic governments) will continue to recoil from risky peacekeeping operations. The U.S. government may even hold back from participation in cases where it is clear that intervention could serve U.S. national security interests.

Viewed properly, peacekeeping is the nation's first line of defense, securing its extended international environment from more serious conflicts and deterioration. A major peacekeeping mission should be incorporated into the defense secretary's Defense Guidance to the forces and into the Joint Strategic Capabilities Planning of the Joint Chiefs of Staff. There should be an adequate budget for Security Council-approved multilateral peacekeeping operations, and peacekeeping contributions should be included in the defense budget, institutionalizing peacekeeping as an integral part of U.S. defense activities. This would not mean extra forces or an additional budget. If the United Nations has its own dedicated financing for peacekeeping, additional national contributions would be required only for major operations.

Upgrading peacekeeping to a national security objective would bolster public support for U.S. armed forces. Deterring large-scale conflict through rapid anticipatory force deployments, as in Kuwait and in Haiti in 1994, is an important benefit of having sizable standing armed forces and an important justification for the U.S. defense budget. If the United States presents lowering the level of conflict in the world as a cooperative international security objective, it will be clear that both preventive deployment of larger forces to *deter* conflict and the deployment of smaller peacekeeping units to *prevent* conflict belong on the same spectrum of conflict-prevention activities. Indeed, if the policy described here is adopted by the administration, peacekeeping activity should in time be viewed by the public as a major justification for defense budgets.

The United States will need to play a major role in improving the capacity of regional security organizations and the United Nations. But this role would be one of political leadership, not one of providing the bulk of troops or finances. Even if this leadership is available, the task of setting up an effective worldwide network of regional organizations dedicated to lowering the level of conflict will take much longer than the span of a single administration. However, if it is pushed energetically and persistently during three or four presidential administrations, there will be real results. Despite their weaknesses, the American political system and the American electorate are mature enough to undertake this long-term task and to carry it through.

Choices

Americans have a decisive choice to make about how to pursue their national defense. They can reject responsibility for establishing a more effective system of conflict prevention, with the probable result that the United Nations and existing regional security institutions will lapse into decades of ineffectual formalism. They can continue to prepare for possible conflict with one or even two as-yet-unidentified regional enemies, with occasional participation in the most urgent of peacekeeping crises, decided on a humanitarian basis. Essentially, this approach means waiting for conflict to erupt and then responding to it as best they can, acting in the spirit of an island nation waiting for its enemies to develop effective means of attack.

Or the U.S. government and the American people can accept that the United States is a state whose size and extended involvements make the absence of conflict a paramount national interest. If they do so, the United States should use the unique conditions of the post–Cold War period to make a real breakthrough in reducing the incidence of armed conflict through more effective conflict prevention and peacekeeping. It should exploit to the full the opportunity to progressively enhance U.S. national security through progressively enlisting the energies, resources, and capabilities of the millions of people and of governments throughout the world who want to increase their own security.

This is adapted from the March/April 1995 *Bulletin*.

V.4 Misreading the Public on Peacekeeping

STEVEN KULL

In December 1992, U.S. military forces entered Somalia as part of a U.N.-mandated operation to deliver food and medicine to desperately hungry people and to create a secure environment in a country that had been ravaged by civil war.

Almost immediately on American television, haunting images of starving children gave way to images of food being given to appreciative Somalis. Early efforts to stabilize the country also seemed promising. The operation enjoyed the overwhelming support of the American public.

But on October 5, 1993, a drastically different set of images came to the

TV screens—bodies of American soldiers being dragged through the streets of Mogadishu by smiling Somalis, members of one of the warring factions.

At that moment, a consensus crystallized in the minds of policy-makers: The American people had no stomach for peacekeeping—humanitarian or otherwise—if it meant that their sons and daughters might be brutalized or killed. Angry phone calls poured into congressional offices. Senators and representatives said the American people wanted out. Editorials and op-eds picked up the theme.

Within 48 hours of the news reports of the deaths, the president addressed the nation: The United States would leave Somalia within six months. Clearly, the announcement was a direct response to the notion that the American people were fed up.

But *are* the American people really that skittish in the face of troop fatalities? Is future American participation in peacekeeping actions virtually impossible, if it puts American sons and daughters in harm's way? Or are panicky politicians, policy-makers, and pundits selling the American people short?

Numerous polls taken at the time of the Somali crisis show that the public was being misread. Two polls, conducted by ABC News and CNN/*USA Today* in the hours just after the American troop deaths were reported, found that, respectively, only 37 percent and 43 percent supported immediate withdrawal of the troops. Three other polls taken over the next few days found similar results.

Furthermore, the same polls found that most respondents wanted *more* involvement in Somalia, at least over the short term. CNN/*USA Today*, ABC, and NBC found that 55, 56, and 61 percent of those polled favored sending in more troops. ABC's poll showed 75 percent favored going after Somali warlord Aideed with a "major military attack" if the American prisoners were not released through negotiations.

A poll taken October 15–18 by the Program on International Policy Attitudes at the University of Maryland presented a three-option question which found that 28 percent wanted the United States to withdraw immediately, 43 percent supported President Clinton's plan to withdraw in six months, and 27 percent wanted U.S. troops to stay as long as necessary to stabilize the country.

Under closer questioning, it appeared that the sentiment in favor of withdrawal, whether immediate or in six months, was not simply a reaction to the fatalities. Two key factors emerged. One was the perception that the Somalis wanted the United Nations to leave. Only a third of the respondents thought the Somalis wanted the United Nations to stay. When asked whether they wanted the United States to remain if a substantial majority of Somalis wanted the United States to stay, 54 percent said they did.

The second factor was that most Americans felt that the purpose of the Somalia operation had already been fulfilled by providing food. Seventy-five percent of respondents found this argument either somewhat convincing or very convincing: "Our purpose in going into Somalia was to deliver food to the starving people. We performed this mission well and this is something we can be proud of. But we can never hope to solve the Somalis' political problems for them. Now that people are eating, our job is done and it is time to bring our boys home."

No doubt the fatalities in Mogadishu contributed significantly to the sentiment in favor of an eventual withdrawal. But the incident did not so much generate this feeling as it simply amplified the already-existing attitude that the job was done. The deaths did not cause most of those polled to conclude that the operation was a mistake. More than 60 percent of those polled by CBS News in October and again in December 1993, believed "the United States did the right thing to send U.S. troops . . . to try and make sure shipments of food got through to the people there."

Taken together, the evidence suggests that a solid core of 45 to 50 percent of respondents consistently supports U.N. peacekeeping in principle and U.S. participation in it; a minority of 5 to 10 percent consistently opposes it; and another 40 to 45 percent forms a "swing element" that can go one way or the other, depending on factors in the situation or the way the question is worded. In most cases, enough of the swing element joins with the solid core to create majority support, and in some cases this majority becomes overwhelming.

Whether majority support is garnered and how strong that majority will be is influenced by whether

- the mission is clearly perceived as part of a U.N. peacekeeping operation, not just as the U.S. acting alone;
- participation is perceived as consistent with U.S. interests; and
- the operation is perceived as having potential for success.

Furthermore, if participation in an operation is favored by the president and Congress, majority public support is all but certain.

If Americans are killed in the course of a U.N. peacekeeping operation, the event will probably focus the public's attention and amplify whatever reservations it may have about the operation. But U.S. fatalities will not necessarily undermine public support. The American public is very sensitive to the loss of American lives abroad, but it also favors the pursuit of certain values that may, at times, require this level of sacrifice.

This is adapted from the March/April 1995 *Bulletin*.

V.5 On Sanctions Think Small

Ivan Eland

Sanctions have a much greater chance of accomplishing symbolic goals than more grandiose objectives like getting the target nation to retreat from aggression or changing its system of government. Therefore, despite the inflated rhetoric of policymakers at the time they impose sanctions, analysts should be realistic about what the measures can accomplish and they should look beyond public statements to explore policymakers' more realistic goals.

Symbolic goals should not be dismissed as insignificant, however. In an anarchic and chaotic international environment, symbolic signaling is vital. Nations watch the behavior of other countries carefully for subtle clues about their intentions and resolve. The sanctions levied by the League of Nations against Italy, after Benito Mussolini invaded Ethiopia in 1935, show just how powerful sanctions can be—particularly when they send the wrong message.

A dispute arose between two of the League's principal nations imposing sanctions. Britain favored strong measures, but France—because it felt it must cultivate Mussolini as an ally against Adolf Hitler's Germany—favored milder steps. The resulting embargo, omitting key items such as oil, coal, and steel, sent a signal that lacked the depth of disapproval that had been intended. According to Albert Speer, a former high-level Nazi official, Hitler interpreted the dispute as showing that Britain and France were too irresolute to stop his further territorial ambitions.

Sometimes the goals of sanctions will vary over time. When sanctions were first imposed against Iraq, they were ostensibly designed to compel Saddam Hussein to withdraw from Kuwait and impede the Iraqi army's readiness for war. Later, the sanctions were justified as an incentive to make Iraq comply with U.N. resolutions ending the Gulf War, which called for routine U.N. inspections of Iraqi weapons facilities and the destruction of Iraq's weapons-manufacturing capabilities. Later, the Bush administration added that sanctions would not be removed until Hussein was ousted from power, although the Clinton administration seemed to be backing away from this latter requirement.

Compliance is a difficult objective to achieve with sanctions, as the Iraqi case bears out. Iraq endured the most universal, comprehensive sanctions in modern history, which were enforced by a tight naval blockade and had a severe effect on that country's economy. Yet the sanctions failed to achieve their goals.

The results in the Iraqi case would seem to validate the pessimistic conclusions of Johan Galtung, who argued that sanctions with severe economic effects could be rendered ineffective by non-economic factors. Galtung coined the term "rally-around-the-flag effect"—arguing that leaders in target nations use the economic pain caused by foreign nations to rally their populations around their cause. Rather than causing political disintegration in the target state, Galtung said, sanctions actually foster political cohesion.

It can be further argued that target regimes that control the media and suppress political opposition can generate even larger rally-around-the-flag effects. This is especially true if the target regime can blame all its economic problems on hostile foreign powers. Fidel Castro has apparently been able to rally Cubans in the wake of the tightened U.S. sanctions against Cuba called for in the recent Torricelli measures.

Thus, Galtung showed that the political success of sanctions is not closely associated with the amount of economic damage they cause. If that is true—if even strong sanctions can be negated by the political cohesion they engender in the target nation—can economically weak effects ever "succeed" politically? Sanctions against South Africa demonstrate that they can.

Selective Use

To use a military analogy, severe comprehensive sanctions with severe economic effects are the equivalent of war by attrition; that is, trying to win a war by materially crippling the opponent. In contrast, more restrained, selective sanctions with the all-important threat of more can be compared with maneuver warfare. In maneuver warfare, the objective is to destroy, by well-timed attacks in key places, the opponent's will to fight. Instead of incurring heavy loses by grinding down the entire opposing army, shattering the opponent's confidence holds friendly casualties to a minimum and shocks the opponent into surrender.

In war and with economic sanctions, the goal should be to induce the termination of unacceptable activities, not to destroy the opponent's society. In fact, trying to destroy the target society may cause the opponent to fight harder. For example, the saturation bombing of Germany toward the end of World War II that was designed, among other things, to crush the German will to fight, may have actually strengthened the resolve of the German population. Galtung would probably agree that the psychology of war is similar to the psychology of economic sanctions.

In the case of South Africa, sanctions by governments (national, state, and local) and private businesses and groups—on selected imports, exports, and financial transactions—were the equivalent of maneuver warfare. Reduced lending and investment and the threat of more sanctions chilled business confidence and induced a long-term drag on the South African economy.

The measures also isolated South Africa politically, making it an international pariah. South African whites, who consider themselves European, were startled when shunned by the West. The South African case also shows that sanctions need not be economically devastating to achieve their desired psychological effect—banning sports-crazy South Africa from international sporting events had a particularly potent negative impact on the psyche of South African whites.

Selectively imposed sanctions gave South Africa a taste of the economic pain that comprehensive sanctions could have brought, but they did not induce a severe rally-around-the-flag effect against foreign meddling that often accompanies severe measures. Some rallying did occur as conservative whites reacted to foreign pressure, but the absence of severe economic hardship mitigated this effect. Wrenching economic dislocation would have forced the business community into an alliance with the South African government, and opposition would have been muted. Severe sanctions would have disproportionately hurt both the white and black opposition, the latter being the group that sanctions were supposed to help.

In most cases, a target government can direct the pain of severe sanctions away from its supporters to its opponents—in many cases the poorest sectors of society. Iraq's Saddam Hussein was able to channel the hardships of sanctions away from the security forces that keep him in power. In Haiti, the poor suffered greatly while the rich were less affected by the sanctions employed against the military junta that overthrew the Aristide government in 1991.

In sum, economic sanctions will rarely result in compliance unless a strong political opposition within the target nation is allied with the sanctioning nation and puts domestic pressure on the target government (the "fifth column effect"). As illustrated by the case of South Africa, the fifth column effect is strongest and the rally-around-the-flag effect is weakest when selective sanctions are imposed but more are threatened. The political benefits of imposing graduated sanctions override their major disadvantage—allowing the target nation time to adjust its economy. This is good news for sanctioning nations because domestic economic costs often make the imposition of severe comprehensive sanctions unlikely. Furthermore, when comprehensive measures are imposed rapidly (the ideal case according to conventional wisdom), even the political opposition in the target nation may become allied with its government for economic survival, thus creating an insurmountable rallying effect.

Friendly Fire

Sanctions imposed by a friendly nation—a nation with well-developed political, economic, and cultural relations with the target nation—will have a greater chance of inducing compliance than measures initiated by an adversary. The target nation's cost of non-compliance—the disruption of close ties—is greater when a friendly nation imposes sanctions. Western sanctions contributed to the South African government's movement toward political reform because that country obtained 80 percent of its trade and all of its capital from six Western nations with which it had extensive political and cultural ties.

The same close ties that make sanctions on friendly nations more likely to be effective, however, can also make them less likely to be imposed. Disrupting ties with friendly nations has greater costs than disrupting them with adversaries.

Multilateral Sanctions

Sanctions do not need to be multilateral to have positive political effects. In 1933, the British government imposed import sanctions and successfully achieved the release of its citizens held in Russia. In 1989, India imposed sanctions on Nepal, a traditional buffer against its adversary, China, because of a pro-China tilt in Nepal's foreign policy. The sanctions reversed the tilt.

Multilateral sanctions, however, can have enhanced political effects, but not necessarily because of their greater economic pressure. Despite the recent examples of severe multilateral sanctions against Iraq and Serbia, which are rarities, it is usually difficult to get many countries to agree to impose harsh, comprehensive measures because of their economic interests. It is easier to win multilateral support for selective sanctions. As more nations impose selective sanctions on the target, the psychological threat of future measures and the potential economic damage caused by this threat are made more credible. Also, the more nations that impose sanctions, the greater political legitimacy the effort has and the greater the international ostracism and isolation the target experiences.

But particular care is needed when seeking multilateral support. Failure to get adequate multilateral cooperation can send a message of weakness rather than a signal of resolve. For example, in the wake of martial law in Poland in 1981, the Western alliance disagreed on an embargo on equipment to be used in constructing a Soviet natural gas pipeline. The dispute made the alliance seem divided instead of sending Moscow an unambiguous signal of protest against the crackdown. As noted before, the quibbling between Britain and France in the League of Nations over the severity of sanctions to be imposed on Mussolini for his invasion of Ethiopia led Hitler to believe that these countries would lack the resolve to stop his expansion in Europe.

Being Realistic

Except in rare cases, the goal of sanctions should not be to destroy the target nation's economy, but to have the maximum political effect by putting maximum psychological pressure on its political leaders and populace. (The sole exception to this might be illustrated by the case of Serbia and Montenegro, when the target state's behavior is so objectionable that severe sanctions are the only punishment suitable to uphold international norms. Sanctioning nations, however, should hold no delusions that strangling the target nation's economy will improve its behavior by compelling compliance with their wishes).

To put maximum psychological pressure on a target nation, selective sanctions should be targeted at vulnerable sectors of the target's economy. If the target nation feels pain in these sectors, its political leaders may tend to overestimate the effects of whatever additional measures are being threatened, either implicitly or explicitly. The threat of future measures may have more psychological effect on the target than their actual implementation because of the many alternative paths of trade and finance—both legal and illegal—that become apparent to the target after imposition. But even if the goal of sanctions is symbolic (for example, to deter, to demonstrate resolve or disapproval, or to show support for allies or the political opposition in the target nation), selected sanctions should at least have a demonstrable economic effect on critical sectors of the economy. Sanctions that are too weak will cause the target nation to dismiss the threat of future measures.

The sanctioning state or states should aim for the type of economic effect that raises the cost of commerce for the target nation, slows its economic growth, and makes credible the threat of future measures. Unless a tight military blockade that completely seals off all of the target nation's borders is instituted (a rare exception), limited economic effects are the most that sanctions can hope to achieve.

In sum, selective sanctions with the threat of more severe measures will have the greatest psychological effect on the target nation and the most chance to induce the target to comply with the sanctioning nation's wishes. Because obtaining compliance is difficult, however, sanctions may have more success in achieving important symbolic goals.

This is adapted from the November 1993 *Bulletin*.

V.6 Who Suffers from Sanctions?

Drew Christiansen and Gerard F. Powers

According to a 1990 study by Gary Clyde Hufbauer, Jeffrey J. Schott, and Kimberly Ann Elliott (*Economic Sanctions Reconsidered*), sanctions were "successful" in about 34 percent of 115 cases studied. The success rate depends on a host of factors. In 52 percent of the cases, sanctions were successful in destabilizing small and shaky governments—one of the objectives in Iraq, Haiti, Yugoslavia, and South Africa. But this success depended in part on using sanctions in conjunction with other measures, such as covert action. Sanctions involving modest goals, such as improving human rights, preventing nuclear nonproliferation, discouraging support for terrorism, and bringing about the release of political prisoners, succeeded about a third of the time.

While sanctions had only a 23 percent success rate in undermining military potential or achieving a surrender of territory or other major policy changes, they were judged successful in a third of the cases involving military adventures short of major wars, as well as in two civil wars: India's war with Hyderabad and Nigeria's conflict with Biafra. The Hufbauer study found that sanctions tend to be most effective when the goal is relatively modest (thus lessening the importance of difficult-to-achieve international cooperation); when the target country is much smaller than the country imposing sanctions; when the target country is an ally and close trading partner of the sanctioning nation; when the sanctions are imposed quickly and decisively to maximize impact; when the imposing nation avoids high cost to itself, and so maintains support for sanctions; and when sanctions are carefully tailored to the objective sought.

The principal moral dilemma posed by sanctions is that the more effective they are, the more likely that they will harm those least responsible for the wrongdoing and least able to bring about change: civilians. Sanctions' impact on the civilian population varies in each case. Are the sanctions being strictly enforced, or has the target country been able to circumvent the sanctions? Can the target country produce food, fuel, medicine, and other basic necessities? Do sanctions allow adequate exceptions for trade in humanitarian goods or for direct relief? Does the target government use its resources to mitigate the suffering of its population? Are the sanctions continued (as is the case in Iraq) after a war has heavily damaged a country's infrastructure, thus exacerbating the impact on the civilian population?

As a general rule, those who impose sanctions are responsible for the harm suffered by civilians. In a blockade against an entire nation, free exit is not plausible. The Haitian refugee situation has been a vivid demonstration of that. The civilian population cannot be presumed to have consented to its government's actions when there is no way for the population to express disagreement short of rebellion. There is ample evidence in Serbia and Iraq, for instance, that a significant minority or even a majority of citizens do not support their government and, in the case of Iraq, have tried to overthrow their government without success.

Assuming adequate provision is made for basic humanitarian needs, do the good ends of sanctions compensate for their unintended bad effects? This question of proportion is firmly rooted in both moral and legal analyses and places an important—albeit inherently difficult to measure—limit on what can be done in the name of sanctions. Among other things, this criterion means that, if the alternative to sanctions is a major war, even a low probability of success could justify sanctions. Moreover, the more sanctions will cause suffering of civilians, the more sanctions should be tied to narrowly defined and tangible objectives; and the longer sanctions remain in place, the less likely they will be proportionate.

A final moral consideration is that economic coercion has historically been used most effectively by big powers to impose their will on weaker states; this should give any moralist pause. Sanctions might well be imposed in a moral way, yet still be subject to the worst kinds of abuse by unscrupulous states. It is unsurprising that the most vulnerable countries of the developing world have frequently sought international condemnation of boycotts and other forms of "economic warfare" in the name of nonintervention, non-discrimination, self-determination and solidarity.

This is adapted from the November 1993 *Bulletin*.

Significant UN Peacekeeping Operations and Economic Sanctions in the 1990s

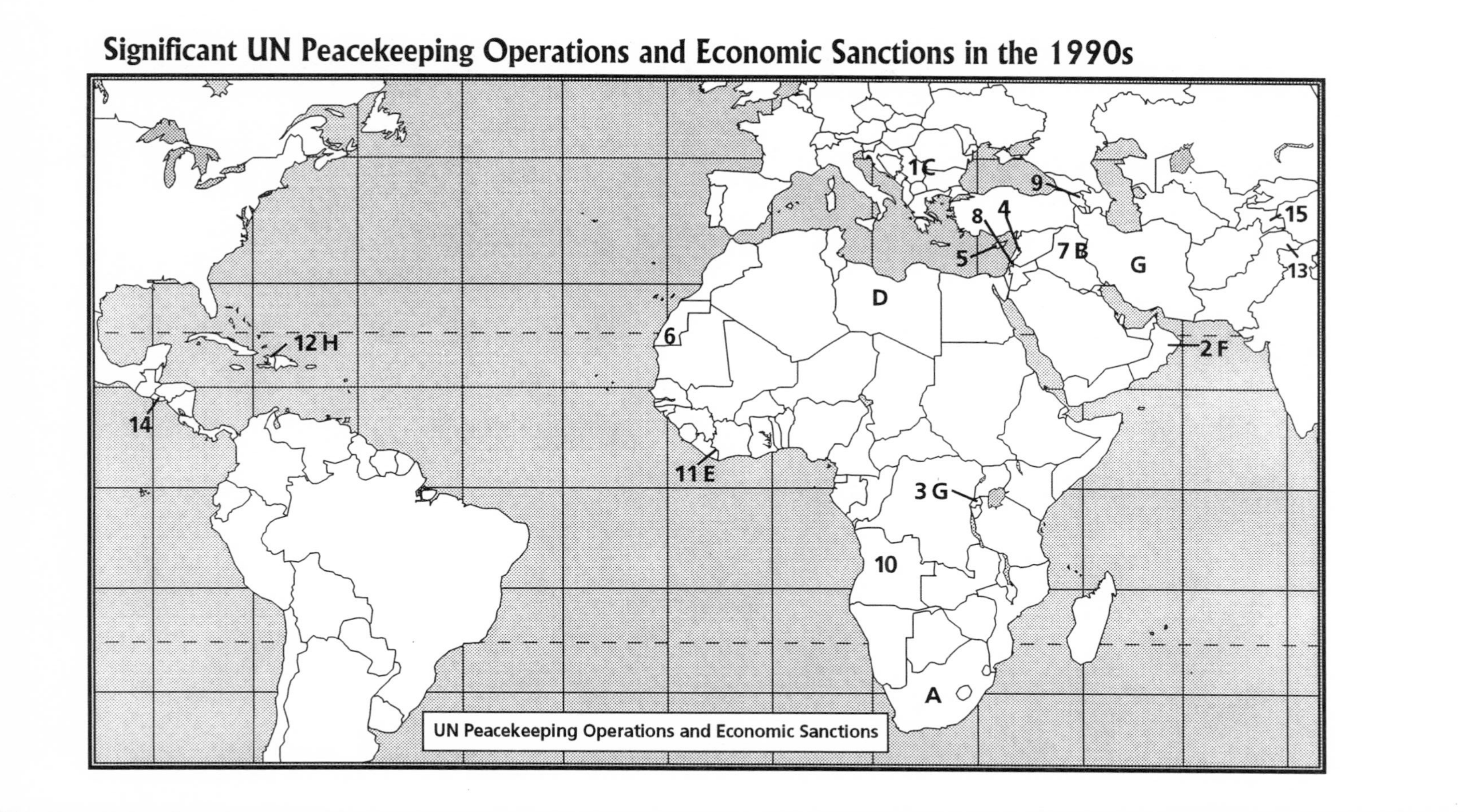

Peacekeeping*

1. FORMER YUGOSLAVIA 1991–
39,789 UN personnel
$1.6 billion annually

2. SOMALIA 1993–95
9,412 UN personnel
$942.4 million annually

3. RWANDA 1993–
5,522 UN personnel
$197.5 million annually

4. LEBANON 1978–
5,146 UN personnel
$142.3 million annually

5. CYPRUS 1964–
1,183 UN personnel
$23 million annually

6. WESTERN SAHARA 1991–
344 UN personnel
$40.5 million annually

7. IRAQ-KUWAIT 1991–
142 UN personnel
$63.1 million annually

*Listed in approximate order of size of operation

8. ISRAEL'S BORDERS
Includes operations since 1948 and Israeli-Syrian border patrols since 1974

9. GEORGIA 1993
134 UN personnel
$10.9 million annually

10. ANGOLA 1991–
138 UN personnel
$26.3 million annually

11. LIBERIA 1993
84 UN personnel
$36.4 million annually

12. HAITI 1993–
74 UN personnel; authorized, 6,567
$5.3 million annually

13. INDIA-PAKISTAN 1949–
39 UN personnel
$7.2 million annually

14. EL SALVADOR 1991–95
34 UN personnel
$29.2 million annually

15. TAJIKISTAN 1994–
17 UN personnel
$1.1 million annually

Sanctions

A. SOUTH AFRICA 1977–94
B. IRAQ 1990–
C. FORMER YUGOSLAVIA 1991–95
D. LIBYA 1992–
E. LIBERIA 1992–(intermittent)
F. SOMALIA 1992–95
G. RWANDA 1994–95
H. HAITI 1993–94

SOURCE: UNITED NATIONS

Chapter V
Discussion Questions

1. Ivan Eland concludes from recent research and policy experience that certain criteria and conditions make sanctions more effective. Drew Christiansen and Gerard Powers contend that sanctions should also be held up to moral and ethical standards. List Eland's generalizations on the factors that make sanctions most effective, and for each one, discuss the ethical issues that it might raise.

2. You have been appointed to chair a committee of experts charged with recommending reforms in U.N. peacekeeping operations. You are to devote special attention to the criteria for deploying peacekeeping forces and the types of actions in which they are permitted to engage in the field. Based on the articles in this chapter, what would you recommend?

3. One fear about the United Nations often heard in American political discussions has been that U.N. actions compromise (at best) or contradict (at worst) policies important to the U.S. national interest. Make an argument for how U.N. policies for peacekeeping and humanitarianism can instead be consistent with U.S. interests.

4. What factors seem to predict when a U.N. peacekeeping or peacemaking operation will be successful? Which of these are under control of the United Nations and its members and which are not?

Chapter VI

Arms and Security at Millennium's End

In Chapter V we focused on U.N. peacekeeping and the use of economic sanctions as part of a global security system based more on international cooperation and less on national military forces. In Chapter VII, we will examine how global civil society is emerging from local initiatives and movements, and the role of global citizenship in promoting peace and security. But no future security system can work without dealing constructively with issues of arms and security—the subject of this chapter.

Few debates bring together so many local, national, and international perspectives on security as do the issues of nuclear arms control and disarmament. Earlier chapters have shown that military spending and the production and maintenance of nuclear weapons have had considerable impact on national economies, the environment, and health. At the same time, a defining question of the Cold War era has been whether nuclear weapons have increased or threatened the security and stability of particular nations, regions, and the world as a whole.

The perspective of this volume is clear:

- The nuclear arms race was excessively costly for the nations that engaged in it. It helped bankrupt the Soviet Union and retarded U.S. international economic competitiveness, infrastructure development, and social programs.
- Cold War competition and mammoth superpower nuclear arsenals generated global and regional insecurity and stimulated the proliferation of nuclear, chemical, and biological weapons.
- Nuclear war between the major foes was avoided through a combination of reason, extraordinary restraint, and a good deal of luck.
- The most viable security systems in the post–Cold War world will be those that reduce or eliminate weapons of mass destruction and that rely

as much as possible on resolving disputes without appeal to military force.

These views are not universally accepted. Some analysts claim that one reason why the post–Cold War world is more prone to internal and regional wars and violence is that the superpower nuclear balance no longer holds such forces in check. But neither past nor present experience suggests clear answers to the question of the future: what will be the relationship between nuclear weapons and security beyond the year 2000?

Throughout the Cold War, both arms production and arms control were pursued in the name of deterrence-based security. In contradictory fashion, the United States and the Soviet Union spent huge sums of money to develop the deadliest of weapons with the most sophisticated delivery systems while trying to limit these advances through arms control agreements.

The assumption of deterrence theory was that danger equaled security. The United States and the Soviet Union made a kind of mutual suicide pact: ordinary people in each country were, in effect, hostages to the weapons of the other nation. If one side attacked, the other would retaliate. If deterrence failed, hundreds of millions on both sides would die.

But deterrence thinking never fully accounted for the fact that each side would try to jump ahead of the other for "strategic advantage"—more weapons, more sophisticated technology. Nuclear arms control agreements represented efforts to address this obvious flaw. Beginning in the 1970s, they tried to establish rough parity in nuclear armaments so that neither side would be tempted to launch a "disarming, preemptive strike" against the other.

Today, of course, the United States and Russia are no longer enemies. But the political situation could change, and huge arsenals still exist in both countries. What to do with these weapons, and whether either nation needs any of them for security, are urgent questions. Another question is the role of nuclear weapons in the other nuclear powers, such as China. Then there is the issue of continuing high levels of military spending in many nations, but especially in the United States.

The articles in this chapter provide viable answers to these questions. As a unit they offer building blocks for a new global security system, based on the following precepts:

- Nuclear weapons and other weapons of mass destruction are illegal according to standards of international law. The task for the near future is to help nations comply with the law.
- The recent nuclear reductions undertaken by the United States and the former Soviet Union are remarkable, but these must continue at an even

faster pace. The time for substantial nuclear disarament is now—and the moment may pass quickly.
- The ultimate goal should be the elimination of all nuclear weapons in the world.
- Taking the lead on nuclear disarmament will enhance U.S. prestige and security. The United States can also exert global leadership by reducing its military budget and aspirations as well as curtailing military research and development.

In the first article, *Bulletin* editor Mike Moore summarizes seven principles that could guide a tight-belted U.S. defense policy. The recommendations, based on the findings of a Washington-based consortium, include "economic conversion" from military to civilian enterprise and diminishing the importance of "worst-case scenarios" in U.S. defense planning.

Dingli Shen's assessment of the Chinese perspective on nuclear disarmament is notable for its frankness. Readers should realize, however, that it would be difficult for someone in Professor Shen's position to deal with even touchier questions such as the size of the Chinese Army and how it should be used.

The final four selections are related to the question of ultimate nuclear disarmament. First, Mike Moore reports on the 1996 World Court decision on the legality of nuclear weapons. Then Michael Krepon shows how world opinion is shifting toward the abolition of nuclear weapons and predicts a major social movement toward abolition in the coming years. William Epstein's article on the recent Comprehensive Test Ban Treaty points out the continuing importance of treaties in the quest for nuclear disarmament. Finally, a group of top-level former military leaders convened by the Stimson Center, a Washington think tank, outline four steps necessary to achieve nuclear disarmament. The chart at the end of this chapter touches on the astonishing tradeoffs Americans have accepted in the pursuit of security based on nuclear weapons.

The Stimson Center statement attracted little attention when it was issued in early 1996. That changed in December 1996, when the group, led by Gen. George Lee Butler, former head of the strategic Air Command, and Andrew J. Goodpaster, a former NATO commander, had expanded to include 60 retired generals and admirals from 17 nations. This time their clarion call for the abolition of nuclear weapons made headlines. Newscasters, talk show hosts, and policymakers paid attention to a phenomenon that has been recorded by the *Bulletin of the Atomic Scientists* from its beginnings: the fact that those closest to nuclear weapons are often the ones to speak out most forcefully against them.

VI.1 More Security for Less Money

Mike Moore

The U.S. military establishment is shrinking. In 1990, at the peak of the Reagan-era buildup, the army had 18 active-duty divisions; the marines had three active-duty divisions; the navy had 16 carriers; and the air force had 24 active-duty tactical wings and 228 long-range bombers.

President George Bush understood that such a force was not necessary in the post-Soviet world, and he proposed a "base force" of 12 active-duty army divisions, three active-duty marine divisions, 13 aircraft carriers, 15 active-duty tactical wings for the air force, and 181 long-range bombers. That force would carry the United States into the next century.

The Clinton administration, however, proposed even greater reductions with its Bottom-Up Review (BUR), issued in September 1993: 10 active-duty army divisions; three active-duty marine divisions; 12 carriers; 13 tactical air force wings; up to 184 long-range bombers.

The centerpiece of the BUR was its two-war strategy: "U.S. forces will be structured to achieve a decisive victory in two nearly simultaneous major regional conflicts and to conduct combat operations characterized by rapid response and high probability of success, while minimizing the risk of significant American casualties."

Further, while the BUR spoke of how the United States might cooperate with its allies in military actions, it also outlined a go-it-alone strategy: "Our forces must be sized and structured to preserve the flexibility and the capability to act unilaterally, should we choose to do so."

In recent years, the political debate over the defense budget has been largely framed by conservatives, who hold the principal levers of power in Congress. It has turned on two questions: Is Clinton cutting the military too sharply compared to the more modest cuts envisioned by George Bush? And even if the force levels presented in the BUR are acceptable, is the Clinton administration asking for enough money—about $1.3 trillion over five years—to insure that the forces will be in fighting trim?

A consortium of citizen groups called the Military Spending Working Group says that these are the wrong questions. In fact, Bush's Base Force plan and Clinton's BUR both argue for fielding forces far stronger than those which are needed to meet the potential post–Cold War threats. An early item on the Working Group's agenda was the drafting of seven "principles," an alternative set of observations that describe the state of the union in the post–

"Well, has anyone *vacationed* recently in a country that could conceivably pose a threat to our national security?" *Frank Cotham*

Cold War world, and which provide guidelines to anyone seeking to craft a defense budget that makes economic as well as military sense. The principles—condensed and paraphrased by the *Bulletin*—follow.

• The Soviet Union is no more. Even if things turn sour between the United States and Russia, the Warsaw Pact is gone and Russia simply doesn't have the economic or military wherewithal to threaten the United States in the foreseeable future. The United States does not need a massive military structure designed to confront a threat that no longer exists.

Under any scenario, the United States will continue to maintain the strongest military in the world—unilateral disarmament is not on the agenda. But the hedge against a new superpower threat, whether from Russia or elsewhere, ought to be well-trained and fully equipped national guard and reserve forces rather than large numbers of active-duty forces.

Continuing ambitious weapons modernization programs conceived in the past decade when there is no advanced rival on the horizon is a bad investment. Selective investment in research and development for critical new weapons technologies makes more sense than producing new weapons systems. Weapons purchased to replace older inventories should come from existing and proven technologies.

Meanwhile, the greatest threat may be the diversion of nuclear weapons or weapons-usable materials from the ex-Soviet arsenal. This can be addressed through U.S. economic support for warhead dismantlement and related activities, as well as through expanded efforts to achieve deep and permanent reductions in the size and readiness of U.S. and Russian nuclear arsenals.

• Ethnic and nationalistic conflicts continue to produce terrible human tragedies while imperiling the security of U.S. allies and U.S. economic interests. And the proliferation of conventional, nuclear, chemical, and biological weapons poses a continuing threat to U.S. citizens and troops.

As instability persists, states pursue advanced conventional arms and weapons of mass destruction. Instead of addressing the causes of regional tensions, the United States has fueled conventional arms buildups by pushing sales of U.S. arms and technologies, making the world more dangerous for everyone. Most arms sales to the developing world are to countries whose citizens do not have the right to choose their governments. These are the future Panamas, Somalias, Iraqs, and Haitis—places where U.S. weapons might someday be used against U.S. troops. U.S. arms sales policies also undercut U.S. efforts to encourage other suppliers to stop shipping arms to states such as Iran and North Korea.

• Smart diplomacy rather than smart bombs should be the rule. Preventive diplomacy and non-violent conflict resolution through the United Nations and other multilateral institutions can help prevent and defuse crises before they spin out of control. With the end of the Cold War, long-standing conflicts in Central America, southern Africa, and the Middle East have ended peacefully.

The United States is not only the dominant military superpower, but also the dominant economic and political actor on the world stage. The end of the Cold War cleared the way for cooperation with the United Nations and other multilateral legal and economic institutions that—if strengthened—can address global problems such as nuclear proliferation, gross human rights violations, drug trafficking, terrorism, environmental degradation, and problems caused by population growth.

Lowering military spending, reducing nuclear weapon stockpiles, and curtailing development of new weapons would encourage other nations to follow suit. The end of the Cold War offers an opportunity to redirect U.S. aid and trade policies to reduce militarization, poverty, and other sources of regional and ethnic conflict. Forgoing a wasteful unilateral strategy and investing some of the money saved in building up multilateral security structures will help insure that the world does not fall back into a system of competing military blocs with its attendant danger of war.

• Size the force to meet the threat. Excessively large forces—designed for another era or for implausible scenarios—cannot be maintained at adequate levels of readiness. While the Bush and Clinton administrations made modest reductions from Cold War force and spending levels, the Pentagon's current plans are ill-conceived and overloaded with excessive—and expensive—capabilities.

The BUR is a poor basis for U.S. force planning. Although it assumes that the United States should be able on short notice to fight two major regional conflicts at roughly the same time, even Defense Secretary William J. Perry called such tandem events "implausible."

The BUR also assumes that the United States should be prepared to act unilaterally, despite opportunities for multilateral action and defense burden-sharing. The review envisions the United States as the world's cop, policing global trouble spots. But U.S. interests in these regions are largely based on threats to friends and allies—and allies would surely aid in their own defense. New regional and security arrangements and cooperative security structures can further reduce the potential for regional military conflict and the requirements for U.S. military efforts.

The Clinton administration plans to buy weapons and sustain force levels that are far in excess of actual requirements. Even so, the spending envisioned by the Clinton administration has engendered the Great Mismatch Debate. Simply put, the Clinton administration is said to be asking for too little money to fund the BUR plan. (The General Accounting Office and the Congressional Budget Office variously estimate the funding shortfall at $50 billion to $150 billion in fiscal 1995–1999.) Underfunding, say Clinton's critics, will lead to skimping on training and the acquisition of materiél. In turn, that equals "hollow forces."

The solution, says the Working Group, is an alternative approach to national strategy that specifies core areas of U.S. national interest, which would result in very different force requirements that could be supported at substantially lower levels of military spending. The United States must understand the nature and the extent of the threats to U.S. national security, for there is danger in overestimating the threats as well as in underestimating them. In times of lower threat, siphoning off too much of our national treasure to maintain excessively large military forces will seriously undermine other avenues of security and compromise the readiness of existing forces.

• Invest in upgrades, not new systems. Many of the major weapons procurement programs in the current defense budget—such as the MILSTAR communications satellite and Seawolf submarine—are Cold War leftovers, designed to meet threats that no longer exist. Tomorrow's potential adversaries have weapons and forces that are far less sophisticated than those of the United States or the former Soviet Union. Thus, they can be overcome with far less effort—and at a lower cost.

In most cases, existing systems are more than adequate to address foreseeable military requirements. U.S. military forces and equipment vastly outnumber and out-perform anything in the armories of potential adversaries. Export controls and nonproliferation efforts can further reduce the dangers of global militarization. For now, the United States should focus on continued research on key technologies rather than on the production of new weapons.

Where new military hardware is needed, it is often best to upgrade an existing platform or to modify a commercial system for military use. Meanwhile, the United States can afford to wait and see which technologies and systems will be best suited for the military requirements of the next century. There is no need to build systems now that may be quickly made obsolete by changing political or military requirements. The huge number of systems purchased in the 1980s and early 1990s will insure that the U.S. arsenal is well stocked, in many cases through the first decade of the next century.

While the United States must maintain a defense industrial base ready to produce the next generation of weapon platforms that may be needed in the future, it is never wise to buy another unneeded weapon today merely to keep a production line going. The efficient way of maintaining industrial knowhow is to consolidate and partially deactivate production facilities while keeping a strong cadre of workers and design teams busy producing prototypes and upgrades.

• Military pork is just as wasteful as domestic pork. Too much military spending is sustained by parochial interests, not by legitimate national security purposes. Over the decades, the military budget became a massive federal program to transfer resources to a few states that disproportionately benefit from military spending. While these states are winners, the rest of the country pays more in taxes to the Pentagon than is returned in military contracts and jobs.

The defense industry has taken hits in the post–Cold War years; but workers and communities have absorbed the heaviest blows. Since 1990, more than 800,000 defense-related jobs have disappeared. But urgent calls to "preserve the defense industrial base" have mostly preserved profits, not jobs. While defense workers continue to face massive layoffs, the stocks of companies responsible for "downsizing" decisions continue to out-perform the stocks of non-defense enterprises. In 1993, for instance, just eight defense companies accounted for half of the direct job loss, while their stock values appreciated 20 to 140 percent.

The job losses have been a boon in another way, however. Military contractors and their protectors in Congress fuel wasteful military spending by promoting weapons as jobs programs, and stuffing pork projects into districts and states. Congress should hold military projects to the same "pork accountability standard" as other government projects. Excessive military contracts not only produce unneeded military equipment, they are also the least efficient way of creating high-skill jobs with taxpayer dollars.

A sustained program of economic conversion and job retraining is needed so that companies and workers currently employed in military projects can make a more productive contribution to society. The Pentagon is a very costly employment agency.

• Reinvest in America—the major challenges are at home. The strength of nations, once defined in military terms, is now also measured by the skills of their workers, the imagination of their managers, and the power of their civilian technologies. Either the United States develops and pursues a national plan for restoring the U.S. economy through a partnership of government, labor, and business, or the United States will slip behind other nations. At stake are American jobs and the American standard of living.

Americans must invest today in the foundations for tomorrow. Nine nations now spend a higher percentage of their income on kindergarten through 12th-grade education than we do. Virtually every country in the world with an advanced economy spends a much higher percentage of their income on infrastructure, on transportation, and on communications than does the United States. The United States must rebuild its railroads, its highways, its bridges, and it must invest in a national information network.

Domestic needs remain unmet in the United States. Poverty is worse, inequality is greater, jobs are scarce. The squalor and brutality of U.S. cities is a disgrace. Low-cost housing is less affordable, college is being priced out of reach, environmental destruction is not a nuisance but a threat. Yet the United States still devotes most of its public research and development money to high-tech weapons, while the nation's economic competitors invest in civilian technologies to capture the markets of the future.

Except in wartime, the United States has always had to choose between military spending and other national priorities. Today, Americans need to take every last dollar by which they reduce defense and reinvest it in an American economy for the twenty-first century. Americans need to create high-speed rail networks, produce new environmental technologies, and develop new technologies that will permit the retraining of defense workers who lose their jobs. The United States must not leave them out in the cold just because they won the Cold War. And more than ever, the people of the United States need to recall the words of President Dwight D. Eisenhower, who said in 1953:

"Every gun that is fired, every warship launched, every rocket fired signifies, in the final sense, a theft from those who hunger and are not fed, those who are cold and not clothed. The world in arms is not spending money alone. It is spending the sweat of its laborers, the genius of its scientists, the hopes of its children."

This is adapted from the September/October 1995 *Bulletin*.

VI.2 A Chinese View on Nuclear Disarmament

DINGLI SHEN

Ultimately we need a nuclear weapons convention that will ban the possession of nuclear weapons. A comprehensive test ban is just one important step toward the goal of a nuclear-weapon-free world. While the Chinese government has said it will take an active part in the negotiating process and work together with other countries to conclude a treaty no later than 1996, at the same time it believes that a pledge by all nuclear weapon states not to use nuclear weapons at all is of even greater significance. It also calls for a commitment to the complete prohibition and thorough destruction of nuclear weapons.

That is the long-term goal. In the more immediate future one has to consider the global and regional disposition of the nuclear weapons currently held by other countries.

First of all, the Chinese government has announced that it will not support, encourage, or engage in nuclear proliferation. This position was presented by the Chinese observer delegation to the fourth NPT review conference in 1990. In March 1992, China became a party to the NPT. Early in 1992

China announced that it would abide by the guidelines of the Missile Technology Control Regime.

Second, it is clear that the possession of nuclear weapons has improved China's national defense, particularly at a time when China perceived threats, first from the United States and later from the former Soviet Union. It is also widely believed that Chinese nuclear weapons have increased China's international prestige.

Third, I think it is in China's interest to protect itself against the eventuality that someday any one of a number of its neighbors might go nuclear. It has been possible for China to prepare itself without creating too much worry for itself or for others. China declared from the very day it became a nuclear weapon state that at no time and under no circumstances would it be the first to use nuclear weapons. It also issued full assurances that at no time and under no circumstances would China use nuclear weapons against any non-nuclear weapon state. In other words, China wishes to be prepared in case of an attack by any other nuclear weapon state—but it would not attack a non-nuclear weapon state with nuclear weapons at any time. With this policy, China has given a maximum security guarantee to the world. In return, China should be able to expect that it might not be a priority target of any other nuclear weapon state.

The Regional Outlook

Is there really any serious risk from the emergence of possible new nuclear weapon states around China? North Korea and Pakistan are friendly countries to China, but they are suspected of developing military nuclear programs. China is careful not to interfere in the internal affairs of other countries. India's reported nuclearization certainly has China's attention, but China can do almost nothing to affect India's independent nuclear pursuit. Japan's potential to go nuclear, which becomes serious as it accumulates large amounts of plutonium, causes concern on the part of its neighbors.

On the Korean peninsula, North Korea's alleged nuclearization might trigger a chain reaction—South Korea and even Japan might follow suit. On the one hand, the Chinese government has made it clear that it will support the de-nuclearization initiatives in this region. China will not support nuclear proliferation pursued by any party on the Korean peninsula. Maintaining peace and stability should be the most important task to be carried out. On the other hand, those relevant parties should have enough patience to tackle the nuclear problem on the peninsula. Sanctions, if they are ever imposed on North Korea, would eventually become counterproductive; sanctions seldom work. In my opinion, providing security assurances would be the most effective way to reduce North Korea's possible incentive to go nuclear. It is now high time for the United States to adjust its "zero-sum" security relations with North Korea and South Korea. It is important to ask that the U.S.–South Korean "Team Spirit" military exercises be permanently stopped. This would significantly reduce tensions on the peninsula and pave the way for better relations.

Japan might be a potential security concern to its neighboring countries, especially as it accumulates a large amount of power-reactor plutonium for purposes that are difficult to understand. But from a more optimistic perspective, if the new Japanese government's policies are fully in accord with the idea of "no war forever," this may relieve concerns over Japan in the nuclear dimension.

South Asia is another area of concern. This is the part of the world where "non-weaponized deterrence" has existed ever since India exploded its nuclear device in 1974 and Pakistan claimed that it had acquired the necessary parts and knowledge for making an atomic bomb. Personally I prefer not to interpret India's nuclear and missile programs as an imminent threat, although India's Agni intermediate range ballistic missiles are reportedly able to hit almost any part of China. The underlying logic might be, "I trust that you will not attack me as long as I do not attack you." Also, it seems that China is not interested in being addressed in the South Asian framework, especially since it does not view itself as being in any sort of rivalry with India.

With regard to China's relations with Pakistan, the United States has accused China of selling missile technology to Pakistan. This has been denied by the governments of both China and Pakistan. I believe that the Chinese government has kept its commitment to observe the Missile Technology Control Regime guidelines. There are several factors to be considered in addressing South Asian missile development. Reducing security concerns and building mutual confidence are of vital importance to de-escalate missile development on the subcontinent. Other countries should help this process.

In sum, China can rightly claim to be against proliferation. The priority given to the ideas of concluding an international convention on unconditional no first use of nuclear weapons is seen as an effective step toward the nonproliferation goal underscored by the NPT. Likewise, the willingness to negotiate a comprehensive test ban treaty could be part of China's policy of working toward the goal of a worldwide prohibition and thorough elimination of all nuclear weapons.

This is adapted from the March/April 1994 *Bulletin*.

VI.3 World Court Says Mostly No to Nuclear Weapons

MIKE MOORE

In an opinion that was simultaneously forthright and ambiguous, the International Court of Justice—usually called the World Court—said in The Hague July 8, 1996, that "the threat or use of nuclear weapons" was "generally" unlawful.

But the court also declared that it could not "definitively" conclude whether the threat or use of such weapons would be lawful or unlawful "in an extreme circumstance of self-defence, in which the very survival of a State would be at stake."

The court's principal findings were embodied in a 37-page advisory opinion to the U.N. General Assembly, which had asked the court for guidance as to whether international law permitted states to threaten or use nuclear weapons.

Given the principles of national sovereignty enshrined in the charter of the United Nations, a World Court advisory opinion cannot compel a nation to do anything it chooses not to do. But legal scholars generally agree that such opinions constitute authoritative interpretations of international law, and that they often carry considerable moral weight.

The vote on the substantive language in the July decision—Paragraph E—was seven to seven. The split decision became the majority opinion because, under the rules of the court, the president of the court, Mohammed Bedjaoui of Algeria, was allowed a tie-breaking "casting vote." In effect, the president voted twice.

However, anti-nuclear activists with the World Court Project, the umbrella organization chiefly responsible for bringing the legality question to the court's attention, noted that three of the "nay" votes were cast by judges who believed that the court had not gone far enough. In effect, said the activists, 10 of the 14 judges had gone on record—either in the main opinion or in dissenting opinions—as condemning the threat or use of nuclear weapons.

In a coda to its opinion, the World Court also endorsed the goal of nuclear disarmament:

"In the long run, international law, and with it the stability of the international order which it is intended to govern, are bound to suffer from the continuing difference of views with regard to the legal status of weapons as deadly as nuclear weapons. It is consequently important to put an end to this state of affairs: the long-promised complete nuclear disarmament appears to be the most appropriate means of achieving that result."

Given that, the judges unanimously concluded: "There exists an obligation to pursue in good faith and bring to a conclusion negotiations leading to nuclear disarmament in all its aspects under strict and effective international control."

The Argument

The court's opinion ultimately turned on the uniquely destructive power of the weapons, which, the court said, "cannot be contained in either space or time. They have the potential to destroy all civilization and the entire ecosystem of the planet."

Further, said the court, "the use of nuclear weapons would be a serious danger to future generations. Ionizing radiation has the potential to damage the future environment, food and marine ecosystem, and to cause genetic defects and illness in future generations."

Those long-lasting and indiscriminate effects, suggested the court, brought the threat or use of nuclear weapons into conflict with a vast body of international humanitarian law relating to armed conflict.

"The cardinal principles contained in the texts constituting the fabric of humanitarian law," said the court, "are the following. The first is aimed at the protection of the civilian population and civilian objects and establishes the distinction between combatants and non-combatants. States must never make civilians the object of attack and must consequently never use weapons that are incapable of distinguishing between civilian and military targets.

"According to the second principle, it is prohibited to cause unnecessary suffering to combatants: it is accordingly prohibited to use weapons causing them such harm or uselessly aggravating their suffering."

After the court determined that humanitarian law applied to nuclear weapons, it asserted that the international principle of neutrality applied as well. That is, belligerents were required to respect the rights of non-belligerents, which meant, in part, that the territory of neutral states could not be violated. Implicit in the court's reasoning was the idea that nuclear war would affect non-belligerents.

While the court said there was little dispute that humanitarian law and the principles of neutrality applied to nuclear weapons, there was controversy over precisely what that might mean in practice.

Britain, for instance, had argued that "nuclear weapons might be used in a wide variety of circumstances with very different results in terms of likely civilian casualties. In some cases, such as the use of a low yield nuclear weapon against warships on the High Seas or troops in sparsely populated areas, it is possible to envisage a nuclear attack which caused comparatively few civilian casualties."

Such arguments apparently were not persuasive to at least ten judges. The court, however, failed to categorically say that nuclear weapons could *never* be used in war. In perhaps the opinion's most controversial paragraphs, the court said:

"Methods and means of warfare which would preclude any distinction between civilian and military targets, or which would result in unnecessary suffering to combatants, are prohibited. In view of the unique characteristics of nuclear weapons . . . the use of such weapons in fact seems scarcely reconcilable with respect to such requirements.

"Nevertheless, the Court considers that it does not have sufficient elements to enable it to conclude with certainty that the use of nuclear weapons would necessarily be at variance with the principles and rules of law applicable in armed conflict in any circumstance.

"Furthermore, the Court cannot lose sight of the fundamental right of every State to survival, and thus its right to resort to self-defence, in accordance with Article 51 of the [U.N.] Charter, when its survival is at stake."

Nor, said the court, could it ignore nuclear deterrence, a policy "to which an appreciable section of the international community adhered for many years."

Deceptive Language

While the court narrowly decided, in Paragraph E of its concluding decision, that the threat or use of nuclear weapons was "generally" unlawful, it could not bring itself to rule out the use of nuclear weapons "in an extreme circumstance of self-defence, in which the very survival of a State would be at stake."

That failure to go all the way in condemning nuclear weapons inspired Judge Christopher G. Weeramantry of Sri Lanka to write an 88-page dissent, which said, in part:

"It would be a paradox if international law, a system intended to promote world peace and order, should have a place within it for an entity that can cause total destruction of the world system, the millennia of civilization which have produced it, and humanity itself.

"A factor which powerfully conceals that contradiction, even to the extent of keeping humanitarian law at bay, is the use of euphemistic language—the disembodied language of military operations and the polite language of diplomacy. They conceal the horror of nuclear war, diverting attention to intellectual concepts such as self-defense, reprisals, and proportionate damage which can have little relevance to a situation of total destruction.

"Horrendous damage to civilians and neutrals is described as collateral damage, because it was not directly intended; incineration of cities becomes 'considerable thermal damage.' One speaks of 'acceptable levels of casualties,' even if megadeaths are involved. Maintaining the balance of terror is described as 'nuclear preparedness'; assured destruction as 'deterrence'; total devastation of the environment as 'environmental damage.'

"Clinically detached from their human context, such expressions bypass the world of human suffering, out of which humanitarian law has sprung."

Almost as if he sought to answer the challenge to the court's decision posed by Weeramantry, President Bedjaoui said in a separate concurring opinion that nothing the court had said could "in any way be interpreted as leaving the way open to the recognition of the lawfulness of the threat or use of nuclear weapons." According to Bedjaoui, in its self-defense language the court merely admitted the existence of a legal uncertainty. Bedjaoui said the self-defense language could not lead to a situation in which a state could exonerate itself from compliance with the "intransgressible norms of international humanitarian law."

It would be very rash, he said, to accord, without any hesitation, a higher priority to the survival of a state than to the survival of humanity itself.

This is adapted from the September/October 1996 *Bulletin*.

VI.4 The Revolt Against Nuclear Weapons

Michael Krepon

Revolutions in nuclear strategy must overcome powerful resistance. As Henry Kissinger wrote in 1957 in *Nuclear Weapons and Foreign Policy*, "Contemporaries are in a peculiarly difficult position to assess the nature of revolutions through which we are living. . . . They will have difficulty understanding that what is most taken for granted may be most misleading because a new order of experience requires new ways of thinking about it." Kissinger was then railing against the official U.S. doctrine of massive retaliation, calling instead for a wide range of flexible nuclear war-fighting options. His critique of the old order prevailed; massive retaliation was replaced by escalation ladders, open-ended requirements, and burgeoning stockpiles.

We are currently living through a counter-revolution in nuclear strategy, one that has received scant acceptance in nuclear weapon states. The counter-revolution is reflected in public demand for a complete end to nuclear weapon tests and by reductions in deployed forces and stockpiles. By narrowing greatly the range of circumstances under which nuclear weapons could be used or threatened, the World Court's ruling reinforces these trends. While the court's decision has downside risks, it should, on balance, help reduce the dark shadow cast by nuclear weapons.

This counter-revolution to diminish military and political utility for nuclear weapons will take many decades to complete, as it is contrary to established thinking among the insular communities within nuclear weapon and threshold states that guard doctrine and employment options. Many impediments stand in the way, including possible acts of terrorism, renewed proliferation concerns, and troubling changes in political leadership, all of which can prompt reaffirmations of the old nuclear order. Revolutions, after all, are hardly linear in nature.

The counter-revolution has been 51 years in the making, but significant construction began only with the waning years of the Cold War. With every year since 1945, the norm against using nuclear weapons has grown. The immediate significance of the World Court's ruling lies in its reaffirmation of this record of restraint, which has survived Cold War crises over Cuba, Berlin, Quemoy and Matsu, Dien Bien Phu, Korea, and other hot spots. The longer this record of restraint continues, the more implausible and counterproductive become threats to use nuclear weapons in other than the most extreme circumstances.

Washington's record in this respect remains deficient. Threats to use nuclear weapons against the Soviet Union and China were a Cold War staple during the 1950s and 1960s. Indeed, the nuclear revolution engineered by Kissinger and his fellow strategists was designed in part to give such threats credibility. While nuclear threats have waned considerably, they have not been entirely abandoned, as was evident in the warnings of senior Pentagon officials in 1996 over a suspected Libyan chemical production and storage complex.

These threats were not only directly contrary to the unanimous opinion of the court, they were also contrary to the legal briefs submitted to the court by the State and Defense Departments' own lawyers, who asserted that nuclear threats might be warranted only in cases of self-defense or in countering acts of aggression, and only in conformity with the requirements of international law, particularly the principles and rules of international humanitarian law. Henceforth, their legal briefs as well as the court's unanimous ruling will be used against national leaders who threaten to use nuclear weapons in anything less than extreme circumstances.

"I'd like to thank everyone who made change impossible." *Frank Cotham*

As the Libyan case suggests, the revolution of diminished roles and missions for nuclear weapons has yet to foreclose hints of nuclear weapons use by the United States against chemical and biological weapons threats. The Clinton administration's nuclear posture review left this option purposely vague, despite its increasing implausibility. Even Washington's signature on protocols to the recent African Nuclear-Weapon-Free-Zone (ANFZ) Treaty included the caveat that it would not exclude the use of nuclear weapons "in response to an attack by an ANFZ party using weapons of mass destruction."

Resistance to the counter-revolution in nuclear strategy has taken other forms, as well. India's bomb lobby has succeeded in reversing four decades of support for a truly comprehensive nuclear test ban treaty. Pentagon officials strenuously oppose early negotiations to reduce deployed arsenals below 3,500 warheads, even though no one can provide a plausible public rationale for more than a few detonations. And Russian officials now place increased reliance on nuclear weapons to offset deficiencies in conventional forces—a calculation that has been tried by others before being discarded as terribly unwise.

Clearly, there is much work to be done to progressively diminish the role that nuclear weapons play in international relations. Old mind-sets die hard, but where they have served to reinforce nonproliferation regimes, traditional ways of thinking require some deference. By narrowly limiting the role of nuclear weapons to extreme circumstances of self-defense, the World Court's ruling must have caused shudders in some capitals that depend on the U.S. nuclear umbrella. There is a risk in yanking away an insurance policy that the owner still values, particularly when the owner can cross the nuclear threshold. Regions that have relied on extended deterrence for many decades cannot change their way of thinking overnight.

Despite this caveat, the World Court's ruling pushes the counter-revolution in nuclear strategy forward. Now comes the hard part: Continued success requires sustained effort against powerful resistance.

This is adapted from the September/October 1996 *Bulletin*.

VI.5 Comprehensive Test Ban Only a Beginning

William Epstein

For most of 1996, the arms control world focused on finally achieving the Comprehensive Nuclear Test Ban (CTB) Treaty, a task that was accomplished in September with great agony, if not angst.

Completion of the treaty was welcome news. But it is a flawed instrument in that India, a "threshold" nuclear weapon state, has said that it will never sign it. Ultimately that could be fatal to the treaty because India is one of the 44 states that must ratify it before it can enter into force.

However, "never" is a strong word. It is possible that India might sign and ratify the CTB within a few years, if the nuclear weapon states get serious about the nuclear disarmament commitment they made more than 25 years ago in Article VI of the Nuclear Non-Proliferation Treaty (NPT), and if the CTB is amended to meet India's objections.

Despite uncertainties regarding the long-range fate of the treaty, the CTB has immediate value. The Vienna Law of Treaties provides that signatories to a treaty must "refrain from acts which would defeat the object and purposes" of the treaty, pending its entry into force. In short, no nuclear tests.

The nuclear powers won an astonishing victory at the NPT Review and Extension Conference a year and a half earlier, when the treaty was extended indefinitely. But to get that extension, the nuclear powers had to reaffirm their commitment to conduct "good faith" negotiations toward nuclear disarmament. Specifically, they made three "binding" political commitments:

- to complete a comprehensive nuclear test ban treaty in time for the fall 1996 session of the U.N. General Assembly;
- to bring to an "early conclusion" a ban on the production of fissile material for nuclear weapons;
- to engage in the "determined pursuit" of "systematic and progressive efforts to reduce nuclear weapons globally with the ultimate goal of eliminating those weapons."

The nuclear weapon powers also agreed that further steps should be considered to guarantee that nuclear weapon states would not use or threaten to use nuclear weapons against non-nuclear parties to the NPT.

The signing of the CTB met one of those commitments, even though the treaty will not enter into force for years, if ever. Meanwhile, it is all the more necessary that the five nuclear powers take additional steps to prove they are really serious about the elimination of nuclear weapons. That would strengthen the NPT, and it might save the CTB.

What the CTB Does Not Do

In contrast to the CTB, negotiations to ban the production of fissile material for weapons—generally called the "cut-off" or "fissban"—have gone completely adrift. The nuclear powers have such excessive stocks of weapons-grade uranium and plutonium that they don't know what to do with it all.

But because of those huge stocks, it is clear to everyone that a cut-off is no longer a disarmament measure, as was originally intended. It's a nonproliferation measure. The nuclear weapon states are awash in weapons-grade material; and they don't want anyone else to obtain it.

Given that, some non-nuclear weapon countries—particularly India, Egypt, Pakistan, and other non-aligned states—insist that the cut-off negotiations should deal with *existing* stocks of weapons-grade material as well as the need for international control of those stocks. The nuclear powers aren't buying that. The cut-off problem seems intractable. Rather than continuing to butt heads over the issue, it makes sense to tuck it into a deep freeze for later retrieval.

Meanwhile, the five nuclear powers could proclaim unilateral moratoriums on the production of weapons-grade material, and they could enter into a cut-off treaty among themselves and open it for signature by other states. This would not solve the existing-stocks problem, but it would at least demonstrate a serious intent to achieve a cut-off.

Although the NPT calls for the nuclear powers to conduct good-faith negotiations toward the goal of nuclear disarmament, they have made very little effort along those lines, although the United States and Russia are now cutting the numbers of weapons back substantially, albeit not as fast as they could.

Further, the nuclear powers systematically blocked all attempts this year, as in past years, to establish a negotiating committee on nuclear disarmament within the framework of the Conference on Disarmament in Geneva. And they have vetoed attempts to include nuclear disarmament as an agenda item at the Disarmament Commission in New York.

Amb. Jayantha Dhanapala of Sri Lanka, the president of the 1995 NPT Conference, has repeatedly warned that failure by the nuclear powers to live up to nuclear disarmament commitments in the NPT might eventually lead some states to exercise their legal right to exit the treaty. Mexico has gone on record as saying that if the nuclear weapon powers do not comply with their agreed obligations, it would review its adherence to the NPT.

The non-nuclear parties to the NPT believe that because they have forsworn the acquisition of nuclear weapons, they are entitled to binding security assurances similar to those made by the nuclear powers to the parties to nuclear-weapon-free-zone (NWFZ) treaties. But the nuclear powers have failed to even discuss the matter.

To be sure, China made such a pledge in 1964, the year it tested its first bomb, and it has repeated the pledge often. The Soviet Union also made a no-first-use pledge in 1982, but Russia withdrew it in 1993.

If all five declared nuclear powers were to make binding pledges of no-first-use, that would provide at least "negative" security assurances to the non-nuclear states until such time as all nuclear weapons are eliminated. (A "negative" assurance means that a nuclear weapon state will not use nuclear weapons against a non-nuclear weapon state. A "positive" assurance is that a nuclear weapon state will come to the aid of a non-nuclear weapon state, if the latter state is attacked or threatened with nuclear weapons.)

Such pledges are compatible with a policy of nuclear deterrence against nuclear attacks. They would be made more credible if they were embodied in a treaty, and if the nuclear powers agreed to take all their nuclear weapons off alert status and remove and significantly separate all warheads and bombs from delivery vehicles.

The five nuclear powers should get on with signing protocols to the South East Asian NWFZ Treaty, which the nuclear powers regard as having security assurances that are too sweeping, even though they are similar to those in other such treaties. Russia has also not yet signed the protocols to the African NWFZ Treaty.

Political Will

It will not be easy for the Conference on Disarmament, when it resumes in 1997, to reach a consensus on a mandate for a committee on nuclear disarmament. The process could take years. Meanwhile, the nuclear powers could and should take a number of steps toward the elimination of nuclear weapons on their own. If so, these measures might be persuasive to India and the other hold-outs on the CTB. Among the steps:

- Pledge no-first-use of nuclear weapons, accompanied by measures to take all nuclear weapons off alert status, and remove and significantly separate all warheads and bombs from their delivery vehicles.
- Sign the protocols to the South East Asian and African NWFZ treaties, and affirm that they would respect any new NWFZ treaties.
- Declare a moratorium on the production of fissile material for weapons, negotiate a cut-off treaty among themselves, and open it for signature.
- Start negotiations leading to an eventual ban on the production, use, and threat of use of all nuclear weapons.
- Begin negotiations on START III after the early ratification of START II by Russia.
- Reaffirm their intention to urgently and fully implement their obligations under the NPT, including the Principles and Objectives of Non-Proliferation and Disarmament adopted at the 1995 NPT Review and Extension Conference.
- Agree to establish a negotiating committee on nuclear disarmament in the Conference on Disarmament.

These measures—which are similar to steps recently recommended by the Canberra Commission on the Elimination of Nuclear Weapons, which called for the unequivocal and demonstrated commitment of the nuclear powers to nuclear disarmament—could be easily undertaken or begun in the immediate future. All that is required is the political will. These actions would give renewed credibility to the NPT and promote nuclear disarmament, even if there is some delay in achieving a legally binding CTB.

This is adapted from the November/December 1996 *Bulletin*.

VI.6 Four Steps to Zero

The Henry L. Stimson Center

The Cold War's end and the dangers of nuclear proliferation demand a fundamental reappraisal of the role of nuclear weapons in U.S. policy and in global politics.

In the changing strategic environment, nuclear weapons are of declining value in securing U.S. interests, but pose growing risks to the security of the United States and other nations. Their only role in this new era—the deterrence of other nuclear threats—could be met with far fewer nuclear weapons. U.S. national security would be best served by a policy of phased reductions in all states' nuclear forces and the gradual movement toward the objective of eliminating all weapons of mass destruction from all countries.

Although nuclear weapons have played a central role in foreign and defense policies for over four decades, there is no military justification in the new strategic environment for current or planned nuclear force levels. U.S. conventional forces can and should counter all conventional threats, and a combination of defensive measures and strong conventional forces are more appropriate responses to any threats of chemical and biological attacks.

The only necessary function for nuclear weapons is to deter nuclear threats to the population and territory of the United States, to U.S. forces abroad, and to certain friendly states. This deterrent function could be met at much lower force levels, as long as other states move in tandem toward smaller nuclear forces.

Deeper cuts would bring important security benefits to the United States. Aside from their direct dollar cost, the continuing existence of nuclear forces entails risks of nuclear accidents and incidents, and of the inadvertent or deliberate use of nuclear weapons in a crisis. Most importantly, continued reliance on nuclear weapons undermines international efforts to persuade other countries not to acquire nuclear weapons—the only weapons that can utterly destroy the United States as a nation and a society. Only a policy that aims at curbing global reliance on nuclear weapons—including our own—is likely to progressively eliminate nuclear dangers.

An "evolutionary" nuclear posture of careful, phased reductions, combined with an up-front, serious commitment to the long-term objective of eliminating all weapons of mass destruction, could enhance U.S. national security significantly.

The United States has committed itself to the elimination of nuclear weapons under Article VI of the Nuclear Non-Proliferation Treaty (NPT), but active governmental efforts to identify and solve the problems associated with achieving this objective have been notably lacking. A decisive commitment at the highest political level would signal to non-nuclear states that the United States' NPT pledge is real, and it would bolster important gains in recent years to devalue all weapons of mass destruction.

The goal of elimination would be achieved in four phases, with each phase corresponding to a new strategic environment and involving changes in nuclear roles, in the operational status and size of nuclear forces, and in arms control arrangements. Alterations in the U.S. nuclear posture would be gradual and conditioned on the cooperation of other states in reducing their arsenals and strengthening nonproliferation regimes for nuclear, chemical, and biological weapons. Progress toward elimination does not imply the creation of a world government.

Phase I. In the current phase, the United States and Russia would work to reduce the importance of mutual assured destruction as a stabilizing element in their relations and would undertake cuts in their nuclear arsenals to roughly 2,000 warheads each. Although the United States must take into account the possibility of a reversal of reforms in Russia, the essential military role of nuclear weapons during this phase—the deterrence of nuclear attack—could be preserved at much lower force levels, and it would be beneficial for both states to undertake deeper cuts in their strategic nuclear arsenals.

Without a commitment to deeper cuts, the reductions mandated under START II will be difficult to implement in Russia. Even if reforms in Russia fail, the United States would be better off if Russia were armed with 2,000 rather than 3,500 or 6,000 deployed warheads. As U.S. and Russian arsenals are downsized, the alert status of each country's nuclear force should be reduced and new measures to increase the transparency of each nation's nuclear forces introduced. Safety issues should be given added emphasis during this phase and steps should be taken to strengthen the nonproliferation regimes for nuclear, chemical, and biological weapons. During this phase, the United States should initiate official studies of the implications of additional cuts for verification regimes and safeguards, U.S. relations with allies, conventional military forces, and the desirability and design of defensive systems.

Phase II. Stable and cordial relations among the declared nuclear weapon states would further ease the requirements for nuclear deterrence, allowing all five states to reduce their arsenals to hundreds of warheads each. As in Phase I, the only military role of nuclear weapons would be to deter nuclear attack. Nuclear weapon states, moreover, would no longer perceive nuclear weapons as contributing positively to their international status.

Cuts in force levels would be accompanied by steps to remove many, if not all, nuclear weapons from active alert status, and by the extension of nuclear transparency and safety measures to the smaller nuclear powers. Elimination of the political roles of nuclear weapons would require significant changes in U.S. defense policy, military strategy, and force posture. The United States and the other nuclear states might facilitate this transformation by deploying national defensive systems during this phase.

Phase III. All nuclear weapon states would reduce their arsenals to tens of weapons each. Achievement of the goals of this phase would require the widespread embrace of new principles and mechanisms for national security and the further marginalization of nuclear weapons in interstate relations.

Although the principle of sovereignty would be preserved, states would rely on regional and global collective security systems for their security. In such a system, nuclear weapons over time might become so devalued, yet entail so many costs, that states might prefer to act as international "trustees" of nuclear weapons. The sole function of nuclear weapons would be to deter threats of mass violence against all states and societies. When the perceived costs of maintaining such a "trustee" arrangement came to outweigh the perceived benefits, the international community would be ready to move into the final phase.

Phase IV. All nuclear weapons would be eliminated from all countries.

The Long View

Most observers find it difficult, if not impossible, to envision a nuclear-weapon-free world. Skeptics argue that the complete elimination of nuclear weapons would require an end to the principle of sovereignty in the global system and the creation of world government. In this view, as long as we live in a world of sovereign states, we are doomed to coexist with the threat of mass destruction.

We disagree. It is not too early to think hard about the issues involved. In our view, the continuation of an international system founded on state sovereignty does not imply a perpetual state of nuclear deterrence. Other outcomes would preserve the state system in recognizable form, yet offer effective alternatives to the threat of mass violence. The slow, if irregular, spread of democracy to formerly authoritarian systems could create a system in which sovereign states would remain the principal actors, but could see so little value in the threat of mass destruction that nuclear weapons and nuclear deterrence would wither away.

In order to achieve the complete elimination of all weapons of mass destruction from all countries, many serious obstacles and problems would have to be addressed and overcome. National and international verification regimes would have to be capable of detecting violations of a ban on nuclear weapons in sufficient time for the United States and the international community to mount an effective response. All relevant materials and technology would have to be subject to stringent controls, and the production of weapons-grade nuclear material and other precursor items prohibited and closely monitored.

Safeguards against the risks of a non-nuclear world would be essential. Critics of the disarmament option have argued that a non-nuclear world would be fraught with instability, since at any time some state or group might aspire to become the sole nuclear power in a world otherwise at peace. Under a worst-case scenario, a clandestine nuclear program would go undetected until a "rogue" state or terrorist group announced that it possessed one or more nuclear devices.

But how great are the risks of such a breakout from a disarmament regime? Might they be countered with alternative military capabilities—both conventional forces and strategic defenses? And what political or military benefits could be extracted from an announcement of nuclear acquisition in any event? Such questions deserve close study.

The safeguards regime would have to provide the international community with the appropriate tools to respond rapidly to any aggressor attempting to extract short-term gain from a position of nuclear monopoly. Under the political conditions envisioned for Phase IV, the detection of a violation against a global ban on weapons of mass destruction would trigger the imposition of severe economic, political, and military penalties on the perpetrator, and would likely lead to the reconstitution of nuclear forces in one or more states.

Although a "rogue" state might threaten other countries with a nuclear, chemical, or biological attack in order to force concessions in the near term, any potential perpetrator would know from the outset that the benefits of blackmail would almost certainly be short-lived. Sooner or later, the violator would face the prospect of severe penalties or certain and massive retribution, depending on its actions; the short-term benefits of nuclear possession would come at the price of sure and certain reversal weeks or months later. If such a system of safeguards could be established, it is far from evident that a position of nuclear monopoly could be used to compel states to make economic, military, or other concessions in the future, although this question deserves further study.

The United States has already committed itself to the long-term objective of eliminating nuclear weapons. As a signatory to the NPT, the United States, under Article VI, is pledged to pursue "negotiations in good faith on effective measures relating to cessation of the nuclear arms race at an early date and to nuclear disarmament." That commitment was reaffirmed and made more explicit during the 1995 NPT Review Conference; tangible steps now should be taken.

Serious attention in official circles to the problems associated with going to very low levels of arsenals or to zero itself has been lacking due to the disapprobation associated with the disarmament option. Only a sustained commitment at the highest political level will legitimate serious discussions of the elimination option and ensure that resources and personnel are devoted to finding solutions to the problems associated with moving to zero, and to crafting appropriate transition strategies. In the absence of such a commitment, the nations of the world may never reach the point at which the desirability and feasibility of a nuclear-free world can be evaluated with greater certainty. To paraphrase Herman Kahn, by contemplating the unthinkable, the boundaries of the feasible might well be stretched.

In contrast, a policy concentrating only on near-term pragmatic options could raise grave dangers to U.S. security. While the existing nuclear nonproliferation regime has been remarkably robust, the status quo is unlikely to be sustainable in the long term.

Despite apocalyptic predictions of widespread proliferation, the spread of nuclear weapons, thankfully, has been contained to a handful of states. But determined countries have proven that it is possible within the current regime to acquire the necessary material and know-how to construct numbers of nuclear devices. Although the NPT was extended indefinitely in 1995, the support of many non-nuclear states was conditioned on tangible, measurable progress toward the Article VI objective of eliminating all nuclear weapons and thus on the abolition of the dual standard that sanctions nuclear possession for five states and condemns the acquisition of nuclear forces by all other participants in the regime.

Without a more radical approach to nonproliferation, the challenges posed to the nonproliferation regime can only mount over time, and the United States, eventually, is sure to face new nuclear threats.

The prospects for a nuclear-free world may be decades over the horizon.

But it certainly could be achieved in one or two generations. The history of world politics since 1945 shows clearly that radical changes are possible in such a time frame. Regardless of the amount of time required, it is virtually certain that the world will never be rid of nuclear risks without a serious political commitment to the objective of progressively eliminating weapons of mass destruction from all countries. The time to start is now.

This is adapted from the March/April 1996 *Bulletin*.

A Sense of Proportion

Rank of United States among countries of the world by military spending: **1**

U.S. military expenditures as a percent of gross national product: **5**

U.S. defense budget as percent of combined military spending of next nine biggest spenders: **120**

U.S. defense budget as percent of military budgets of all "regional adversaries" (Cuba, Syria, Iran, Iraq, North Korea, Libya) combined: **1600**

Size of Defense Department–controlled land compared to that of "regional adversary" North Korea: **1:1**

Rank of Defense Department by size among U.S. cities if its employees—civilian, active military, and reserves—were considered the population: **3**

Number of Defense Department finance and accounting employees: **14,000**

Years of government funding for arts and humanities (*All Things Considered*, Big Bird, classical music, ballet, etc.) that could be paid for by eliminating one year of Pentagon waste, as calculated by the Government Accounting Office: **13**

Cost of weapons not requested by the Defense Department but added to its 1996 authorization by the House National Security Committee: **$4.5 billion**

Cost of unrequested weapons that will be built in or near House National Security Committee members' districts: **$3.35 billion**

Cost of the Manhattan Project to build the first nuclear weapons (through August 1945): **$20 billion**

Annual cost of U.S. nuclear weapons activities, 1995: **$33 billion**

Cost of U.S. nuclear testing in 1985 (16 tests): **$825 million**

Cost of testing in 1995 (0 tests): **$410 million**

Total land area occupied by U.S. Defense and Energy Department nuclear weapons installations: **12,603 square miles**

Total combined land area of Maryland, Delaware, and the District of Columbia: **11,834 square miles**

Number of U.S. nuclear bombs lost in accidents and never recovered: **11**

Number of secret facilities built for presidential use during and after a nuclear war: **more than 75**

Currency stored until 1988 in Culpeper, Virginia, by the Federal Reserve to be used after a nuclear war: **more than $2 trillion**

Minimum number of pages still classified as secret by the Energy Department: **280 million**

Annual cost of U.S. Defense Department for each U.S. citizen: **$1,100**

Annual cost of United Nations and U.N. peacekeeping for each U.S. citizen: **less than $4**

All costs are converted to 1995 dollars. Some material is adapted from the Nuclear Weapons Cost Study Project. Adapted from the September/October 1995 and November/December 1995 *Bulletin*.

Chapter VI
Discussion Questions

1. Do you believe that nuclear disarmament has a realistic chance of happening in your lifetime? What reasons and factors influence your thinking on this question? Do any of the ideas offered in this chapter influence the way you think about this issue?

2. Military spending in nations and arms races between nations have been based on the notion that more spending and more arms produce more military security. Discuss how and why the United States might achieve more security by spending less and producing fewer arms.

3. It is often claimed that in order for nuclear disarmament to occur, a variety of developments must unfold. These include realistic steps for demilitarizing nations without generating security crises and the emergence of legal and organizational building blocks for disarmament. Based on the readings in this chapter, describe elements of these steps that are in place now and those that need to be created or strengthened in the future.

4. You have been appointed U.S. assistant undersecretary of state for nuclear policy in an administration that was elected on a platform favoring nuclear disarmament. What specific steps would you recommend in U.S. weapons and defense policy to begin to fulfill the promise to achieve U.S. nuclear disarmament?

Chapter VII

The Emergence of Global Citizenship

Consider these illustrations of changes in everyday life that have occurred since the parents of today's students were students themselves:

- The CNN telecast we watch while sipping morning coffee is broadcast to over 115 million locations around the world. It might describe how scientists and military personnel of Russia and the United States are collaborating to dismantle nuclear warheads.
- The actions of an exploitative lumber company in one country can touch off a series of protests from rain forest activists worldwide.
- It is no longer possible to know where many products we buy were "made"—because components from different corners of the globe are assembled in yet another.
- With a personal computer, a modem, a telephone line, and the most rudimentary skills, we can communicate with social and political groups anywhere in the world on issues as diverse as gay/lesbian rights, economic development, and soil enhancement.

"Globalization" sums up a multitude of processes that touch all phases of life at the end of the twentieth century. In recent years, the increase in interaction across national borders has intensified dramatically not only for those engaged in international business, but also for ordinary people. For the first time in the modern nation-state system, a wide range of international actors involved in exchanges of information, goods, and services are bypassing national governments.

Even the long-standing mechanisms for linking people internationally for political or social actions are changing rapidly. At the level of "high politics," many international governmental organizations (IGOs) such as the United Nations and its agencies, which are formed by cooperative agreement among nation-states, are no longer simply extensions of national governments. They have become major transnational governing units addressing issues from peacekeeping to weather prediction.

But it is in the "low politics" of citizen movements that real changes have occurred. Before globalization, citizens had one model for non-violent political change: the democratic electoral and lobbying model. Now there are new ways for citizens to participate in politics and exert influence on their governments. Through transnational social movements (TSMOs) and international non-governmental organizations (INGOs), citizens are working behind the scenes in multiple ways to bring pressure on their own governments, to forge treaties, and to effect change. Diverse clusters of cosmopolitan change agents have been responsible for recent progress in arms control, environmental cleanup and protection, and human rights. These range from ad hoc networks of experts and concerned citizens to formal institutions.

This has occurred in the context of other trends that have transformed the relationship between the citizen and the nation-state, undermined traditional notions of sovereignty, and given new significance to the notion of global citizenship. Global economic processes now outpace the ability of national governments to harness them. Because of rapidly developing technology, national elites can no longer control the flow of communication—as Chinese leaders learned in 1989, when student dissidents used faxes and videos to keep the world abreast of the Tienanmen Square protests and repression.

When the Cold War ended, these trends diversified and intensified around the globe. The result has been a rare combination of processes: while global activities, organizations, and movements have expanded, local situations and norms have received increasing attention. The global and local trends have sometimes merged, at other times, diverged. Moreover, the processes of global peace and security are changing in ways that make global citizenship more central than ever before. How and why that has happened is the focus of this chapter.

We revisit the story that began in the first chapter of this volume, the dawn of the nuclear age. Some of the "atomic scientists" who developed the bomb became some of the first and most noteworthy global citizens of this era. They were a transnational group, many of them Europeans who fled Nazism to England and the United States. They were patriotically dedicated to defending against the Nazi threat; however, as soon as the dreadful implications of their work became apparent, many became part of what *Bulletin* founder Eugene Rabinowitch calls, in the first article in this chapter, "the conspiracy to preserve our civilization." This loyalty to humanity, above the bounds of nationality, is a mark of global citizenry.

That story is brought full circle in the last article of the volume, the 1995

Nobel Peace Prize acceptance speech delivered by Joseph Rotblat. Rotblat was the only scientist who walked away from the bomb project when he learned, in early 1945, that Germany's effort to develop an atomic bomb had stalled—and that Allied scientists were therefore working under false premises. Rotblat presides over the Pugwash Conferences, an international coalition of scientists that has been meeting since the 1950s to promote nuclear arms control and disarmament. Even during the most frigid stages of the Cold War, the Pugwash Conferences, which shared the 1995 award with Rotblat, included scientists from the Soviet Union.

The other essays address a range of influences on, and outlets for, global citizenship today. George Lopez and his colleagues examine the process of globalization and its implications for peace and security. Russian journalist Nadezhda Azhgikhina shows how the collapse of the Soviet Union led to a new women's movement in that country. Unlike the heavily ideological women's movement sanctioned by the communist regime, these spontaneous organizations often concentrate on local governance and improving their own lives. At the same time, they find much in common with women in other hard-pressed nations who work for peace and economic justice. Mary Kaldor—university professor and peace activist—documents how the European antinuclear movement of the early 1980s developed into a movement for a "civil society" throughout Europe by the end of the decade. The call for nuclear disarmament was combined with insistence on respect for human rights, and it was thoroughly transnational.

Many analysts believe the best example of what a broad-based, transnational citizens group can accomplish with time, energy, strategy, and commitment is the successful campaign to establish majority rule in South Africa. Jennifer Davis, a longtime activist in the anti-apartheid campaign, describes that multinational effort, which was based on a sophisticated strategy combining economic persuasion with coercion; lobbying of transnational corporations with lobbying of governments; and the control of investments with control of trade.

The chronological listing of Nobel Peace Prize winners from 1945 to 1996 illustrates how ordinary citizens can be agents of peace and change in their own locales and thereby have a global impact. The array of recipients also illustrates the interplay among arms control, peacekeeping, conflict resolution, and human rights in the building of a peaceful world.

VII.1 Scientists as Public Educators: 1945–50

EUGENE RABINOWITCH

The first issue of the *Bulletin of the Atomic Scientists* appeared on December 15, 1945. It was born of a combination of gloom and hope. Standing around under the first nuclear fire lit under the West Stands of the Athletic Field of the University of Chicago in December 1942, and, two-and-a-half years later, in July 1945, watching the flash of the first atomic bomb explosion at Alamogordo, the scientists had a vision of terrible clarity: They saw the cities of the world, including their own, falling into dust and going up in flames.

Some of us walked the streets of Chicago vividly imagining the sky suddenly lit by a giant fireball, the steel skeletons of skyscrapers bending into grotesque shapes and their masonry raining into the streets below, until a great cloud of dust rose and settled over the crumbling city.

From this vision arose the weak and inadequate attempts that groups of scientists made to stop the hands of the clock before it struck the first hour of the atomic age—the memoranda and petitions, asking that the use of the atomic bomb in the war against Japan be foregone. The news of the Hiroshima strike was a terrible blow to many who had contributed most toward making the atomic bomb possible; the news of the bombing of Nagasaki was received by an even larger group with dismay and gloom. To some of us, it seemed at that time that with this unimaginative and ruthless introduction of atomic energy to mankind, America had initiated a chain of events that would inexorably lead to the same fate visited, sooner or later, upon her own cities, and the cities of Europe.

Hope

A glimmer of hope appeared in the darkness. Was there not a chance—an off-side chance perhaps, but still a chance—that the fate of Hiroshima and Nagasaki would cause Man to turn a new leaf? Could we not spur this decision by buttonholing all who would listen and preaching to them our message of doom and our precept for survival: live in peace or perish? And did not atomic energy offer an incomparable chance for nations to become partners in a venture into uncharted new fields, instead of eternal competitors for the limited known wealth and power of the earth? The founding of the *Bulletin of the Atomic Scientists* was a part of the conspiracy to preserve our civilization by scaring men into rationality.

How often did we hear at that time that we were dreamers? Men wise in history, or practical politics, or proud of their common sense, told us that wars have always been—and will always be; that national and ideological enmities cannot be made to lapse simply because physicists have found that certain nuclei will fission in a chain reaction. The scientists were supposed to be so naive politically as to ignore this! They were also accused of not understanding that the Soviet Union is a totalitarian dictatorship, out to convert the world to its ideology, and, if opportunity appears, to conquer those who refuse to be converted; and that it was unrealistic, to say the least, to plan the development of atomic energy as a common enterprise with this dictatorial regime. As if we did not know this, too!

To a rational mind—and the scientific mind must try to remain rational even when dealing with the emotion-laden facts of social and international politics—it was clear at the time that overwhelming historical probability pointed to a new power contest, to be waged between the victors in the contest just won against Germany. The fact that one of the victors was a ruthless, totalitarian state, founded on a belief in the wickedness of the "capitalist" world outside its borders, and the inevitability of a mortal conflict with this world, made it obvious that to avoid the traditional clash between victorious allies would be even more difficult this time than in the past. The threat of atomic destruction, if not banished by some immediate settlement, was bound to make the contest more bitter and irrational than ever.

We knew all this, and yet we have tried to work against the all but inevitable trend, because we saw only too clearly what the consequence of letting this trend take its course would be. As time went on, the odds against success grew higher and higher. What was most likely to happen, happened. Men of common sense and of practical politics can be satisfied; the patient is steadily getting worse.

Failure

Scientists—whose profession requires a recognition of facts, however unpleasant—cannot but admit the fact that their campaign has failed. Even in America the success of their educational efforts fell far short of persuading the majority of the nation that with the emergence of atomic weapons the meaning of national security and national sovereignty, national sacrifice and national prosperity, had radically changed. Even more decisive in determining the failure has been the fact that all attempts scientists have made to establish contact with Russian colleagues have been in vain. Several dozen copies of the *Bulletin* regularly go to addresses in the Soviet Union; but we doubt if any Russian is permitted to read these copies, except agents gathering material for military intelligence or political propaganda.

[Years later, Soviet scientists reported that the *Bulletin* was highly valued in the Soviet underground and influenced Soviet moves toward arms control.—*Editors*]

Was there something American scientists could and should have done—and have left undone? Have they been too sparing in their efforts? Have they been wrong in trying to keep up with their professional work, and—with few exceptions—devoting only a small fraction of their time to the education of American people and their leaders in the "facts of life" of the atomic age? Should they have made less timid attempts to reach their Russian colleagues, enlisting, for this purpose, the public opinion of the free world? Should they have tried to mobilize the intellectuals of Europe and Asia for peace—instead of leaving this mobilization to Soviet agents and communist dupes? What would have been the result if they had adopted some spectacular methods of propaganda through mass action, such as a demonstration strike, or a refusal to do any military work?

Such radical plans have been occasionally suggested by individuals, but never seriously considered by responsible groups. It could not have been otherwise: Scientists are too individualistic for any concerted action of this kind; few of them have the temperament of political fighters.

The intrusion of scientists into public affairs undoubtedly has produced some undesirable results. It has made, in some instances, for more and not less passion and confusion, and has made some rational solutions more and not less difficult.

The popular and congressional backing of the concept that American military planning should be based on atomic weapons, and the vociferous popular support for the President's decision to go "all-out" for the development of the hydrogen bomb—both decisions of doubtful strategic soundness—have been expressions of the same "half-educated" public opinion.

The Soviet propaganda for the prohibition of atomic weapons would never have achieved the success it has achieved in many countries of the West, if scientists had not convinced so many people that atomic weapons are in a different class from all the other implements of war. The emphasis scientists have put on the destructive potentialities of atomic weapons has permitted communist propaganda to shift the moral indignation of thousands of well-meaning people from aggressive war, and the mass extermination of civilian populations as such, to the one weapon whose threat now restrains the Soviet Union.

While trying to frighten men into rationality, scientists have frightened many into fear or blind hatred. This was inevitable. The question is whether, in the final reckoning, the despair and confusion which scientists have helped to create will prove to be more significant than the understanding of the impact of modern science and technology (and of atomic energy, in particular) on the world political situation that we have been able to impart to those—in America and elsewhere—who are able to face the facts, and to act rationally to meet the challenge. These are the men on whom free society must depend to organize its defenses without sacrificing its basic principles of individual freedom and responsibility; to match the relentless drive of totalitarianism by an all-out defense mobilization of the industrial and military potential of the free world.

These men will have to find a way to organize peace on a permanent, stable basis, to keep the competition between national, political, and economic interests, and the clash of conflicting ideologies within limits set by a world law; and to provide the framework for the rational utilization of world resources for the benefit of all mankind, so as to assuage the social and national unrest that breeds in hunger and poverty.

Whatever little scientists have done in the last five years to help form the minds of such future leaders, and to influence the feelings and ideas of the thousands who will have to support these leaders if their efforts are to succeed through a democratic process, is the justification of our efforts. This is also the only reason why we do not think we should cease these efforts now, when we have so manifestly failed in our first purpose—to stop the trend toward war by bringing West and East together in an organization dedicated to the prevention of an atomic arms race and the development of atomic energy for the benefit of all mankind.

Patience

While the present emergency continues—and it may continue for many years—scientists—and others who think in terms of rational reorganization of the world—will have to be patient and humble. For the time being they will have to be content with contributing to the solution of day-to-day problems. In every choice American policies will have to make, scientists should be able to contribute important arguments that may escape those not fully and continuously aware of the implication of scientific progress for the problems at hand.

Because of this possible contribution to the formation of national and local policies, the continued political activities of scientists will remain worthwhile even in the dark years ahead, when the dominant question will be, how to avoid defeat in the already raging power contest, and, if and when this problem is successfully solved, how to terminate this power contest without resort to the ultimate irrationality of war.

In the background of their minds, giving direction to their thinking on all the practical decisions at hand, scientists, more than anybody else, should and, we believe, will preserve the fundamental conviction, born of close acquaintance with the powers liberated by modern science for the destruction of mankind or for its progress toward greater security and freedom: the conviction that mankind is ready and must be willing to terminate the endless sequences of wars, and to create new forms of social organization under which the limitless human capacities for effort and sacrifice will be directed in a rational way toward constructive ends.

This is adapted from the January 1951 *Bulletin*.

VII.2 The Global Tide

GEORGE A. LOPEZ, JACKIE G. SMITH, AND RON PAGNUCCO

In the 1970s, babies in Third World nations were dying when they might have been thriving. The apparent culprit: ersatz mother's milk made from powder. The Nestlé Company, a Swiss-based multinational, had identified Third World mothers as a high-growth marketing opportunity. Nestlé baby formula was aggressively pushed as the "modern" way to feed infants.

In the developed world, baby formula works fine. It may not be as good as mother's milk, but it's reasonably close. As long as the bottles and rubber nipples for the formula are properly sterilized, the mixing water reasonably pure, and the mixing proportions right, babies do well on it.

But in Third World villages in the 1970s, pure water was the exception, not the rule, and the need for sterilization was hard to explain and seldom practiced. Beyond that, the formula was cheap by First World standards, but expensive by Third World reckonings. That made it fatally tempting to stretch the powder by diluting it too much, thus degrading the nutritional value.

Health care professionals and missionaries working in the Third World were outraged, and they communicated their sadness and anger to Nestlé, which did nothing, and to governments, which didn't seem to care. Nestlé had threatened no nation's security, broken no laws.

But nutritionists and activists in the industrialized world did care, and condemnation of Nestlé's marketing practices became widespread. As word got out, the cause was taken up by nearly 100 private organizations in 65 nations. A transnational economic boycott of Nestlé products was launched, coordinated by a U.S.-based transnational citizen coalition, the Infant Formula Action Committee (INFACT).

Whether the boycott had much economic effect on Nestlé's bottom line is hard to pin down. But it became a public relations nightmare for a company that liked to be known for its warm and cuddly hot chocolate and its candy-counter Crunch bars. The INFACT-led transnational campaign ultimately forced Nestlé to abandon its Third World marketing practices, and it also led to the passage in 1981 of a World Health Organization code of conduct governing the marketing and sale of infant formula.

The Nestlé boycott was arguably the first activist campaign of its type. It attracted cross-border participants who organized outside traditional diplomatic or political channels in an attempt to accomplish reform in an area outside the immediate interests of international politics. The success of the boycott, and the apparent influence of two other transnational movements of the early 1980s—the campaign against the deployment of intermediate-range missiles in Europe and the divestment campaign to end apartheid in South Africa—have inspired citizen groups around the world to organize around common cross-national interests.

Transnational social movements are one aspect of "globalization"—a term pundits use to describe the rapidly increasing cross-border economic, social, and political interactions that are not originated by national governments.

Although theorists argue about when the trend toward globalization began, few would deny that the process has been accelerating for more than two decades.

Phase 1: Interdependence

It was in the 1970s that Americans discovered—with a jolt—that the world's economy had become highly interdependent. In 1971, President Richard Nixon withdrew the dollar from the gold standard. From then on, the dollar floated against other currencies, thus facilitating—in theory—worldwide free trade.

When the Organization of Petroleum Exporting Countries (OPEC) restricted oil production and distribution in 1973, it sent a series of shock waves through Western economies. The OPEC oil embargo demonstrated that the Western nations had become shockingly vulnerable to external pressure, and their governments could do little about it.

At first, only the economies of advanced industrial states were thought to be closely interconnected, but when the entire world felt the effects of the debt crises in developing countries in the post-OPEC world, opinions were revised.

Phase 2: Intensification

Danish analysts Hans-Henrik Holm and Georg Sørensen define globalization as the intensification of economic, social, and political interaction across national boundaries. Noting the dramatic increase that has occurred in both the breadth and depth of cross-border activity, they label the 1970s the decade of interdependence, and the 1980s the decade of intensification.

Superpower détente was one of the conditions that favored the increase in transnational activities that began in the mid-1970s. International contacts were no longer limited to diplomats or globe-trotting businessmen. And many of the issues that stimulated new transnational associations went beyond the political-economic and military-security issues that states traditionally concerned themselves with.

In the social and political spheres, it was becoming clear that many modern social problems were not confined within boundaries, nor did ways of dealing with issues like human rights, refugees, and environmental concerns fit neatly with notions of national sovereignty. Many of those committed to solving modern social problems were citizen-activists unaffiliated with their governments.

In the 1980s, as national leaders continued to initiate state policies and administer them through traditional diplomatic avenues, a new and diverse set of international actors gradually made their appearance in matters of "low politics," as dealing with the environment, human rights, and related issues came to be called.

The decline in price and the widening distribution of personal computers, fax machines, and modems meant that private citizens in one corner of the world could communicate readily with others in another corner of the world. It became nearly impossible for governments to prevent the transmission of information by jamming broadcasts, instituting embargoes, or other means of control. Human rights activists and academics were among the first to grasp that computer networks and fax machines were "technologies of freedom" that could be used to enhance democracy.

Agents of Change

To Robert Keohane of Harvard University, "globalization is fundamentally a social process, not one that is technologically predetermined." Keohane argues that the global economy and new communications technologies are necessary components of globalization, but they do not alone explain global social change. The critical component is the growing number of individuals with a transnational conscience who are committed to solving the pressing social and political problems of our age.

The aspirations and motives of these individuals differ from those of the international business community, as well as from those of their governments. And the activities of these private citizens are now changing the way citizens and the state relate to one another, and how each relates to the international political arena.

Of course, some mechanisms linking political and social activists outside the governments of nation-states have been with us for some time. International organizations have been created as extensions to international agreements. The oldest of these groups, the International Labor Organization, and the newer organizations created within the U.N. family, are institutions that began as agents of national governments.

Since World War II, the progress made on complex and sensitive issues such as arms control, environmental cleanup, and human rights has increasingly involved the efforts of transnational groups ranging from ad hoc networks of experts and concerned citizens to these more formal institutions.

Stifled by the unwillingness of nations and international governmental organizations to share decision-making, and frustrated by the failure of political institutions to bring about reform, activists began to form their own cross-border coalitions in the 1970s and 1980s. As noted earlier, three of these movements—the Nestlé boycott, the anti-apartheid campaign for South Africa, and the campaign against nuclear missile deployment in Europe—inspired, and continue to inspire, transnational social organizations today. The influence of these "non-governmental organizations"—or NGOs as they are called—should not be ignored. And these groups now number in the tens of thousands.

"Tiz-moes" Do It Best

More than any other social or political entity, transnational social movement organizations—TSMOs, or "tiz-moes"—may be the fullest embodiment of globalization. The majority of TSMOs are coalitions or formal federations of national or regional non-governmental organizations. While some TSMOs, such as the International Fellowship of Reconciliation, have been promoting peace and security issues for most of this century, most are new to the global arena. Some 94 percent of all TSMOs were formed after 1945,

A TSMO at work: A health worker from CARE inoculates a Bolivian baby. *CARE photo by Carolyn Watson*

and their numbers have doubled since the early 1980s. Today, there are nearly 600.

A significant proportion of TSMOs are organizations of professionals committed to global betterment—Medicins Sans Frontières (Doctors Without Borders), for instance. There is even a TSMO—and an increasingly influential one, at that—for legislators, Parliamentarians Global Action. The organization has 900 members from more than 74 nations, and through its newsletter, meetings, and briefing kits, it works for enlightened policies on disarmament and security issues.

TSMOs provide the organizational structures needed for mobilizing disparate peoples who share a common political agenda. They engage in education, lobbying, and the framing of issues in ways that would not be open to citizen groups, were they to work through the diplomatic services of their own nation-states. On human rights and environmental issues, TSMOs have played major roles in the drafting of resolutions and legal conventions for consideration by nation-state delegates to the United Nations and other international forums. Beyond that, they are widely regarded as reliable monitors of national compliance with international codes and legal agreements. In short, TSMOs are a fundamental element of a new and yet to be fully defined global governance structure that is now emerging.

Good or Not So Good?

Whether the rise of transnational agents of change benefits all humanity equally is open to debate, in part because the effects of globalization are not evenly distributed, and in part because the hub of globalization is in the West.

One concern about globalization is raised by those opposed to the dominance of Western ways of thinking and organizing. Sometimes we imagine that all critics of Western culture resemble the most extreme portrayals of Islamic fundamentalists presented in the Western news media. But even in cultures friendly to the West, concerns are expressed about the singular lens through which the "desirable" political, economic, and social life is portrayed in the global media. At its best, globalization should produce a synthesis of cultural views, not the triumph of one over all others.

Unfortunately, even in transnational movements that are committed to peace and justice, the goal of cultural synthesis is more frequently expressed than realized. More than three-quarters of transnational citizen groups are headquartered in Geneva, where these organizations have ready access to the U.N. community. At some point, however, more organizations should probably be located in Nairobi, Lima, or New Delhi.

A number of Western-based citizen-activists carry with them a set of assumptions that has little relevance to problems "on the ground." Often they compound the problems caused by their initial bias with a less-than-adequate willingness to listen to local groups' approaches to the problems at hand. Even old hands at transnational organizations sometimes show less sensitivity to local expertise than might be expected. Apologists say that, like their official diplomatic counterparts, many "issue and network" experts simply were not prepared for the press of work that has come their way since 1989, when the Berlin Wall came down and the Cold War ended. Many of yesterday's activists are today globe-trotting consultants—on environmental issues, human rights monitoring and advocacy, or nonviolence and conflict resolution. They had little time to prepare for their new roles.

These problems may reflect the growing pains of the transnational movement, but they provide ample ammunition to local factions who are only too willing to reject efforts to protect human rights, campaigns for demilitarization, or sustainable development under the guise of rejecting Western imperialism.

Globalization's greatest strength lies in its potential to improve the economic, social, and political life of all people. But globalization should unfold in ways that allow local groups to participate as equal partners. They are the resident change agents who understand the opportunities and obstacles in their own local-global nexus.

Globalization, Politics, and Peace

Before globalization, the single non-violent route to political change involved citizens petitioning their local and national leaders for the changes they desired. Now, through transnational organizations, citizens can bring political pressure on national officials from two new directions.

"Lateral" pressure may be applied through NGOs in other countries, especially through those organizations based in countries where the "home" government is favorably disposed to the desired change.

"Downward" pressure may be exerted by transnational organizations. This occurs most often when these organizations have successfully appealed to other transnational institutions about the lack of compliance with global norms or commitments. As more private citizens in many nations take advantage of these options, it will have profound implications.

Despite the new tools that private citizens can use to influence governments, it would be wrong to conclude that the nation-state will be a less critical actor in international relations. The emergence of citizens with a transnational conscience does not guarantee that broad social movements or international non-governmental organizations will continue to thrive. These associations may be expected to be part of the changing order, but, as Keohane points out, they are still dependent on the willingness of nation-states to empower them with resources and to allow them to enter into many areas that traditionally have been the province of sovereign states. What the global citizen movements have produced is a redefined equation for how issue-based politics may be pursued and a consensus reached.

One of the most compelling questions asked about globalization is whether it will lead to a truly global civil society, which many believe is the key to world peace.

Both in reality and in its prescriptive allure, globalization is appealing. But its long-term consequences are the subject of spirited debate. Some analysts, like John Naisbitt, predict that one outcome will be more direct democracy at the local level. Others, like international relations expert James Rosenau, believe that globalization is already being counterbalanced by other forces. Rosenau asserts that globalization brings with it its own self-correcting, if not countervailing, tendencies, such as fragmentation and localism. For every pressure that pushes people to be or do the same things—to "act globally"—there is a distinctly local counterpressure. For example, the former superpowers and their citizens may seek new forms of global security, but local rivalries, hatreds, and wars continue.

Those whose working framework is "think globally, act locally" probably believe that Rosenau has missed the forest for the trees. What he considers a tension or a contradiction, globalist-localists are likely to see as synergy and mutual reinforcement. They believe that the transnational movements have become so powerful, and the benefits of affiliation so clear, that many groups with strictly local problems now reach out to global organizations first, because a global strategy is more likely to produce results. Today, for example, if the population living near New York's Love Canal faced the same environmental problems they encountered 20 years ago, many local citizens would be likely to seek to enlist the aid of international environmental groups like Greenpeace, Friends of the Earth, and the Natural Resources Defense Council before lobbying the New York State legislature or suing the local companies that dumped chemicals in the area.

Because citizen action is now global, there are new ways of doing politics and, as always, political structures must be adapted to economic and social change. Interdependence in the 1970s revealed the porous nature of borders. Intensification in the 1980s revealed the see-through nature of sovereignty. The 1990s may be regarded as the decade of intentionality, a time when those inclined to think globally have routes for action that were never before available.

The availability of new routes of action means that recruitment and membership in existing transnational organizations should increase dramatically, and the rate at which new groups are formed will also increase. Those who share a sense of global citizenship will be free to participate in a wide range of regional and global political and social entities.

This is adapted from the July/August 1995 *Bulletin*.

VII.3 A Movement Is Born

NADEZHDA AZHGIKHINA

In 1990, in the midst of perestroika, an American colleague asked me about the future of feminism in the new, democratic Russia. Without hesitation, I told her that feminism had no future whatsoever in my country—that women's problems had been solved long ago, in Lenin's time, by the earliest Soviet decrees. I told her that, if anything, Soviet women suffered from an excess of the rights Western feminists were fighting for, and that they would be happy to share their excess of independence with others.

My acquaintance tried to argue with me. She talked about the difficulties of life for women in the Soviet Union, the existence of international women's organizations, and their various initiatives like working for peace. I replied that the main task of the new democratic forces in Russia was not to single out women, retirees, or the handicapped from the rest of the citizens, but to achieve real freedom of speech and real democracy. I told her that as far as international initiatives were concerned, we had only to elect a wise government from the ranks of the democratic intelligentsia. That government would then make well-considered decisions on domestic and foreign affairs.

And of course, I continued, everything would be all right when we got a real market economy, which would bring the prosperity and renewal we deserved.

In other words, I repeated to my American colleague every cliché of perestroika that all members of the Soviet intelligentsia with more or less liberal inclinations whole-heartedly believed. Especially the part about the renewal that a market economy would bring on its young wings.

"State Woman"

Of course, there was a women's movement before perestroika—the official women's movement, born with the Soviet system. It was closely connected to the Communist Party and it followed party ideology. It was financed by the government, answered to the government, and functioned in ways similar to other Soviet structures. Naturally, wives and other relatives of Soviet apparatchiks served at the headquarters of the Committee of Soviet Women. Members of the committee enjoyed the same advantages as the rest of the Soviet *nomenklatura*: food from special shops not accessible to ordinary citizens, vacations at prestigious resorts, and trips abroad.

Like other official Soviet organizations, the Committee of Soviet Women had branches in all regions of the country. It maintained a close relationship with all the women's committees of workers' unions and collectives. The committee helped to keep in place the women's *nomenklatura*. By law, a third of all deputies had to be women, and those who served in various elected bodies as representatives of the Soviet people were selected from among the ranks of the official women's organizations.

It should be no surprise that the Committee of Soviet Women was not popular among the intelligentsia—or with any other sensible person. The image of the "state woman" originated with a famous phrase of Lenin's in which he said that, in the Soviet state, every cook (a feminine noun in Russian) had to know how to rule. "State woman" represented the interests of the *nomenklatura* and the ruling party, not the interests of ordinary women, whose lives were very difficult in Soviet times. In response, an alternative female ideal—that of a completely apolitical woman concerned only with family matters—became very popular in Soviet society.

Freedom—to Despair

During perestroika, the intelligentsia in Moscow and Leningrad began to pay some attention to feminist ideas, in part because of the increased access to West European and American theoretical works on the topic. Women philosophers read Simone de Beauvoir and Gloria Steinem; women linguists and art critics discussed and translated the works of Julia Kristeva and Ann Isaac. However, these efforts were intellectual and elitist, and feminist ideas did not gain tremendous popularity or exposure.

The end of perestroika and the introduction of market reform, with all its ensuing problems, altered the situation profoundly. Life became more difficult every day, especially for women. Russia's 1992 census revealed that more than 70 percent of the country's unemployed were women, and that did not include hidden unemployment or those women who failed to register at labor exchanges.

In pre-perestroika years, women's wages were approximately 70 percent of

New freedoms for women in Russia bring a combination of hardship and opportunity, and a rediscovery of traditional culture. A women's folk choir greets an important Western businessman in the snow outside Moscow. *Mark Shteinbock*

men's; by the early 1990s, the percentage had fallen to 40. Only 5 percent of the new entrepreneurs were women, and only 7 percent of elected officials were women.

As it turned out, it was extremely difficult to include women in the new economy. New entrepreneurs preferred to hire men. Business schools and other professional courses also exhibited a marked preference for men. In the classified sections of the papers, ads for lawyers or accountants for new enterprises commonly specified that "only men need apply."

About 15 percent of all Russian mothers are unmarried; they were especially affected by the new economic realities. Consumer services, which were already miserable in Soviet times, broke down completely. Health care and primary education met the same fate. The chief victims of this breakdown again were women. The feminization of poverty in the country led to sub-standard living conditions for many children. Today, more than 40 percent of Russian children reportedly live in poverty.

Taking Charge

But out of this desperation, a new women's movement was born, despite the overwhelming prejudice of the former Soviet people to all types of supposedly social organizations and coerced "cooperation." The first to come together were women who were suffering most from economic hardship—the unemployed and women who anticipated the loss of their jobs. These groups appeared primarily in cities and in regions with large concentrations of the defense industries that have traditionally employed a significant number of women.

With the conversion of some defense industries, and the general reduction of production in others, these women were the first candidates for the unemployment line. In response, they began to organize data banks of job vacancies and business schools, and they sought out economic experts to help them start their own enterprises and companies. They opened clubs for women's initiatives and mental health centers. It is a mystery how they have managed to do all this without government aid. I suppose action came from the knowledge that no one would do it if they didn't do it themselves.

When they come to Russia, Western activists always want to meet "the new feminist elite." Yet the strongest and most interesting groups in Russia are not involved with theory, but with the pressing economic and social problems of the day.

These groups include unions of mothers of soldiers (who in the middle of the Chechen conflict somehow found a way to go to Chechnya and arrange an exchange of imprisoned and wounded soldiers), groups that deal with aid to retirees and the handicapped, organizations of university women, women facing defense conversion, and many others.

These local women's groups have learned how to work efficiently, and how to set and fulfill specific, realizable goals—skills the Russian government would do well to emulate. As a result, in some towns and provinces they have acquired authority and have a real influence on policymaking. Leaders of the new generation are emerging from among their ranks.

One group of women in particular has been my personal inspiration. My colleagues and I organized a meeting of non-governmental organizations in Sergiev Posad, a small town near Moscow. Participants came from Sergiev Posad and nearby villages. A group from one small village was especially interesting. It was made up of refugees from different conflict zones of the former Soviet territory: Central Asia, Azerbaijan, the northern Caucasus.

These women of different nationalities and religions, who had lived through tragedy and disaster, had been resettled, some with their families, in the remote village of Samotovino, "where a sober man had not been seen since the First Coming."

Most of these women were professionals with university degrees—engineers, teachers, and journalists. Unable to work at their professions, they managed to find some kind of work. Then they proceeded to work together to create some semblance of normal life for themselves and their families. They established a club and began to have social gatherings and musical evenings. They arranged to have performances at the local school.

The inhabitants of Samotovino, who had long ago stopped expecting anything new in life, began to notice a decline in the consumption of vodka, an increase in the construction of new homes, and even the revival of the chorus at the old "club of culture." The natives describe the effect the newcomers have had on their lives very simply: "These refugees have been for us what the Decembrists were for Siberia."

A Broader Meaning

It may seem that these examples are isolated, particular—that they have nothing to do with high-stakes politics or solving global problems.

But if we look closely at some of the world's most significant political developments of the past several years, and at their contexts, the activities of the women's groups I have cited are not as isolated as they may seem.

For instance, before the peace agreement between Israel and the Palestinians was signed, Palestinian and Israeli women's organizations invested many years of ground-breaking work to create an emotional space conducive to future political dialogue. These women conducted a number of very difficult meetings—between wives of leaders, members of political groups, activists, and ordinary concerned citizens.

Not everyone recognizes that the meetings helped to create an atmosphere of peace, but they established precedents for the future. These Israeli and Palestinian women also managed to humanize complicated political issues by debating them with one another and with their families at home. Although it would be an exaggeration to say that the efforts of these women brought peace, their contribution should not be underestimated.

Their dialogue became especially real for me during a roundtable discussion, "Transcaucasian Women's Dialogue," which brought together women from Georgia, Armenia, and Azerbaijan—countries torn by ethnic conflict and civil war. That meeting this year was the first of its kind: a discussion between women of those regions and Russian women and journalists.

The conversation was extremely difficult. But statements of resentment and pain were followed by insistent expressions of the need for dialogue, and the desire to look for solutions together. The participants did not stop at agreeing on the need for a sustainable dialogue or "future cooperation." They proposed to start with action—creating centers for the child victims of the ethnic conflict from the three republics, and organizing an information clearinghouse on peacekeeping initiatives and the women's groups involved in conflict resolution.

The group included deputies, leaders of political blocs, scientists, writers, and ordinary women who never thought they would become involved in a social movement. But these women from the Caucasus realized that if they didn't initiate the dialogue—if they didn't start building new bridges where the old ones had been burnt—no one would.

Diplomacy has been a domain from which women have been excluded for centuries. But women possess a number of qualities that allow them to find solutions when men can't.

Women truly hear out the other party, whether that party is their child or an opponent. Their problem solving is geared to finding compromises, not escalating a conflict with pride and posturing.

And the amazing thing is that this is what is happening in the former Soviet Union, and without party decrees. Women, who a few years ago couldn't agree, and wouldn't have separated themselves from the destructive forces that have turned their countries into bleeding "hot spots," are coming together today to create a new fabric of life, to insure the future of their children.

They understand that war and the political ambitions of the new reformers of their countries are infinitely removed from their interests. If you called them feminists, they might still be insulted. What they are tackling is survival, but in the process they are working together as women. They have come together with their common sense and the willingness to accept one another. They have come together outside the traditional political structures of power. And they will effect change.

This is adapted from the July/August 1995 *Bulletin*.

VII.4 The Revolutions of 1989

MARY KALDOR

There is something strange about the way the 1989 revolutions in Eastern Europe have been interpreted in the West. It is said there were no new ideas—that the people who gathered in the streets of East European cities simply wanted to live like their Western counterparts. The revolutions have been treated as spontaneous outbursts, as though they had no history.

But commentators who hold this point of view—people like Francis Fukuyama, Jeffrey Sachs, and Ralf Dahrendorf—had little involvement in Eastern Europe before 1989. (Timothy Garton Ash is an honorable exception.) Their opinions have prevailed because the "experts" on Eastern Europe were discredited when they failed to predict the revolutions, and those who took part in the revolutions were too busy constructing new democracies to write about their experiences.

In fact, the 1989 revolutions had a history and were responsible for new ideas. One of the most important was the idea of transnational civil society that emerged from the intensive dialogue between West European peace movements and the developing peace and human rights groups in Eastern Europe. The West's failure to grasp the significance of this idea is one reason for its inability to come to grips with the challenges of the post–Cold War world.

The role of peace movements in shaking the status quo in Europe seems to have been more or less written out of accounts of the 1980s. In the early 1980s, the peace movement in the West was considerably larger than the movements that eventually toppled the East European regimes. Five million people demonstrated in the capitals of Western Europe in 1981 and 1983. The movement was unprecedented in scale and in its transnational character.

The immediate stimulus to the 1980s peace movement was NATO's decision to deploy a new generation of nuclear missiles in Europe. Together with the Soviet invasion of Afghanistan, this decision marked the beginning of what became known as the "new Cold War."

The new Cold War followed a period of détente that culminated in the 1975 Helsinki Accords. A new generation of West Europeans, now free to travel in Eastern Europe, no longer feared a Soviet invasion nor felt they needed an American military presence. At the same time, they were more acutely aware of the reality of Soviet oppression in Eastern Europe than earlier generations.

The new Cold War seemed like a return to the 1950s in terms of the nuclear threat and the fate of East Europeans. As one young Hungarian put it, "I am against Reagan's nuclear policies, not because I am afraid of dying in a nuclear war, but because I am afraid of a return to the 1950s with closed borders. That would be unbearable."

What made the peace movement of the 1980s different from earlier movements was the explicit link between peace, and democracy and human rights. E. P. Thompson, the eminent historian whose writings inspired the new movement, called for a transcontinental movement of citizens. The Euro-

Peaceful demonstrations led to the revolutionary changes in Eastern Europe—and eventually to the downfall of the Soviet Union. In 1990, Moldovan nationalists called for a general strike to insure justice and independence from Russia. *Mark Shteinbock*

pean Nuclear Disarmament (END) Appeal of 1980, signed by millions of people all over Europe, called on its signatories, who included Vaclav Havel, Olof Palme, and George Konrad, not to "be loyal to East or West, but to each other." From the beginning, this new movement sought links with individual dissidents and groups in Eastern Europe.

Something parallel was happening in Eastern Europe. The period of détente gave rise to new forms of opposition. The most important new movement was Solidarity in Poland. But other groups, like Charter 77 in Czechoslovakia and the Democratic Opposition in Hungary, were also significant. The starting point for Charter 77 was the Helsinki Accords and the commitment to human rights contained in the Final Agreement.

The initial dialogue between Eastern and Western movements was characterized by deep suspicion. The East's suspicions were admirably recorded in "Anatomy of Reticence," an essay by Havel that was addressed to the West European peace movements. With the word "peace" divested of meaning by its use in Soviet propaganda, peace activists were widely regarded as agents of the Kremlin. Western peace activists, for their part, found it hard to cope with Eastern enthusiasm for Ronald Reagan and Margaret Thatcher.

Gradually, these suspicions were dispelled. The fact that Western peace activists were prepared to risk arrest and expulsion was important in the development of mutual trust. A turning point came with the Prague Appeal, addressed to the END Convention of 1985, in which Charter 77 called for a bloc-free Europe and the removal of weapons of mass destruction.

Solidarity leaders like Janusz Onyskiewicz and Jacek Kuron attended END conventions, and Polish writer Adam Michnik publicly acknowledged the importance of the peace movement and transnational links among social movements. For Western peace activists, supporting the struggle for democracy in Eastern Europe came to be seen not just as a tactical maneuver—a way to convince people in the West that peace activists were not pro-Soviet—but as an end in itself, and the most realistic strategy for overcoming the Cold War and bringing about nuclear disarmament.

Even more important than the shift in opinion was the emergence of a new generation of peace and human rights groups in the East. These young people were greatly influenced by Solidarity. But they also were influenced by the peace movement, especially its culture, and by the notion that peace offered a potentially acceptable space in which to organize independently.

The earliest movements were the Dialogue group in Hungary and Swords into Ploughshares in East Germany, which sprang up under the umbrella of the Protestant churches. "We watched your demonstrations and we thought, why can't we do it here?" said Pastor Rainier Eppelmann. "It was very important that you visited us and talked to us." When the missiles were first deployed in 1983, both of these movements were crushed.

In the late 1980s, other movements developed. In Poland, Freedom and Peace, a movement of young men who refused to swear allegiance to the Warsaw Pact or to join the Polish army, pioneered new forms of theatrical political action and argued that they took non-violence seriously (to Solidarity, non-violence was only a tactic). The Independent Peace Association was formed in Czechoslovakia. In Hungary, a new West–East dialogue group was created that later became the Association of Young Democrats. Out of this dialogue there emerged a new discourse and a new practice.

Those of us engaged in the peace movement in the West found that East European intellectuals were articulating ideas that expressed what we ourselves were trying to do. Their ideas about how to confront the totalitarian character of modern states as well as their concepts of civil society and anti-politics seemed both new and relevant.

In the peace movement, we had always argued that our aim was not to capture power, but to change the relationship between state and society, to create an environment in which states were more responsive to independent political debate. We always said that we would win when our ideas were adopted, not when our people achieved power positions.

What the East Europeans meant by civil society was not just the eighteenth-century concept of the rule of law (which was how it was interpreted by orthodox Western commentators), but the notion that self-organized groups, movements, and institutions can limit the power of the state by constructing a democratic space independent of the state. Adam Michnik first expounded this theory in "The New Evolutionism," an essay written in 1978. Anti-politics, as developed by Vaclav Havel and George Konrad, meant a non-political space in which public affairs could be discussed honestly and openly without self-interested concerns about power. The dialogue with the peace movement added a European and transnational dimension to these concepts.

By the 1980s, the impossibility of closing societies off to the outside world was becoming evident. Trade, travel, and communication increasingly eroded the efforts of East European countries to insulate their societies from foreign influence. Links at the level of civil society helped to provide the independent space that movements in both East and West needed. For the Western groups, links with East Europeans helped to establish their integrity, to demonstrate once and for all that they were not agents of the Kremlin. The endless pressure West European peace activists brought to bear on East European officials and the Western publicity they achieved for East European movements helped to protect these new movements and their activities. For example, the Dialogue group in Hungary was allowed to exist because Western peace activists convinced Hungarian officials that the existence of an independent peace movement in the East would help in the campaign against new missile deployments. After the missiles were deployed, the group was broken up.

The ideas expressed in difficult meetings and confrontations with officials slowly had an impact on official thinking. "It's like water dripping on a stone," one Soviet official told me privately after a particularly disheartening and unpleasant meeting. But after Mikhail Gorbachev came to power, the impact became evident in "new thinking."

It was the very groups and individuals who had been engaged in the dialogue that were to organize and inspire the 1989 revolutions. The revolutions had a history. They would not have been possible without the emergence of those groups and individuals who had developed the capacity to mobilize.

Those of us who were engaged in the dialogue knew that change was on the way in Eastern Europe. By the spring of 1989, it was clear that Solidarity would be legalized in Poland and that there would be a multi-party system in Hungary. Something was bound to happen in Czechoslovakia and East Germany, although it was less clear what it would be.

Everyone was surprised by the swiftness of the revolutions, but not by the fact that they took place. That we were more aware of what was happening than the "experts" or the politicians was not due to the fact that we were cleverer or had some special insight. The experts studied the behavior of governments; we got our information from intellectuals and non-governmental groups. They regarded the states as independent actors. We put more emphasis on political processes, on the way in which the behavior of states reflected changes in the relationship between states and societies.

This is adapted from the July/August 1995 *Bulletin*.

VII.5 Squeezing Apartheid

JENNIFER DAVIS

In 1959, Albert Luthuli, then president of the African National Congress, urged the international community to impose an economic boycott of South Africa to "precipitate the end of the hateful system of apartheid." South Africa's white-controlled economy was potentially very vulnerable to economic sanctions because it relied heavily on foreign capital. In the late nineteenth century, capital for the first growth industries, diamond and gold mining, came from Britain and Europe. U.S. capital arrived later, after World War II, and played a key role as manufacturing assumed increasing importance. In general, the 1960s and 1970s were boom years for the South African economy. From 1964 to 1974, foreign investment contributed 8 percent of the country's gross domestic investment. Foreign investment averaged 14 percent during the first five years of the 1970s and peaked at 24.5 percent in 1975–76, before collapsing to 2 percent during the unrest after Steve Biko was killed in 1977.

Foreign investment brought with it technical expertise. Some economists attributed much of South Africa's annual growth during the 1960s and 1970s (which averaged 4.5 percent and sometimes topped 5.5 percent) to this infusion of technical know-how. South African whites enjoyed a rapidly rising standard of living, a benefit denied to the country's black population.

By 1981, U.S. direct investment totaled more than $2.6 billion, nearly triple the book value of investments made during the previous decade. U.S. investors, like other foreign investors, had been drawn to South Africa by very high rates of return—29 percent in 1980 and 19 percent in 1981, several percentage points higher than the average rates of return worldwide.

When the U.N. General Assembly passed its 1962 resolution calling for a ban on exports to or imports from South Africa, three countries—Britain, the United States, and Japan—were absorbing 50 percent of South African exports; West Germany, Belgium, France, and Italy accounted for an additional 25 percent. South Africa's import sources were similarly concentrated. In 1966, Britain, the United States, West Germany, and Japan accounted for 62 percent of South Africa's total imports; Britain alone accounted for 28 percent.

Twenty years later, a report by the U.S. General Accounting Office revealed a very similar pattern. Most of South Africa's foreign trade was still with the United States, Britain, West Germany, France, Italy, and Japan. These countries sold South Africa 79 percent of its $8.2 billion worth of imports and bought 78 percent of its $12.4 billion worth of exports.

South Africa imports heavy machinery and high-tech goods like computers, chemicals, and oil. It exports raw materials, mainly minerals, and some agricultural products. Gold has always played a key trading role, often accounting for 40–50 percent of foreign exchange earnings. The fall in the price of gold from an annual average price of $613 an ounce in 1980 (and a high of $800 an ounce in 1984) to an average price hovering in the $350 range caused considerable pain.

Citizens Step In

As repression intensified in South Africa throughout the 1960s and 1970s, proponents of sanctions argued for international mandatory sanctions. However, only the U.N. Security Council had the power to impose mandatory economic, diplomatic, and cultural sanctions, as provided in Chapter VII of the U.N. Charter, and the three Western nations that are permanent members of the Security Council vetoed all such efforts. In 1977 these powers finally agreed to impose a mandatory arms embargo, but they continued to block all economic action.

It was left to citizens of the Western countries to take up the issue, and increasingly they did so, in a great variety of ways. The breadth of these campaigns and the long-term involvement of many thousands of people in an incredibly drawn-out struggle not directly their own is the more remarkable because it was achieved in the face of great obstacles. The media reported little on South Africa and less on anti-apartheid actions in small towns in Europe and North America.

There were anti-apartheid movements in all countries doing business with South Africa. Strong challenges were mounted to the British banks that stood at the center of South Africa's capital market. From the Netherlands, home of Shell Oil, which did considerable business with South Africa, came the impetus and direction for a powerful international "Boycott Shell" campaign. In many countries consumer boycotts were organized against easily identifiable products like South Africa–produced Outspan oranges.

In the United States, early protest after the Sharpeville massacre in 1960 focused on the consortium of 10 banks—led by Chase Manhattan—that provided South Africa with $40 million in rescue loans, thus making available funds to compensate for capital leaving the country because of political brutality. There were few easily identifiable consumer products to boycott, but a lively campaign was developed against the South African gold coin, the Krugerrand. And Polaroid Corporation workers waged an early, dramatically successful campaign, risking their jobs to stop their employer from continuing to supply the South African government with film for its notorious identification-card system.

The movement focused on ending U.S. corporate and financial engagement with apartheid South Africa. Practicalities, rather than the relative size of the several areas of U.S.–South Africa economic involvement, determined this choice. By 1982, when the campaign was accelerating, overall U.S. financial involvement in South Africa amounted to some $14 billion, excluding trade. Direct investment by several hundred corporations was estimated at $2.8 billion. U.S. financial institutions had $3.6 billion in outstanding loans to South African borrowers, and U.S.-based investors held some $8 billion worth of shares in South African mines.

The divestiture movement sought to make institutions such as universities, churches, unions, municipalities, and states sell their holdings in all corporations with direct investments in, or with loans to, South Africa.

When the campaign started, many supporters believed in its educational value—that it would heighten public awareness of the repressive apartheid system and lay the groundwork for eventual federal sanctions. But it seemed to others that the corporate interconnection in U.S. life might be useful; these connections provided levers to exert pressure on the corporations. Every union had a pension fund, and every university and even most colleges had some form of accumulated funds, often invested in "blue chip" corporations. Most of these corporations did business in South Africa. On state campuses and in Ivy League schools, students drew administrators into intense debate about the morality of investing in apartheid. After the Soweto student uprising of 1976, the U.S. student movement grew. By 1982, more than 30 colleges and universities had withdrawn more than $100 million from banks and corporations operating in South Africa, and these divestitures brought new consciousness to hundreds of campuses.

Churches were early participants in the debate and the campaign, with activists struggling for years to get their own boards to divest. Sometimes churches chose to retain their stock and use it to exert pressure on the companies via shareholder resolutions, but by the early 1980s, major Protestant denominations had voted to withdraw funds from banks and do no business with corporations operating in South Africa. Many national, regional, and local churches took special action against Citibank, the largest U.S. lender to South Africa.

By the beginning of the 1980s, the divestiture campaign was beginning to win more than propaganda victories. Activists made new alliances and took their issue to city and state legislatures. By 1982, legislatures in Massachusetts, Michigan, Connecticut; and the cities of Philadelphia, Wilmington, and Grand Rapids had approved measures to withdraw amounts up to $300 million.

The movement accelerated in the mid-1980s after the South African United Democratic Front gathered more than a million members and then was effectively banned by the South African government. In the United States, a growing number of states, counties, and cities moved to intensify their pressure on the corporations. By the end of 1991, 28 states, 25 counties, and 91 cities had taken economic action against corporations with investments in South Africa, reportedly at a cost to South Africa of some $20 billion. A further economic lever was the use of selective purchasing—preference was given to companies not doing business in South Africa.

Grassroots activities contributed to a major 1986 victory in Washington, D.C. The Comprehensive Anti-Apartheid Act was passed with enough votes to override a Reagan veto. This act imposed selective sanctions, including bans on new investment, on sales to the police and military, and on new bank loans. It included specific measures against trade, prohibiting the import of agricultural goods, steel, coal, iron, uranium, and the products of state-owned corporations.

The 1987 Rangel Amendment to the Budget Reconciliation Act further extended federal sanctions and eliminated U.S. firms' tax credit deductions for taxes paid in South Africa.

Counting the Costs

In the 1960s, a Union Carbide advertisement that appeared in South Africa read, "We've been in South Africa a long time; we like it here." By the 1970s, no company dared say that in public, and by the end of the decade, companies were seeking to ward off public pressure by adopting a code of corporate behavior: the Sullivan principles. Soon companies began to talk about the "hassle" factor; in 1982, General Electric pulled out of a $138 million joint venture with a South African mining company, admitting that public pressure in its Connecticut home base had influenced the decision.

Such examples multiplied, and corporations found themselves having to choose between doing business and making loans in New York City and California—or in South Africa. By 1989, key companies like Mobil were pulling out. At the end of the decade, some 200 companies had eliminated their investments in South Africa (although their methods varied greatly, and many continued to do business through licensing, franchising, and distribution agreements).

It is difficult to quantify the costs of sanctions to the South African economy. If the books are opened in a more democratic era, a precise analysis will be possible. Factors such as the drop in the price of gold, which eliminated South Africa's safety net, complicate the task. South Africa's long-vaunted high growth rate, still significantly over 3 percent annually in the 1970s, dropped to an average of 1.3 percent in the 1980s, and slipped into negative numbers in 1990, 1991, and 1992.

A 1990 *Washington Post* article noted South Africa's declining growth rate and 1986–88 capital outflows, and reported that the country "had sustained net capital outflows of $4 billion not so much because of trade sanctions but because of a cutoff of U.S. and European investment and the calling in of outstanding loans." The *Post* cited a bankers' study showing that sanctions cost South Africa $32–40 billion between 1985 and 1989, "including $11 billion in net capital outflows and $4 billion in lost export earnings."

South African business confidence collapsed, along with internal investment. Sanctions clearly inflicted some losses on South African exports such as iron, steel, uranium, clothing, fruit, and coal.

The context within which sanctions were imposed is important. At no time did sanctions supporters believe the sanctions by themselves could achieve the desired end—bringing human equality and political democracy to South Africa. Rather, the imposition of sanctions was a strategy to provide direct support for an active and ongoing struggle for liberation.

This is adapted from the November 1993 *Bulletin*.

VII.6 Remember Your Humanity

Joseph Rotblat

At this momentous event in my life—the acceptance of the Nobel Peace Prize—I want to speak as a scientist, but also as a human being. From my earliest days I had a passion for science. But science, the exercise of the supreme power of the human intellect, was always linked in my mind with benefit to people. I saw science as being in harmony with humanity. I did not imagine that the second half of my life would be spent on efforts to avert a mortal danger to humanity created by science.

The practical release of nuclear energy was the outcome of many years of experimental and theoretical research. It had great potential for the common good. But the first the general public learned about this discovery was the news of the destruction of Hiroshima by the atom bomb. A splendid achievement of science and technology had turned malign. Science became identified with death and destruction.

It is painful to me to admit that this depiction of science was deserved. The decision to use the atom bomb on Japanese cities, and the consequent buildup of enormous nuclear arsenals, was made by governments, on the basis of political and military perceptions. But scientists on both sides of the Iron Curtain played a very significant role in maintaining the momentum of the nuclear arms race throughout the four decades of the Cold War.

The role of scientists in the nuclear arms race was expressed by Lord [Solly] Zuckerman, for many years chief scientific adviser to the British Government: "When it comes to nuclear weapons . . . it is the man in the laboratory who at the start proposes that for this or that arcane reason it would be useful to improve an old or to devise a new nuclear warhead. It is he, the technician, not the commander in the field, who is at the heart of the arms race."

There is no direct evidence that nuclear weapons prevented a world war. Conversely, it is known that they nearly caused one. The most terrifying moment in my life was October 1962, during the Cuban missile crisis. I did not know all the facts—we have learned only recently how close we were to war—but I knew enough to make me tremble. The lives of millions of people were about to end abruptly; millions of others were to suffer a lingering death; much of our civilization was to be destroyed. It all hung on the decision of one man, Nikita Khrushchev: would he or would he not yield to the U.S. ultimatum? This is the reality of nuclear weapons: they may trigger a world war; a war which, unlike previous ones, destroys all of civilization.

As for the assertion that nuclear weapons prevent wars, how many more wars are needed to refute this argument? Tens of millions have died in the many wars that have taken place since 1945. In a number of them nuclear states were directly involved. In two they were actually defeated. Having nuclear weapons was of no use to them.

To sum up, there is no evidence that a world without nuclear weapons would be a dangerous world. On the contrary, it would be a safer world, as I will show later.

We are told that the possession of nuclear weapons—in some cases even the testing of these weapons—is essential for national security. But this argument can be made by other countries as well. If the militarily most powerful—and least threatened—states need nuclear weapons for their security, how can one deny such security to countries that are truly insecure? The present nuclear policy is a recipe for proliferation. It is a policy for disaster.

To prevent this disaster—for the sake of humanity—we must get rid of all nuclear weapons.

Achieving this goal will take time, but it will never happen unless we make a start. Some essential steps towards it can be taken now. Several studies, and a number of public statements by senior military and political personalities, testify that—except for disputes between the present nuclear states—all military conflicts, as well as threats to peace, can be dealt with using conventional weapons. This means that the only function of nuclear weapons, while they exist, is to deter a nuclear attack.

All nuclear weapon states should now recognize that this is so, and declare—in treaty form—that they will never be the first to use nuclear weapons. This would open the way to the gradual, mutual reduction of nuclear arsenals, down to zero. It would also open the way for a nuclear weapons convention. This would be universal—it would prohibit all possession of nuclear weapons.

We will need to work out the necessary verification system to safeguard the convention. A Pugwash study produced suggestions on these matters.

Joseph Rotblat outside his office on Great Russell Street in London. *Photo © James Lerager*

The mechanism for negotiating such a convention already exists. Entering into negotiations does not commit the parties. There is no reason why they should not begin now. If not now, when?

So I ask the nuclear powers to abandon the out-of-date thinking of the Cold War period and take a fresh look. Above all, I appeal to them to bear in mind the long-term threat that nuclear weapons pose to humankind and to begin action towards their elimination. Remember your duty to humanity.

Stop Making Weapons

My second appeal is to my fellow scientists. I described earlier the disgraceful role played by a few scientists, caricatured as "Dr. Strangeloves," in fueling the arms race. They did great damage to the image of science.

On the other side there are the scientists, in Pugwash and other bodies, who devote much of their time and ingenuity to averting the dangers created by advances in science and technology. However, they embrace only a small part of the scientific community. I want to address the scientific community as a whole.

You are doing fundamental work, pushing forward the frontiers of knowledge, but often you do it without giving much thought to the impact of your work on society. Precepts such as "science is neutral" or "science has nothing to do with politics," still prevail. They are remnants of the ivory tower mentality, although the ivory tower was finally demolished by the Hiroshima bomb.

Here, for instance, is a question: Should any scientist work on the development of weapons of mass destruction? A clear "no" was the answer recently given by Hans Bethe. Professor Bethe, a Nobel laureate, is the most senior of the surviving members of the Manhattan Project. On the occasion of the fiftieth anniversary of Hiroshima, he issued a statement that I will quote in full.

"As the director of the Theoretical Division of Los Alamos, I participated at the most senior level in the World War II project that produced the first atomic weapons.

"Now, at age 88, I am one of the few remaining such senior persons alive. Looking back at the half century since that time, I feel the most intense relief that these weapons have not been used since World War II, mixed with the horror that tens of thousands of such weapons have been built since that time—one hundred times more than any of us at Los Alamos could ever have imagined.

"Today we are rightly in an era of disarmament and dismantlement of nuclear weapons. But in some countries nuclear weapons development still continues. Whether and when the various nations of the world can agree to stop this is uncertain. But individual scientists can still influence this process by withholding their skills.

"Accordingly, I call on all scientists in all countries to cease and desist from work creating, developing, improving and manufacturing further nuclear weapons—and, for that matter, other weapons of potential mass destruction such as chemical and biological weapons."

If all scientists heeded this call there would be no more new nuclear warheads; no French scientists at Mururoa; no new chemical and biological poisons. The arms race would be over.

But there are other areas of scientific research that may directly or indirectly lead to harm to society. This calls for constant vigilance. The purpose of some government or industrial research is sometimes concealed, and misleading information is presented to the public. It should be the duty of scientists to expose such malfeasance. "Whistle-blowing" should become part of the scientist's ethos. This may bring reprisals; a price to be paid for one's convictions. The price may be very heavy, as illustrated by the disproportionately severe punishment of Mordechai Vanunu. I believe he has suffered enough.

The time has come to formulate guidelines for the ethical conduct of scientists, perhaps in the form of a voluntary Hippocratic Oath. This would be particularly valuable for young scientists when they embark on a scientific career. The U.S. Student Pugwash Group has taken up this idea—and that is very heartening.

At a time when science plays such a powerful role in the life of society, when the destiny of the whole of mankind may hinge on the results of scientific research, it is incumbent on all scientists to be fully conscious of that role, and conduct themselves accordingly. I appeal to my fellow scientists to remember their responsibility to humanity.

Abolish War

My third appeal is to my fellow citizens in all countries: Help us to establish lasting peace in the world. I have argued that we must eliminate nuclear weapons. While this would remove the immediate threat, it will not provide permanent security. Nuclear weapons cannot be disinvented. The knowledge of how to make them cannot be erased. Even in a nuclear-weapon-free world, should any of the great powers become involved in a military confrontation, they would be tempted to rebuild their nuclear arsenals. That would still be a better situation than the one we have now, because the rebuilding would take a considerable time, and in that time the dispute might be settled. A nuclear-weapon-free world would be safer than the present one. But the danger of the ultimate catastrophe would still be there.

The only way to prevent it is to abolish war altogether. War must cease to be an admissible social institution. We must learn to resolve our disputes by means other than military confrontation.

The quest for a war-free world has a basic purpose: survival. But if in the process we learn how to achieve it by love rather than by fear, by kindness rather than by compulsion; if in the process we learn to combine the essential with the enjoyable, the expedient with the benevolent, the practical with the beautiful, this will be an extra incentive to embark on this great task. And above all, remember your humanity.

 This is adapted from the March/April 1996 *Bulletin*.

Nobel Peace Laureates, 1945–1996

1945	Cordell Hull, former U.S. secretary of state; an initiator of the United Nations
1946	Emily Greene Balch, USA, president of the Women's International League for Peace and Freedom; and John Raleigh Mott, USA, president of the World Alliance of Young Men's Christian Associations
1947	The Friends Service Council, London; and The American Friends Service Committee
1948	none awarded
1949	Baron John Boyd Orr of Brechin, UK, director general of the UN Food and Agricultural Organization, president of the National Peace Council and the World Union of Peace Organizations
1950	Ralph Bunche, USA, director of the UN Division of Trusteeship, mediator in Palestine in 1948
1951	Léon Jouhaux, France, international trade union leader
1952	Albert Schweitzer, France, physician and missionary, founder of the Lambarene Hospital in Gabon
1953	George Catlett Marshall, USA, former secretary of state and defense, originator of the Marshall Plan
1954	Office of the UN High Commissioner for Refugees
1955, 1956	none awarded
1957	Lester Bowles Pearson, former Canadian foreign minister, president of the UN General Assembly
1958	Georges Pire, Belgium, head of the aid organization for refugees, L'Europe du Coeur au Service du Monde
1959	Philip John Noel-Baker, UK, member of Parliament, campaigner for international cooperation and peace
1960	Albert John Lutuli, president of the South African liberation movement, the African National Congress

1961	Dag Hammarskjöld, Sweden, UN secretary general (awarded posthumously)
1962	Linus Carl Pauling, USA, chemist, campaigner for an end to nuclear weapons tests
1963	International Committee of the Red Cross and The League of Red Cross Societies
1964	Martin Luther King, Jr., USA, campaigner for civil rights
1965	United Nations Children's Fund (UNICEF)
1966, 1967	none awarded
1968	René Cassin, France, president of the European Court of Human Rights
1969	The International Labor Organization
1970	Norman Ernest Borlaug, USA, led research at the International Maize and Wheat Improvement Center, Mexico City
1971	Willy Brandt, former West German chancellor, initiator of "Ostpolitik" embodying a new attitude toward Eastern Europe
1972	none awarded
1973	Henry A. Kissinger, USA; and Le Duc Tho, North Vietnam (declined the prize); jointly negotiated the Vietnam peace accord
1974	Sean MacBride, Ireland, president of the International Peace Bureau, Geneva, and UN commissioner for Namibia; and Eisaku Sato, former prime minister of Japan
1975	Andrei Sakharov, Soviet Union, campaigner for human rights
1976	Betty Williams and Mairead Corrigan, co-founders of Northern Ireland's Peace People
1977	Amnesty International
1978	Mohammad Anwar Al-Sadat, president of Egypt; and Menachem Begin, prime minister of Israel; jointly negotiated peace between Egypt and Israel
1979	Mother Teresa, India, leader of the Order of the Missionaries of Charity

1980	Adolfo Pérez Esquivel, Argentina, architect, campaigner for human rights
1981	Office of the United Nations High Commissioner for Refugees
1982	Alva Myrdal, Sweden, diplomat and delegate to UN disarmament conferences; and Alfonso García Robles, Mexico, diplomat and disarmament campaigner
1983	Lech Walesa, Poland, founder of Solidarity, human rights campaigner
1984	Desmond Mpilo Tutu, South Africa, bishop, interfaith leader
1985	International Physicians for the Prevention of Nuclear War
1986	Elie Wiesel, USA, author, humanitarian
1987	Oscar Arias Sánchez, president of Costa Rica, initiator of peace negotiations in Central America
1988	The United Nations Peacekeeping Forces
1989	Tenzin Guatso, Tibet, the 14th Dalai Lama, religious and political leader of the Tibetan people
1990	Mikhail Sergeyevich Gorbachev, president of the Soviet Union, helped end the Cold War
1991	Aung San Suu Kyi, Burmese oppositional leader and human rights advocate
1992	Rigoberta Menchú Tum, Guatemala, campaigner for human rights for indigenous peoples
1993	Nelson Mandela, South Africa, leader of the African National Congress; and Frederik Willem de Klerk, president of the Republic of South Africa
1994	Yasir Arafat, chairman of the Palestine Liberation Organization; Shimon Peres, foreign minister of Israel; and Yitzhak Rabin, prime minister of Israel; awarded for their efforts to create peace in the Middle East
1995	Joseph Rotblat, UK, and Pugwash Conferences on Science and World Affairs for their efforts to diminish the role of nuclear arms in international politics
1996	Carlos Felipe Ximenes Belo, bishop, and José Ramos-Horta, both of East Timor, for their work toward a solution to the conflict between Indonesia and East Timor

Chapter VII
Discussion Questions

1. What are the characteristics of the new global citizenship? How well do scientists and journalists typify these characteristics? Do other professions or lifestyles lend themselves well to global citizenship? How well do you think your own career and life choices will lend themselves to global citizenship?

2. In "The Global Tide," the authors discuss how citizens of different countries cooperate on particular global issues through transnational organizations. Using the categories of daily life listed below, list transnational organizations in which you participate, even tangentially.

Aspect of daily life	*Organizations* (examples)
Where you live (city, community, state, nation)	Sister Cities International
Religion	Southern Baptist Church
Hobbies	World Chess Federation
Sports	International Olympic Committee
Charity	Save the Children
Activism	Amnesty International

Other:

3. Suppose you were interested in mounting a worldwide campaign to end a particular practice, such as the U.S. export of tobacco products to countries of the so-called Third World. What lessons and strategies for organizing and targeting such a campaign do you learn from the articles in this chapter?

4. From the vantage point of 1951, Eugene Rabinowitch noted that the past five years had been a time of failure and of hope regarding the control of atomic weapons. On the basis of the social movements and global actions discussed in this chapter, discuss how your era is a time of both failure and hope regarding peace and security.

Index

ABM. *See* antiballistic missile systems
A-bomb. *See* atomic bomb
Academic Assistance Council, 9
accidents, nuclear, 103, 105–14
Adamsky, Victor, 22
AEC. *See* Atomic Energy Commission
African National Congress, 248
African Nuclear-Weapon-Free-Zone Treaty (ANFZ), 210–11, 214
aircraft, 29
Aleksandrov, Anatoli, 20–21
alliances, 42–44, 46–49, 79–86, 129–31, 183–87, 202–4
Almaty, Kazakhstan, 139, 142
Altshuler, Lev, 19, 22
An Agenda for Peace (Boutros-Ghali), 163–66
ANFZ. *See* African Nuclear-Weapon-Free-Zone Treaty
animals, 152
Annabi, Hedi, 165
antiballistic missile systems (ABMs), 43; Antiballistic Missile Treaty, 44
anti-politics, 247
apartheid, 248–53
Armenia, 148–54
arms control. *See* arms reduction; disarmament; nonproliferation
arms race: costs of, 5; social impacts of, 89; stockpiles chart, 50
arms reduction: Comprehensive Test Ban, 211–15; global politics, 215–20; Soviet, 34; U.S. defense policy, 196–202. *See also* disarmament; nonproliferation
Army Corps of Engineers. *See* Manhattan Project
Arzamas-16, 18–22, 74
asbestosis, 99
Askarov, Tulegen, 145
Association of Young Democrats, 247
atomic bomb: development of, 3, 6–7, 9–18; Hiroshima, 253. *See also* defense spending
Atomic Energy Commission (AEC), 27
atomic veterans, 93

B-2A Spirit (Stealth), 29
B-29, 29
Baghdad, Iraq, 65
ballistic missile defense. *See* antiballistic missile systems
Baltics, 132–39
Belarus, 108–14
Belopukhov, Sergei, 71
Beria, Lavrenti, 18–21
Berlin Wall, 48
beryllium disease, 99, 101
Bethe, Hans, 256
black-market nuclear materials, 68–75
Bohr, Niels, 14
Bosnia, 167–74
Bottom-Up Review (BUR), 196, 199
Boutros-Ghali, Boutros, 160–61; *An Agenda for Peace*, 163–66
Bravo nuclear test, 93
Briggs, Lyman J., 16
Briquemon, Francis, 168
Bulletin of the Atomic Scientists, 226–27; doomsday clock, xiii, 5, 37–49

BUR. *See* Bottom-Up-Review
Bush, George: arms reduction, 36, 196; Gorbachev and, 49; military policies, 125, 177; sanctions against Iraq, 183

Canberra Commission on the Elimination of Nuclear Weapons, 215
CARE, 234
Carter, Jimmy, 45
Castro, Fidel, 184
Central Intelligence Agency, 83
centrifuges, 64–68
cesium contamination, 110
Chalmers, Thomas, 12
Charter 77, 246
Chelyabinsk-40, 20, 21
Chelyabinsk-65, 74
Chernenko, Andrei, 70
Chernobyl, 28, 90, 105–14
Chiang Kai-shek, 40
children, 110–13
China, 40, 202–4
cholera, 111
C³I. *See* command, control, communications, and intelligence
Clinton, Bill, 173; arms reduction, 196; BUR, 196, 199; national security interests, 176–77; Russian Foreign Policy, 130; sanctions against Iraq, 183
Closing the Circle on the Splitting of the Atom (U.S. Energy Department), 94
Cold War, 26; end of, 48; impacts of, 89–91; new, 244; strategic planning, 32
Columbia University, 13, 15
command, control, communications, and intelligence (C³I), 30
Committee of Soviet Women, 239
Comprehensive Test Ban (CTB) Treaty, 7, 211–12
Compton, Arthur Holly, 17
Conference on Disarmament (Geneva), 213
contamination, radioactive, 98–101, 105–14. *See also* toxic materials
cooperative threat reduction. *See* Nunn-Lugar funds
counter revolution, nuclear strategy, 208–11
countervalue. *See* defense spending
CTB Treaty. *See* Comprehensive Test Ban Treaty
Cuban missile crisis, 41, 254

decade of intensification, 232
decade of interdependence, 231–32
defense spending (U.S.): atomic bomb development, 24–26; bomber aircraft, 29; Manhattan Project, 28; nuclear secrecy, 35; Reagan administration, 28–29; wasteful, 36; weapons reduction, 33
defense workers, displaced, 100
de Gaulle, Charles, 102
de Klerk, F. W., 82
Demidchik, Evgeni, 111
Democratic Opposition, 246
d'Estaing, Valéry Giscard, 103
détente, 37–49
deterrence, 4, 33–37, 41–49, 57, 61–64; theory, 194. *See also* nonproliferation
diptheria, 111
disarmament, 41, 211–20; China, 202–4; European Nuclear Disarmament Appeal, 244–46; globalization and, 236–38; North Korea, 79; nuclear weapon states and, 86; Russian efforts, 34–35; South Africa, 79. *See also* arms reduction; nonproliferation
Disarmament Commission, 213
discourse, technostrategic, 114–22
disease: infectious, 111; toxic materials and, 99, 104
doomsday clock, xiii, 5, 37–49
downwinders, 93
Dr. Strangelove (Stanley Kubrick), 42
dual-use technology, 64–68
Dulles, John Foster, 163

Economic Sanctions Reconsidered (Hufbauer, Schott, and Elliot), 188

Einstein, Albert, xiii–xiv, 6, 10, 13, 15–16
Eisenhower, Dwight D., 4, 40, 202
Elektrostal, 73, 74
Elliot, Kimberly Ann, 188
Elugelab Islet, 39
END. *See* European Nuclear Disarmament Appeal
energy crisis, Armenia, 148–54
environment, harm to, 92–93. *See also* contamination; toxic materials
environmental disasters: Chernobyl, 105–14; Cold War, 89–91
Eppelman, Rainier, 246
Estimating the Cold War Mortgage (U.S. Energy Department), 94
Estonia, 69–75
European Bank for Reconstruction and Development, 152
European Nuclear Disarmament Appeal (END), 244–46
export controls, 64–68, 82

Fail Safe (Sidney Lumet), 42
fallout: Chernobyl, 108; French nuclear testing and, 101–4. *See also* toxic materials
Feld, Bernard T., 44–45
feminism: nuclear strategic practice and, 114–22; Soviet, 238–40
Fermi, Enrico, 6, 15, 39, 94
Fermi effect, 13
Fernald Plant, 93
fifth column effect, 185
Flügge, Siegfried, 14
France: atomic test sites, 101–4; U.S. foreign policy and, 36
Fuchs, Klaus, 18

Gale, Robert, 111
Galtung, Johan, 184–85
General Electric, 252
Germany, 64–68
glasnost, 126
globalization, 223, 232
Goldhaber, Maurice, 12
Gorbachev, Mikhail, 47–49, 106, 125–26, 136–37, 248
Gosatomnadzor, 77–78
Grey, Robert T., Jr., 166
Groves, Leslie R., 6, 38
Gulf War, 61, 62, 82–83; Iraq's nuclear weapon program, 80; U.N. inspectors and, 67; U.N. sanctions, 183; U.N. Security Council, 159–60

The Hague, 103. *See also* World Court
Hahn, Otto, 6, 14
Haiti, 160
Hanford Site, 94
Havel, Vaclav, 247
hazardous materials. *See* toxic materials
H-bomb, 27, 39
Helsinki Accords (1975), 244
Hiroshima, 6, 18, 23, 27–28, 90–91, 111, 122, 226, 253
Holm, Hans-Henrik, 232
Hufbauer, Gary Clyde, 188–89
humanitarian law, 206, 208–11
Hussein, Saddam, 56, 183, 185
hydrogen bomb, 27, 39

IAEA. *See* International Atomic Energy Agency
Independent Peace Association, 247
India: Comprehensive Nuclear Test Ban Treaty, 211–12; as nuclear threat, 203
INFACT. *See* Infant Formula Action Committee
Infant Formula Action Committee (INFACT), 231
infectious diseases, 111
information selling, 64–68
INGOs. *See* international non-governmental organizations
injection experiments, 93
Institute for Disease Control and Prevention, 93
intelligence: Central Intelligence Agency, 83; National Reconnaissance

Office, 31; spy systems, 30; strategic planning, 33
interdependence, 231–32
Intermediate Nuclear Forces Treaty, 34, 47
International Atomic Energy Agency (IAEA), 54, 61, 79, 82–84; Iraq, 67–68; Medzamor, 153; Soviet delegation, 106
International Atomic Energy Association, 110
International Fellowship of Reconciliation, 232–35
international force, United Nations, 164
international law: humanitarian, 208–11; nuclear weapons, 205–8
International Monetary Fund, 146
international non-governmental organizations (INGOs), 224
international nonproliferation regime, 80
international relations, postwar, 18
international security system, 166
international women's organizations, 238–40
intervention, 162–67
Iran, 62
Iraq: nuclear weapon program, 62, 80; sanctions against, 159–60, 183; technical assistance to, 64–68
Isinaliev, Mikhail, 145
Islamic bomb, 56, 57
isotopes, 12–13
Israel, 36, 58, 242
Italy, 183
Ivan the Terrible, 129

Japan, 203, 226; Hiroshima, 6, 18, 23, 27–28, 90–91, 111, 122, 226; Nagasaki, 6, 27–28
Joliot-Curie, Frédéric, 14

Kahn, Herman, 219
Kazakhstan, 139; business, 140–44; energy resources, 144–48
Kazhegeldin, Akezhan, 146
Kennedy, John F., 40, 79
Keohane, Robert, 232
Khariton, Yuli, 18–22
Khrushchev, Nikita, 254
Kissinger, Henry, 208–9
Konrad, George, 247
Korean War, 40
Kubrick, Stanley, 42
Kunayev, Dinmuhammed, 141–42
Kurchatov, Igor, 18

Lange, Fritz, 11
Langsdorf, Alexander, 38
language abstractions, 114–22
Latvia, 69–75
launch on warning, 30–33
Lawrence, Ernest O., 17
Leach, James, 164
Legasov, Valery, 106
Lehrer, Tom, 79
leukemia, 111
Libya, 160
Los Alamos National Laboratory, 6
Lumet, Sidney, 42
Luthuli, Albert, 248

Manhattan Engineer District. *See* the Manhattan Project
Manhattan Project, 3–4, 6, 18, 27–28
MAN Technologie, 64
Marshall Islands, 27, 92–93
Martyl, 38
masculinity, 114–22
McKenzie, Louis, 168
McMahon, Brien, 24
McNamara, Robert S., 43
media, 180–82
Medicins Sans Frontières, 235
Medzamor, 148–54
Meitner, Lise, 6, 11
Meitner-Frisch experiment, 11, 14
Mendiluce, Jose-Maria, 173
Michnik, Adam, 246–47

Milic, Goran, 170
military spending. *See* defense spending
Military Spending Working Group, 196–202
miners, 92
Minsk Children's Hospital No. 3, 111
Minsk Thyroid Tumor Clinic, 111
MIRVs. *See* multiple independently targetable reentry vehicles
Missile Technology Control Regime, 203
Mogadishu, 182
Morillon, Philippe, 167–70
Moruroa atoll, 101–4
Moscow, Russia, 132–33; Center of Radio Analysis Control, 72
Moscow (Russia), Raw Materials Exchange, 72
multiple independently targetable reentry vehicles (MIRVs), 43–44
Muslims, 56–63
Mussolini, Benito, 183

Nagasaki, 6, 90–91, 226
Naisbitt, John, 237
National Committee for Radiation Protection of the Ukrainian Population, 108
National Preventive Program of Genetic Consequences of the Chernobyl Accident, 111
National Reconnaissance Office, 31
NATO. *See* North Atlantic Treaty Organization
Nazarbaev, Nursultan, 140, 142, 145
Nazi Germany, 11
Nestlé Company, 230–31
Netherlands, 250
Nevada-Semipalatinsk environmental movement, 146
New Zealand, 35
Nixon, Richard, 231
Nobel Peace Laureates, 259–61
Nobel Peace Prize, 253
no-conflict zones, 177
no-first-use strategy, 213–14
nonproliferation, 7, 57, 62–64; initiatives, 79–86; regime, 54; Sweden, 80. *See also* arms reduction; disarmament; Nuclear Nonproliferation Treaty
North Atlantic Treaty Organization (NATO), 46–47
North Korea, 83–84; deterrence and, 203; disarmament, 79
NPT. *See* nuclear Nonproliferation Treaty
NSG. *See* Nuclear Suppliers Group
nuclear accidents, 105–14
nuclear allergy, 35
nuclear chain reaction, 6, 9–13; experiments, 12; first, 6, 18; patent of, 11
nuclear fallout, 27
Nuclear Nonproliferation Treaty (NPT), 7, 42, 53–54, 62, 79–82, 85–86, 212; Chinese delegation, 202–4; four phases of, 216–17; review conference, 214, 219
nuclear reactors, spent fuel, 95–96
nuclear research, secrecy of, 16–18
Nuclear Suppliers Group (NSG), 61, 79
nuclear terrorism, 84
nuclear testing, 7; Bravo, 93; French, 101–4
nuclear waste storage, 94. *See also* toxic waste
nuclear-weapon-free-zone (NWFZ) treaties, 213–14
nuclear weapons: arms control, 44; capability, 7–8; competition, 5; counterrevolution, 208–11; environmental impact of, 92–93; foreign policy, 208–9; government spending, 5; launch on warning, 32; production of, 7, 28–29; retirement of, 33; role in new era, 215–20; Soviet dismantlement, 34; theft of materials, 76–79
Nuclear Weapons and Foreign Policy (Kissinger), 208–9

nuclear weapon states, 7; legitimate, 81
nuclear weapons workers, 98–101
Nunn, Sam, 132
Nunn-Lugar funds, 34, 55, 132
NWFZ. *See* nuclear-weapon-free-zone treaties

O'Leary, Hazel, 94, 98
On-Site Inspection Agency (OSIA), 34
OPEC. *See* Organization of Petroleum Exporting Countries
Oppenheimer, Robert, 6
Organization of Petroleum Exporting Countries (OPEC), 231–32
OSIA. *See* On-Site Inspection Agency
Ozolos, Romualdas, 137–38

Pakistan: nuclear weapons program, 62, 82, 203; U.S. foreign policy and, 36
Parliamentarians Global Action, 235
Partial Test Ban Treaty, 34, 41
peace, 215–20
peacekeeping: public opinion, 180–82; U.N. Charter Chapter VII, 162–67
Peace of Westphalia, 165–66
Peper, Carlo, 98–101
perestroika, 126, 238–40
Peter the Great, 129–30
plutonium, 6; cost, 28; implosion bomb, 18; injection experiments, 93; production reactor, 20; Russian stocks, 84; toxic waste, 33–34, 96–98
pollution, radioactive, 26
Presidential Decision Directive 25, 176
President's Advisory Commission on Human Radiation Experiments, 93
Principles and Objectives of Nonproliferation and Disarmament, 214
Program on International Policy Attitudes, 181
Project Sapphire, 34
Prunskene, Kazimiera, 138–39
public opinion, 180–82
Pugwash study, 254

Rabi, Isidor, 13, 39
Rabinowitch, Eugene, 38–42, 226–30
radiation exposure, 26, 92–93, 98–101; Chernobyl, 105–14. *See also* toxic materials
Radiation Exposure Compensation Act, 92–93
radioactive fallout, nuclear tests, 101–4
radioactive materials, black market for, 68–75
radioactive waste. *See* toxic waste
rally-around-the-flag-effect, 184–85
Rangel Amendment to the Budget Reconciliation Act, 252
Reagan, Ronald, 26, 28–29, 46, 47–48, 115; arms reduction, 196; Cold War, 45; SALT II, 45
research, 111. *See also* scientists
Rhodesia, 160
Rocky Flats workers, 98–101
Romanenko, Anatoli, 111
Roosevelt, Franklin D., 6, 16
Rose, Michael, 168
Rosenau, James, 237
Rotblat, Joseph, 225, 253–58
Russia: allies, 131; Atomic Energy Ministry of Russia, 75; black-market nuclear materials, 72; Chernobyl, 108–14; nuclear security problems, 84; State Institute of Rare Earth Metals, 72; voters, 128. *See also* Soviet Union
Russian Revolution, 129
Rutherford, Lord Ernest, 9
Rwanda, 160, 164–65

Sakharov, Andrei, 20, 22–24
SALT. *See* Strategic Arms Limitation Talks
sanctions, 185, 186
satellites, spy, 30–31
Schott, Jeffrey J., 188
scientists, 225; export control on know-how, 64–68; as public educators, 226–30

secrecy, 16–18, 35–36
security: Armenian, 148–54; nuclear allergy, 35; Russian, 76–79, 84; United States, 77
Semipalatinsk, 145–46
Serbs, 167–73
sexism, 114–22
Slavophiles, 130
Somalia, 159, 176, 180–82
Sorensen, Georg, 232
South Africa, 160, 251, 252; disarmament, 79; Union Carbide, 252; United Democratic Front, 251
South Asia, 203
South East Asia, 214
South Korea, 203
sovereignty, 165–66
Soviet Union, 128; black-market nuclear materials, 68–75; independence of Soviet republics, 132–44; post-Soviet government, 128; research, 19; Soviet Academy of Medical Sciences, 111. *See also* Russia
spies, 18, 30
Stalin, Josef, 18, 21, 129
START. *See* Strategic Arms Reduction Treaty
Star Wars. *See* Strategic Defense Initiative
State Institute of Rare Earth Metals (Russia), 72
Stemmler, Bruno, 64–68
Strassmann, Fritz, 6, 14
strategic arms control, 31
Strategic Arms Limitation Talks (SALT, SALT II), 43–45
Strategic Arms Reduction Treaty (START), 34, 49, 86, 214, 216
Strategic Defense Initiative (Star Wars), 26, 46
Supplement to an Agenda for Peace, 160–61
Sweden, 80
Swords into Ploughshares, 246
Szilard, Leo, 4, 6, 9–18
Szilard-Chalmers effect, 13

technical knowledge, 64–68
technostrategic discourse, 114–22
Ter-Petrosian, Levon, 150
testing: French sites, 101–4; H-bomb, 27, 39; Nevada Test Site, 26; nuclear, 93; thermonuclear device, 39; underground, 103
theft of nuclear material, 76–79, 84
Thompson, E. P., 244
threat inflation, 36
threat of attack to U.S., 87
thyroid cancers, 111
toxic materials: cleanup crew's risk, 111; environmental damage and, 101–5; human exposure to, 92–93, 98–101, 105–14, 122; wildlife and, 101–5. *See also* contamination
toxic waste, 94; Chernobyl, 105–14; disposal, reprocessing, and storage of, 94–96; plutonium, 96–98; transuranic, 96
transnational social movement organizations (TSMOs), 224, 232–35
transuranic waste. *See* toxic waste
treaties, 34; nuclear-weapon-free-zone (NWFZ) treaties, 213–14. *See also specific treaties*
Truman, Harry S., 38
TSMOs. *See* transnational social movement organizations
tuberculosis, 111
Turajlic, Hakija, 167

Ukraine, Chernobyl, 108–14
U.N. *See* United Nations
underground testing, 103
unemployment, 239
United Nations: army, 163–64; Charter Chapter VII, 250; General Assembly, 205, 249; inspectors, 67–68; peacekeeping, 173–82; sanctions, 159–69, 183–91, 250; Security Council, 61, 83, 159–60, 163–64, 183–87, 250; Special Commission on Iraq, 62; United Na-

tions Protection Force (UNPROFOR), 167–73
United Nations Charter Chapter VII, 162–67
United States: Anti-Apartheid Act, 251; Budget Reconciliation Act, 252; Energy Department, 28, 35, 93, 94–95, 99; foreign aid to Israel, 36; Los Alamos National Laboratory, 6; Nunn-Lagar funds, 34, 55, 132; Presidential Decision Directive 25, 176; President's Advisory Commission on Human Radiation Experiments, 93; Rangel Amendment to the Budget Reconciliation Act, 252. *See also* defense spending; *specific presidents*
UNPROFOR. *See* United Nations Protection Force
uranium, 6; cost, 28; injection experiments, 93; nuclear fission in, 6, 14; production of, 64–68; Russian stocks, 84; spheres in graphite, 15; storage, recycling, and disposal of, 33–34
uranium miners, 92
Urenco machine, 66
Urquhart, Brian, 163
Vienna Law of Treaties, 212
Vilnius, Lithuania, 138

The Washington Post, 252
waste disposal, 95–96
Waste Isolation Pilot Plant (WIPP), 96
weapons reduction, 55. *See also* arms reduction; nonproliferation
Weeramantry, Christopher G., 207–8
"Who's Next" (Lehrer), 79
Wigner, Eugene, 6, 11
WIPP. *See* Waste Isolation Pilot Plant
Wohlstetter, Albert, 80
women, 238–40
women's organizations, 242
World Association of Nuclear Operators, 153
World Court, 205–11
World Heath Organization, 231

Yeltsin, Boris, 126, 128, 130–31, 136
Yugoslavia, 160

Zaire, 174
Zeldovich, Iakov, 20
zones of no-conflict, 177
Zyuganov, Gennadi, 128, 130–32

About the Contributors

Len Ackland, a former *Bulletin* editor, directs the environmental journalism program at the University of Colorado.

David Albright is president of the Institute for Science and International Security.

Nadezhda Azhgikhina is a journalist at the newspaper *Nezavisimaya Gazeta* and co-chair of the Association of Women Journalists in Moscow.

Kirill Belyaninov, a former *Bulletin* fellow, conducted this investigation for *Literaturnaya Gazeta* and now heads the investigative department of *Ogonyok* in Moscow.

Oleg Bukharin is a staff member at Princeton University's Center for Energy and Environmental Studies.

Drew Christiansen, S.J., is director of the Office of International Justice and Peace at the U.S. Catholic Conference in Washington, D.C.

Nina Chugunova, an editor at *Elle*'s Moscow bureau, was a *Bulletin* fellow.

Carol Cohn teaches at Bowdoin College in Maine.

Bengt Danielsson is an anthropologist who first came to the South Pacific with Thor Heyerdahl's Kon-Tiki expedition in 1947.

Jennifer Davis is executive director of the American Committee on Africa and the Africa Fund in New York City.

Former Amb. **Jonathan Dean** is adviser on international security issues for the Union of Concerned Scientists, in Washington, D.C. He has participated in East-West arms control negotiations and worked with U.N. peacekeepers in the field and in the State Department.

Ivan Eland is a national security affairs analyst with the Congressional Budget Office. The views expressed in his essay are his own.

William Epstein, who long represented the United Nations in arms control negotiations, is the Pugwash representative to the United Nations. The views expressed in his essay are his own.

David Holloway is a professor of political science and co-director of the Center for International Security and Arms Control at Stanford University.

Pervez Hoodbhoy is a professor in the physics department at Quaid-e-Azam University in Islamabad, Pakistan.

Mary Kaldor, co-chair of the Helsinki Citizens Assembly, is a reader in Contemporary European Studies at the University of Sussex, Brighton, UK.

Michael Krepon is president of the Henry L. Stimson Center in Washington, D.C.

Steven Kull is director of the Program on International Policy Attitudes of the Center for International and Security Studies at the University of Maryland, College Park.

William Lanouette is a senior energy and science policy analyst for the U.S. General Accounting Office.

Richard C. Longworth is a senior writer at the *Chicago Tribune*.

George A. Lopez is professor of government and international affairs and fellow at the Kroc Institute for International Peace Studies at the University of Notre Dame.

David R. Marples is professor of history and director of the Stasiuk program on Contemporary Ukraine at the Canadian Institute of Ukrainian Studies, University of Alberta.

Dzenita Mehic, a research assistant at the Center for Strategic and International Studies in Washington, D.C., was a radio and TV journalist for the independent Studio 99 in Sarajevo.

Mike Moore is editor of the *Bulletin*.

Kevin O'Neill is a research assistant at Institute for Science and International Security.

Ron Pagnucco is an assistant professor of sociology at Mount St. Mary College, Newburgh, Maryland.

William Potter directs the Center for Nonproliferation Studies at the Monterey Institute of International Studies.

Gerard F. Powers is a policy adviser for the Office of International Justice and Peace at the U.S. Catholic Conference in Washington, D.C.

Eugene Rabinowitch was co-founder of the *Bulletin* and its chief editor from 1945 until his death in 1973.

Joseph Rotblat, who is president of the Pugwash Conferences, resides in London, England. On behalf of Pugwash, he accepted the 1995 Nobel Peace Prize.

Linda Rothstein is managing editor of the *Bulletin.*

Dingli Shen is an associate professor at the Center for American Studies at Fudan University in Shanghai and co-chairs the university's Program on Arms Control and Regional Security.

Jackie G. Smith is an assistant professor of sociology at SUNY, Stony Brook.

Viktoria Tripolskaya-Mitlyng, former international programs director at the *Bulletin,* writes for the Russian and Western press.

Mikhail Ustiugov, a journalist in Almaty, Kazakhstan, was a *Bulletin* fellow.

Astghik Vardanian, a journalist in Armenia, was a *Bulletin* fellow.

Leonid Zagalsky is a journalist and television producer who works in New York and Moscow.